AN INTRODUCTION TO
FINANCIAL PRODUCTS AND MARKETS

Also available from Continuum:

Bradburn: *Understanding Business Ethics*
Evans: *Supervisory Management*, 5th edition
Forsyth: *Career Skills*
Goddard: *Informative Writing*, 2nd edition
Hamilton: *Passing Exams*
Robson: *Essential Accounting for Managers*, 6th edition

An Introduction to

Financial Products and Markets

LINDSAY FELL

CONTINUUM
London and New York

Continuum

Wellington House
125 Strand
London WC2R 0BB

370 Lexington Avenue
New York
NY 10017-6503

First published 2000

British Library Cataloguing-in-Publication Data
A catalogue record for this book is available from the British Library.

ISBN 0-8264-4886-0

Designed and typeset by Kenneth Burnley at Irby, Wirral, Cheshire
Printed and bound in Great Britain by Redwood Books, Trowbridge, Wiltshire

Contents

Preface

FINANCE, FOR MANY PEOPLE, is a complex and baffling subject. This world of unimaginably large sums of money, buzzing dealing rooms and echoing, marbled halls of long established institutions can seem far removed, to say the least, from everyday life. Then there is the financial jargon which has to be coped with, seeming perhaps to have been deliberately designed to exclude all but the most financially literate from understanding the workings of the financial sector. At the same time though, many of us have to get to grips with the way finance works. For almost all of us, there will be a benefit in doing this simply in order to be able to manage our personal financial affairs better. For others, understanding how financial products and markets work will be important for the jobs they do, whether those jobs be in finance *per se* or in other industrial, commercial or even charitable areas.

Finance need not, however, be complicated or baffling. It is essentially a logical subject based on a few clear and relatively straightforward principles. Once these basic principles have been explained and understood, then an understanding of the workings of most parts of finance will automatically follow. Perhaps that makes the study of finance sound banal or boring, but it certainly should never be that. Although finance is essentially logical and, I would argue, for the most part straightforward, what makes it really fascinating as a subject is that interweaved into it is a good bit of 'oddity'. What I mean by 'oddity' is that what happens in different aspects of finance cannot always be explained totally by logical financial principles. Some parts of finance are odd because traditions may have been retained which have outlived their original logical basis, or because laws may be in place which distort otherwise logical financial behaviour. In other parts of finance we come across oddities because finance is, in the end, about people, often acting collectively, and people, of course, do not always act logically. So to understand finance we have to get to grips with the logic but also look behind that to find the human and historical or other environmental factors which have their influence too.

Overall, what I have set out to offer in this book is an introduction to the study of financial products and markets which is broad and detailed, yet assumes no prior financial knowledge and requires no financial valuation or other techniques. The book aims to explain what can at first seem to be complex aspects of finance in a straightforward but uncompromising way, bringing clarity rather than confusion to an area of study which I know from experience can often prove difficult. Fundamental principles of finance are applied, but account is also taken of the wider influences on finance, those 'oddities' that I mentioned above. For instance, the theoretical valuation of financial assets is explained in some detail throughout the book; this is done without resort to complicated formulae or diagrams which some readers might have insufficient experience to cope with or otherwise might find difficult. Wider influences on valuation are also discussed; for example, the issue of whether some share values can be justified by fundamental factors or whether we have to look outside financial principles to explain them. Throughout the book there are activities for readers, to make studying this text a more participatory experience. The activities are designed to emphasize the practical nature of the material studied, with readers being encouraged to apply theory discussed to numerical problems or to financial data that they find themselves.

The subject matter of this book has been focused deliberately on the financial products available to end users of the financial sector and to financial markets in which some of those products are traded. The make-up of institutions which participate in financial markets or provide some financial products has not been discussed in detail. This is because this is a subject in its own right and one that, I would argue, is relevant principally only to those who want to work in the financial sector rather than to a wider readership who may, instead, be interested just in using it. The coverage of financial products and markets, while being in many aspects universal in approach, is, where a particular country's system must be chosen to discuss a point, predominantly from a UK standpoint. Variations from the UK position in other countries are in many cases noted.

A number of institutions and individuals have been instrumental in the writing of this book by providing material and or support. My thanks go particularly to the *Financial Times*, the London Stock Exchange, the Bank of England, National Westminster Bank in Hull and John Murphy of the University of Lincolnshire and Humberside.

To my family:

Tim, Matthew, Nicola and Emily

1

The role of the financial sector within the wider economy

LIKE IT OR NOT, the financial sector affects all our lives every day.

If you are an avid investor in shares or bonds and follow the markets personally, this will probably come as no surprise. But what if you do not have any investments you actively manage – what has the financial sector got to do with you then? Most of us, even if we do not take an active interest in financial markets and products, end up using them in one way or another. In some cases we make investments through the financial sector. We might have deposits in a bank or savings institution, or might have a pension organized through a pension fund. At other stages in our lives (for example, when we are students), the financial sector is likely to be a means of raising funds rather than investing them. Anyone with personal borrowings, whether that be in the form of an overdraft or a mortgage or some other loan, is participating in the financial sector, and events within the sector, such as changes in interest rates, are going to affect them.

The influence of the financial sector on our lives is not, however, limited to our personal investment or borrowing. This is because changes in the value of financial assets or the rate set for other financial variables can affect the whole level of activity in an economy. The amount people spend on goods and services depends, at least in part, on how wealthy they feel and on their overall level of confidence. Significant changes in the value of shares or the level of general interest rates can affect both wealth and confidence, and can thus have a notable impact on how well an economy performs.

In this first chapter we are going to consider what the overall function of a financial sector should be. In doing this, we are going to look particularly at how the sector interacts with other sectors in the economy. Having obtained this overview of the position of the financial sector, we will then go on in subsequent chapters to study the structure of the sector itself and the detailed workings of individual parts of it.

Learning objectives

This chapter covers the function of a monetary system, which facilitates the making of payments, and a financial system, which facilitates lending and borrowing, within an economy. A number of important points to grasp are:

- the function of money and how it is measured;
- the role of the financial sector in smoothing the payments mechanism;

- how the need for borrowing and lending arises;
- the role of the financial sector as a channel for funds around the economy;
- the risk, return and liquidity aspects of investment.

Money

What comes to mind when you see or hear the word 'money'? Notes or coins that you keep in your pocket, purse or wallet might be one of the first things you think of. But money can be much more than that. It might include your credit cards or cheque book, because you can use them to buy things too, or it could represent to you how much you get paid every month, in whatever form, because that is your real spending power.

Money is in fact a surprisingly difficult concept to tie down, and even the highest financial authorities in the world have had problems defining, measuring and, in some cases, trying to control it. How shall we define money?

> Money is a product used in an economy to express the value of other goods and services, to make payments for those other goods and services and to allow people to store wealth so that they can buy goods and services in future periods.

All developed societies use money, and even less developed ones tend to have products which serve at least some of the functions of money.

Money as a unit of account

Money acting as a 'unit of account' means the value of all other goods and services being expressed in terms of money in order to allow a comparison of their worth. This greatly assists the exchange of different goods and enables people to plan their expenditure more easily.

For instance, suppose bananas are selling for 60p each and apples for 30p. The valuation of both products in money enables us easily to conclude that bananas are worth twice as much as apples on an individual basis. Without money as a unit of account, in order to compare apples and bananas we might need to collect a great deal more information. We might need to find, for example, the precise numbers of apples and bananas recently exchanged for each other or even look at third products for which either bananas or apples had been traded.

Money as a medium of exchange

Money as a 'medium of exchange' allows goods and services to be traded for a money payment. The payment of money avoids the need for goods to be 'bartered', i.e. for one good or service to be traded directly for another.

To return to apples and bananas, imagine that we are in an economy with no money and I have more apples than I want and you have more bananas than you want. If we manage to find each other and I just happen to want your surplus bananas in exchange for my apples and vice versa, then we can trade satisfactorily. What, though, if you want my apples but I want oranges rather than bananas? In order for us to trade with each other, we need to find a third person who has surplus oranges and wants bananas. Then the trade can take place: you and I exchange apples for bananas and then I trade bananas for oranges. Needing to find someone who has just the goods that you want and wants to exchange them for just the goods that you have as a surplus is referred to as 'the double coincidence of wants'. Coincidences tend not to happen reliably and thus trade in the absence of money is likely to be restricted.

Now imagine the same opportunities for trade as described above, but this time imagine that there is a product, money, which everyone is prepared to receive in exchange for goods. In order to sell my surplus apples, all I have to do now is find someone who wants apples and is prepared to pay me money for them. Armed with my money, I can then look for someone with surplus oranges and pay him or her money for the goods I want. Overall, trade has been much simplified because surplus goods are being traded for an intermediary product – money.

Money as a store of value

The third main function of money is to allow people to store their wealth so that they do not have to spend all their income now and can instead save up and purchase extra goods in future. People could, if they wished, store wealth in the form of goods rather than money. Returning again to the example of fruit traders above, if I had surplus apples, I could save these to sell in future and then look to spend the proceeds from my apples in some time to come. Apples could be a problematic store of value, however. They could be costly to store and could deteriorate in quality if kept too long. Ideally we would want a product in which to store value that would maintain its worth and not be costly to maintain in the storage period. An efficient form of money should achieve this.

Desirable attributes of money

We have noted above what functions money needs to perform. A number of different products might be selected to fulfil the money role and the question arises of how we can tell which products will make good forms of money and which less so.

Activity 1

Taking into account the different functions of money as a unit of account, medium of exchange and store of value, suggest different characteristics that money should possess in order to carry out its role efficiently.

Thinking of money as a unit of account, we would want our money product to be denominated in a variety of amounts so that we could express the value of different products precisely. For example, it would be no good having a money product whose smallest denomination was, say, £10 if we wanted to express the value of a banana as 60p. The need for money to be denominated in small amounts is termed a need for 'divisibility'.

The function of money as a medium of exchange requires that people should be readily prepared to take money in exchange for goods. We would want one unit of money to be equally acceptable as compared to another unit of money; otherwise someone trading goods would need to spend time and effort studying the units of money carefully in order to determine their quality. We would also want units of money to be easily recognizable, again to save on research costs, and to be easy to carry around in view of their likely use to make future purchases. These are the qualities of money expressed formally as 'homogeneity', 'recognizability' and 'portability'. Homogeneity and recognizability in turn lead to a third desirable quality, and that is that money should be 'acceptable'. What this means is that a person taking money in exchange for goods and services should be confident that the money will then be accepted by someone else when he or she in turn offers it for goods and services at another place or time.

The qualities of money required to make it a suitable store of value have already been touched on above. Money needs to be cheap to maintain, and resistant to physical deterioration over time. We would also want it to retain its purchasing power for future periods. These attributes are together referred to as the 'durability' of a money asset.

Types of money

Various different types of product have been used as money in societies around the world. In some societies, animals, such as cows, are used as a store and measure of wealth. In others, shells, beads or even dried leaves have been used as a money product.

The most common forms of money in developed countries are coins, made of either precious or cheaper metal, and notes of a variety of denominations. Payments are also made using cheque books, which access current accounts at a bank, debit and credit cards. If we think of money just as a store of value rather than a medium of exchange, many more assets perform the function of money. Longer-term interest bearing bank deposits, referred to as 'sight' or 'time' deposits, are a store of value and we could even include market traded assets, such as shares or bonds.

Activity 2

How do notes and coins measure up to the qualities of money that we have noted as desirable in the preceding discussion? Do they have any shortcomings?

Notes and coins have been specifically designed to perform as money and should, therefore, exhibit its desirable characteristics to a high degree.

Considering UK money, notes and coins are denominated in small enough sums to be able fully to express the value of different assets. Different units of money are also sufficiently homogeneous for us not to concern ourselves about the quality of one unit as against another. Recognizability is generally also achieved, with thought being given to making the different denominations easily discernable (the shape of the 50p and 20p pieces being a case in point, designed to be recognizable even to people with impared vision). There is, however, increasingly a problem with forgery; high tech printing facilities make the copying of even the most intricate bank notes a possibility. With good forgeries about, users of money have to concern themselves with the authenticity of any cash offered to them, and this involves time and cost. Generally though, notes and coins are sufficiently homogeneous and recognizable to be wholly acceptable as a means of payment for goods and services. The only exception to this is when there are so many forged notes circulating in an area that some sellers of goods refuse to take any notes of the relevant denomination in exchange for their products. Portability can also be a problem, this time of coins, which are heavy and bulky.

As a store of value, notes and coins score less well than as a medium of exchange or unit of account. The assets are reasonably physically durable (as anyone will know who has put a bank note through a washing machine!). Cash kept for long periods tends, however, to erode in purchasing power because of inflation, which is the increase of the price of goods and services over time. It may also involve storage costs because it needs to be protected against theft.

Assets which perform all the functions of money are termed formally 'money assets'. Assets which perform some of the functions of money but not all of them are called 'near-money assets'. Bank time deposits are an example of the latter, in that they act as a store of value but cannot be used to make payments directly, since they have no cheque book facility attached to them.

Measuring money

We have thought above about what money is, but how can we measure the total amount of money in an economy? Perhaps before we get to this, however, we should ask a preliminary question, and that is: *why* should we want to measure money in the first place?

Authorities in a country seeking to control or at least influence an economy want to measure money because the amount of money is believed to have an effect on inflation. Inflation in turn is believed to have an influence on other economic variables, such as the growth of the economy and the amount of employment, and these are the key factors in terms of which most governments express their economic goals. These ideas are discussed in more detail in Chapter 3, but for our purposes here the important point to note is that measuring money gives authorities some indication of whether an economy is in a position where inflationary pressure is high or low. The authorities can then take action to try either to stimulate or cool down the economy to keep inflation at the rate desired. One possible course of action would be to take measures to try to change the amount of money in the economy directly. Other measures might be directed towards influencing the level of activity in the economy, but would not be targeted towards controlling the amount of money directly.

The amount of money in an economy is normally referred to as 'the money supply', and the financial authorities in most countries have a number of different measures for it. The principal measures used in the UK at present are shown in Table 1.1.

The different measures of money can be divided into two categories, 'narrow' and 'broad' definitions of money. Narrow measures of money seek to measure the immediate purchasing power in an economy, and include, in the UK, M0 and M2. The assets included in these definitions are all money assets and perform the full functions of money as set out above. The broad measures of money (M4 and M5) include near-money as well as money assets. The function of money as a store of value is being considered here, as well as its role as a medium of exchange.

Which measure of money is the most relevant for financial authorities? Remember that

Table 1.1   Some UK measures of money

M0	Notes and coins outside the Bank of England + the balances held by banks with the Bank of England
M2	Notes and coins + private sector bank and building society current account deposits and National Savings ordinary accounts of the non-bank private sector
M4	Notes and coins + private sector bank and building society deposits (current and time) and certificates of deposit[a]
M5	M4 + private sector holdings of other short term financial assets, such as Treasury bills[a]

[a]Certificates of deposit are, in essence, tradable short-term bank deposits. Treasury bills are also short-term financial assets. They are promises by the UK government to repay a given amount on a particular date in the future. Both these assets are discussed in more detail in Chapter 6.

the authorities' purpose in measuring money is to assess inflationary pressure in an economy. Will inflation be influenced more by people's immediate spending power, in which case the narrower definitions will be the most important, or will people spend according to their wider money wealth, in which case the broader definitions should be considered most closely? In many countries this puzzle has never been worked out. The relationship between inflation and money supply measures has tended to be unclear and unreliable; in these countries (the UK included) money supply is not used as a precise inflationary indicator or monetary tool, and instead is just one of a number of pieces of evidence showing how the economy is performing. In other countries, notably Germany, money supply has been measured and targeted successfully, and monetary policy is framed very much in terms of controlling the money supply.

The role of the financial sector

So far we have looked at money and the functions it needs to perform in a society, but this has not brought in the financial sector. What we are going to consider in this section is how the financial sector operates with the various forms of money in essence to make money work to its full potential.

The role of the financial sector can be broken down into two main elements. Parts of the sector operate to make the system for payments in the economy as smooth as possible. The financial sector is in this way assisting money to perform its function as a medium of exchange. We can call the institutions and procedures which work together in the payments process 'the monetary system'. Other parts of the financial sector are not concerned with smoothing the system for payment for goods and services with money. Instead, their role is to facilitate the function of money as a store of value. Institutions and markets operate to help people to shift their ability to spend money on goods and services between different periods. The part of the financial sector concerned with this transfer of funds over time is termed 'the financial system'. The two systems are illustrated in Figure 1.1, which shows illustrative exchanges of real and monetary assets between two 'units' in an economy; a 'unit' in an economy is any independent user of money, be that an individual or a company.

On the left-hand side of Figure 1.1, we see the operation of the monetary system element of the financial sector. Unit 1 sells goods and services to Unit 2; this exchange is a non-monetary one and the financial sector is not involved. However, the payment by Unit 2 for the goods and services is shown routeing through the financial sector. Unit 2 might be making payment using a bank cheque, and this involves a number of systems and institutions, as described below. On the right-hand side of Figure 1.1, we see the involvement of the financial system element of the financial sector. Unit 1 has a surplus of funds in the current period and lends it, via the financial sector, to Unit 2. In a future period, Unit 2 will return the funds, again through the financial sector, to Unit 1.

Figure 1.1 The monetary and financial systems

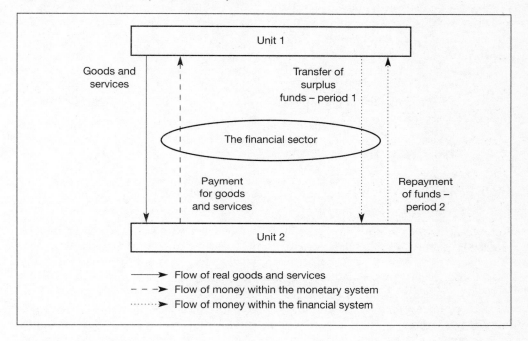

The monetary system

The financial institutions predominantly involved in the monetary system are the 'clearing' banks. These are the banks with which you will be familiar, with branch networks on most high streets. They assist with the payment mechanism by offering current accounts against which the account holder can write cheques or use a debit card in order to pay for goods. In the absence of such facilities, people would need to carry sufficient cash about with them in order to meet their requirements for purchases.

The use of a cheque book or debit card has some advantages over the use of cash. In Activity 2 above, you considered some of the shortcomings of cash, and these were some lack of portability, recognizability and durability. Payment facilities offered by banks overcome some of these difficulties. Portability is certainly not a problem, and there is less exposure to theft than in the case of cash. What cheque books and debit cards sometimes fall down on is divisibility and acceptability. Sellers of some products are unwilling to take such means of payment for small items because of the administration involved in authenticating and presenting the payment. In other cases sellers simply do not have the facilities to accept anything other than cash.

Banks involved in the monetary system are called clearing banks because they participate in a procedure for administering payments called 'the clearing system'. The clearing banks in the UK all hold accounts with the central bank, The Bank of England. The way the clearing system works is that, after each day, when cheques will have been written by many customers with accounts at Bank X in favour of people with accounts at Bank Y and vice versa, a single adjustment is made through the accounts of Banks X and Y at the Bank of England. To take an example, suppose customers of HSBC write cheques totalling £20 million on one day in favour of customers with accounts at Barclays Bank. On the same day, Barclays customers write cheques totalling £18 million in favour of HSBC customers. Although the banks will need to make individual entries in their customers' accounts to reflect all the transactions made, the state of play between the two banks is reflected in a single transfer of £2 million from HSBC's account to Barclay's account at the Bank of England. The £2 million represents the net amount (£20 million – £18 million) paid by HSBC customers to Barclays customers.

The financial system

What this book is primarily concerned with is the function of the financial sector in enabling people in an economy to transfer funds over time. The parts of the sector concerned with the financial system are thus of most interest to us.

In any particular period, some people in an economy will wish to spend more on goods and services than the income earned in the period allows, and at the same time other people will have more income than they wish to spend and will therefore want to save the surplus for expenditure in future periods. This situation was represented in Figure 1.1, where Unit 1 had surplus funds in a period and provided these to Unit 2 to spend. Unit 2 then repaid the funds to Unit 1 in the following period. We can also consider the principle through a flow of funds diagram, which shows different units in the economy, this time grouped into economic sectors, and how their income and expenditure leads to surpluses or deficits in a period.

In Figure 1.2, the personal sector, which represents individuals in the economy, receives income in the form of wages, dividends and government transfers. Wages are paid to individuals by commercial and industrial firms in return for time supplied performing work. Dividends and other returns on financial investments are sums paid, also by companies, for capital invested in previous periods. The personal sector's other source of income, transfers, are benefits paid by the government to individuals in respect, for example, of the individuals being unemployed, aged or disabled. From these various sources of income, tax is deducted, and the net amount becomes 'the disposable income' of the sector, i.e. the income available to spend by households. Some of this money is spent on goods and services which are consumed in the current period. Another part of this income is spent on capital goods which last for more than one period, such as houses. A further part is taken by taxes on expenditure, Value Added Tax (VAT) in the UK. Anything left over is the 'financial surplus' of the personal sector, or if expenditure, including tax, were more than disposable income, the sector's financial deficit.

Figure 1.2   A flow of funds diagram

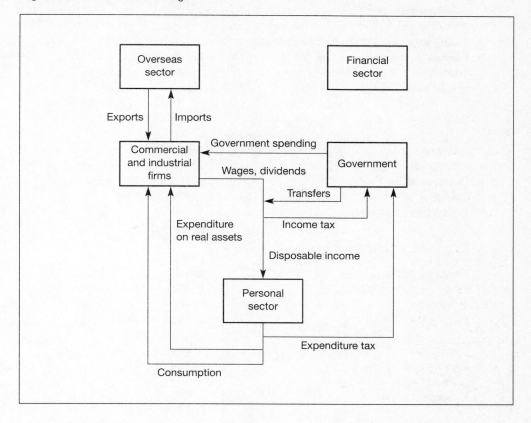

Activity 3

Calculate the financial surplus or deficit for each of the sectors shown in Figure 1.2,
assuming the following supporting data for the period represented:

	£ billion
Exports	20
Imports	23.4
Government spending	190.7
Wages and dividends	593
Transfers to individuals	179
Income tax	178
Expenditure tax	177
Expenditure on real assets by individuals	32
Consumption	364.8

The position of each sector on the basis of the data above and showing inflows to
the sector as positive numbers and outflows as negative numbers is:

Overseas sector	£ billion
Imports	23.4
Exports	−20
Surplus	3.4

Commercial and industrial firms	£ billion
Government spending	190.7
Consumption	364.8
Expenditure on real assets by individuals	32
Exports	20
Imports	−23.4
Wages and dividends	−593
Deficit	−8.9

Government	£ billion
Income tax	178
Expenditure tax	177
Transfers	−179
Government spending	−190.7
	−14.7

Personal sector	£ billion
Wages and dividends	593
Transfers	179
Income tax	−178
Disposable income	594
Expenditure on real assets	−32
Consumption	−364.8
Expenditure tax	−177
Surplus	20.2

The surpluses and deficits of different sectors calculated in Activity 3 are, in fact, the actual surpluses and deficits for different sectors in the economy in the UK in 1997 (*Economic Trends*, March 1999). The only exception to this is the overseas sector, which is reported as having a deficit of £7 billion. The surpluses and deficits then sum to zero, which is what we would logically expect, if we take into account the surplus made by firms in the financial sector (8.7 billion) and also a statistical error figure (£1.6 billion).

The statistics from 1997 in the UK show a fairly typical position for the sectors to find themselves in. Governments often run a funding deficit because they spend more on public services than they receive in taxation. Companies are often net borrowers too, as they typically raise money to invest in longer-term projects. The personal sector is often the 'banker' for the other two domestic sectors, with individuals, taken together, earning more than they consume currently or invest in 'real' fixed assets, such as housing.

So far the financial sector has stood in splendid isolation in our picture of the economy, apparently taking no part in the flow of funds around the economy. Where does the sector come in? This is shown in Figure 1.3, where the financial surpluses for different sectors in 1997 are shown being channelled through the financial sector to finance any financial deficits.

Figure 1.3   Flow of funds diagram representing UK data from 1997. Source: *Economic Trends*, March 1999, Table 2.10.

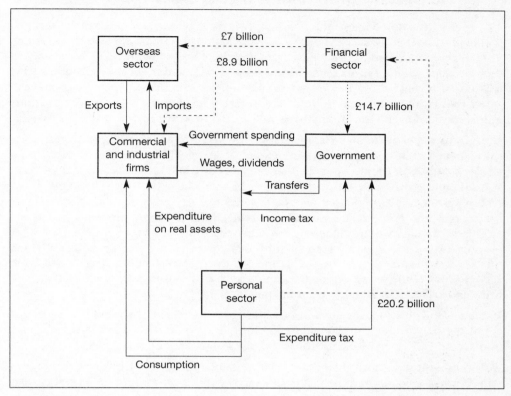

Why are financial surpluses routed through the financial sector rather than being supplied directly to sectors with a financial deficit? This is discussed in more detail in the next chapter, but is explained in essence by the financial sector making lending and borrowing more attractive to all involved by the services it offers.

Let us consider what in practice the role of the financial sector as a conduit for funds means. Suppose that you as an individual have a financial surplus for a period. This has arisen because your income, after income tax has been deducted, has been greater than you need to pay for things you want to buy to consume currently and the investments you want to make in other real assets. You could lend your financial surplus directly to, say, a company which needs the money in order to invest in a capital project. This would involve you contacting the company personally and coming to an individual agreement on the terms on which your money would be provided. What is more likely to happen is that you would invest your financial surplus through the financial sector. You would either put the money in a financial institution, such as a bank, or buy assets such as shares or bonds traded in a financial market. The institution or market would in turn use your money in order to provide funds to someone with a funding deficit. Either way, you would be using the financial sector to channel your money to an ultimate borrower, in this case the company which needs extra current funds.

The nature of financial investment

We have noted above that, for people in an economy with a financial surplus, the financial system is likely to have a role in channelling that surplus to deficit units in the economy. When people place their financial surplus with the financial sector, they are undertaking financial investment, and as we noted in the example above, this is likely to involve either buying financial products in a market or buying financial assets created by an institution. Individuals do not have to use their financial surplus in this way, however. One alternative would be to hoard any financial surplus as cash.

What induces people to make financial investments through the financial sector rather than holding cash? Our consideration earlier of the attributes of cash leads us to an answer to this. One of the principal drawbacks of cash, and its closest alternatives such as current accounts, is that its value tends to be eroded over time by inflation. For this reason cash is not a good store of value. In order to preserve purchasing power over time and thus improve the maintenance of value, financial surpluses need to be invested in assets which will produce a *return*. The return on an investment is the amount of money someone is paid for providing funds now which will be paid back at some time in the future. Return comes in many forms; it could be interest on a bank account, dividends on shares or the capital gain made from buying an asset at one price and selling it at a higher price at some time in the future.

While anyone investing surplus funds is likely to be crucially interested in return, this is not the only important characteristic of an investment. Two other factors to take into account when assessing any financial investment are *risk* and *liquidity*.

Risk is present in an investment whenever the outcome of the investment is not certain. For example, if you buy a share, you may expect, on average, to earn a certain return for investing your money in this way. You may build your expectation from data on how shares have performed in the past or from reports produced by experts predicting how the share price will move in the future. However, as prospective investors should always be warned in material advertising share investments, the performance of shares is in no way guaranteed. The share price may end up at quite a different point to that expected and the income paid on the share may also vary. Investing in a share is thus a risky venture, and in general people do not like taking on risk. People are still prepared to invest in risky assets, though. Why? The answer is something known as 'the risk–return trade-off'. In order to induce people with financial surpluses to invest in risky assets when there may be other less risky or riskless assets around, risky ventures have to offer a higher return to compensate. Thus company shares, which are some of the more risky financial assets available, have on average produced a higher return than other less risky assets, such as bank time deposits.

Risk comes in a variety of forms. 'Capital risk' is the chance that the amount you invest in a financial asset will be wholly or partly lost. The loss could arise because the person who borrows from you does not pay you back, which is called 'defaulting', or because the value of your investment falls in terms of the price it will fetch if sold on the open market. 'Income risk' is the chance that the income that you expect on your investment will not materialize, or will turn out to be less than at first thought. 'Inflation risk' is the chance that your overall return on investment will be eroded by inflation. The last gives an interesting and somewhat under-acknowledged view of risk. Many people would regard putting their money in a bank account as a virtually risk-free investment. There is virtually no capital or income risk because banks (at least the major clearing ones) are such substantial instititions that their not honouring deposit obligations is almost unthinkable. Anyone putting their money in a bank account does, however, run inflation risk. If the interest rate paid on the account is not sufficient to cover inflation, the purchasing power of the money saved will actually deteriorate and the person investing will be receiving a negative real return for saving. Other investments, such as shares, which have more capital and income risk, have proved in the past to have a better record of beating inflation.

The third principal attribute of a financial investment is its liquidity. The liquidity of an investment is determined by how quickly the investment can be turned into cash and with what capital certainty. The most liquid financial asset is cash itself and its closest substitutes, such as bank current accounts. If you want to withdraw money from a current account, you can get cash instantly and you receive exactly the amount in notes and coins that you held in the account. Other financial assets are less liquid. Shares of quoted companies, for instance, can be turned into cash in a matter of days by selling them through a stock market. The amount of capital that will be received for the shares is, however, uncertain because the value of shares changes from day to day and because costs will be incurred in the selling process. Shares are thus a less liquid asset than bank current accounts.

Investors normally prefer more liquid assets to less liquid ones, other things being equal. This is because, when you invest a financial surplus, thereby giving up current purchasing power, there is always a chance that you will find that you need the invested funds now after all. It will always be a good thing to have access to funds invested if there is no cost in doing so. In order to induce people with financial surpluses to invest for longer periods and give up some liquidity, an incentive in the form of extra return will tend to be offered on less liquid investments. You can see a practical example of this in most high street banks. Higher rates of interest will almost always be offered on deposits made for longer periods than on those for shorter periods or withdrawable on demand.

Summary

The financial sector has an influence on the lives of everyone in an economy, whether through direct activity as investors or borrowers, or through the sector's wider impact on the level of activity in the economy as a whole.

Money serves three main functions in an economy, acting as a unit of account, a medium of exchange and a store of value. In performing these functions, money enables the worth of different goods to be easily compared, promotes the trading of goods without the need for direct barter and permits surplus income to be saved in one period in order to be spent in another.

Different goods can be used to serve as money. In order to carry out the functions of money efficiently, money assets need to have a number of qualities, such as divisibility, acceptability and durability. The notes, coins, cheque books and debit cards used in most developed societies exhibit most of the desirable qualities of money, though they do have some shortfalls. Assets which fulfil all the functions of money are called money assets while those that fulfil only some of the functions are called near-money assets.

The financial authorities use different measures of the amount of money in an economy in order to monitor or try to influence the performance of the economy. Narrow money measures include money assets only, while the broader measures include near-money assets as well.

The financial sector can be divided into the monetary system, which smooths the payment mechanism in an economy, and the financial system, which facilitates the transfer of funds over time. The role of the financial sector in channelling funds from sectors in the economy with a funding surplus to those with a funding deficit can be represented on a flow of funds diagram. The typical situation in an economy like the UK is for the private sector to have a funding surplus and for this to be channelled through the financial sector to meet the funding deficits of the government and corporate sectors.

People with surplus funds in a period are induced to invest those funds in financial assets rather than just hoarding them as cash by the prospect of a financial return. Return is not the only element of an investment to be taken into account, however. The other important elements are risk, which is variability in the expected outcome of an investment, and liquidity, which is the speed and capital certainty with which the investment can be turned into cash.

Questions

Note: suggested solutions are provided for questions marked *

*1. Imagine you are spending an afternoon in your nearest town centre. You wander around a number of gift shops considering what to buy as a present for a friend. You have a limit of £10 in mind for the present and compare what you can get for this amount in different shops. You then buy some food at a supermarket; the prices are shown on the supermarket shelves and you use your bank debit card to pay for the items. Finally you drop into your bank at which you have a deposit account and pay in a birthday cheque.

Analyse the activities set out above in terms of the functions that money is being required to perform. Support your analysis with a full explanation of what each function entails.

*2. Different goods have been used in a number of cultures to perform the functions of money. Consider to what extent the following forms of money exhibit the desirable characteristics of money as discussed in the chapter:
   a) shells
   b) cattle
   c) gold, jewellery and precious stones
   d) cigarettes
   e) an 'IOU' (i.e. a note promising future payment) for a large sum of money, say £100,000.

3. Explain the difference between the monetary and financial systems within the financial sector.

*4. Consider the following financial data with respect to different sectors within an economy:

	£bn
Exports	30
Imports	25
Government spending	250
Wages and dividends	600
Transfers to individuals	150
Income tax	200
Expenditure tax	170
Expenditure on real assets by individuals	40
Consumption	450

Calculate the financial surplus or deficit of each sector in the economy and then represent your results on a flow of funds diagram. In your diagram, show financial surpluses being channelled to fund financial deficits via the financial sector.

5. Explain what is meant by the return, risk and liquidity of an investment. How would these investment attributes be exhibited if the investment made was in the shares of a quoted company?

2

An overview of financial products and markets

WE ESTABLISHED IN CHAPTER 1 that the principal role of the financial system in an economy is to channel funds from units in the economy with a funding surplus to those with a funding deficit. How, though, is this financial system constituted? How, precisely, does its existence ease the transfer of funds within an economy? And what makes the financial sector in one economy more efficient than that in another economy? These are the questions that we are going to answer in this chapter, where we take a closer look at the structure and function of a financial system as a whole. Then, in subsequent chapters, we will look at individual parts of the financial system and at their particular roles within the whole.

Learning objectives

This chapter considers the make-up of the financial sector and its overall function in easing the transfer of funds between saving and investing units in the economy. The focus is then principally on markets and products rather than institutions, with a consideration of their general characteristics and role within the financial system. Particular points to note are:

- the structure of the financial system in terms of a number of financial markets and institutions;
- how the financial sector eases the transfer of funds by providing a brokerage and transformation service;
- the function of financial markets in fund raising and secondary trading;
- the main types of financial product and their use within the financial system.

The structure of the financial sector

In Figures 1.2 and 1.3, 'the financial sector' was represented as a separate part of the economic system, channelling funds between different sectors in the economy, such as the private sector, or households, and the company sector. What exactly does this financial sector consist of? The financial sector is a collection of institutions and markets, the prime purpose of which is to perform this channelling of money around the economy.

Financial institutions

Let us consider the institutions that form part of the financial sector first. We can divide these bodies, which are collectively referred to as 'the financial institutions', into two broad categories. Some financial institutions are first and foremost involved in direct lending and borrowing of funds, and this is their financial function. Examples of such institutions are the banks and building societies in the UK.[1] These institutions also provide monetary, as opposed to financial, services, in enabling payments for goods to be made with cheques and credit cards.

The other category of financial institutions is the 'investing institutions'. These institutions channel funds to deficit units in the economy by acquiring 'financial securities' which the deficit units issue; these securities are among the financial products discussed further towards the end of this chapter, and include shares issued by companies. Examples of investing institutions are pension funds, insurance companies and unit and investments trusts.[2]

Some investing institutions have as their primary role the provision of a service other than the channelling of funds within an economy. The main role of a pension fund, for example, is to provide pensions for its members once they reach retirement age or are unable to work for other reasons. As a spin-off from their pension providing role, however, the pension funds have huge sums of money to invest, because pension contributions are made throughout a working person's life and the pension payouts are only required at a later date on retirement. Insurance companies, similarly, have as their primary role the transfer of risk, be that of death or illness or of some unexpected damage to an asset. The insurance companies incidentally, however, find themselves with funds to invest because of the timing difference between receiving insurance premia and paying out on any insured event. In the case of other investing institutions, however, their sole purpose is to ease the transfer of funds within the economy. Unit and investment trusts are institutions which attract money from individuals and then invest it in larger amounts in securities issued by companies or public bodies requiring funds. Collecting funds together and investing them as a larger amount in this way has attractions for both borrowers and lenders, as we shall discover further below.

It should be noted that although we have split the institutions into broad categories of lending and investing institutions, there are increasingly overlaps between the two. Banks, for instance, have traditionally been involved in taking deposits from people wishing to save, and then lending to people wishing to borrow. In the past thirty or so years in the UK, however, banks have also actively traded financial securities; many also have insurance and investment product businesses within them which make it increasingly difficult to distinguish between them and investment institutions. In Germany and many Far Eastern countries, banks have traditionally lent to companies but also bought shares in them as long-term investments, so here the distinction is even more blurred.

Financial markets

As well as a number of financial institutions, the financial sector also consists of several financial markets. What exactly do we mean by the word 'markets'? A layman thinking of a market might conjure up a picture of a street market with stall-holders offering different products and customers wandering around the market and considering what to buy. This would be an example of a 'physical' market, in that it would be a place you would actually have to go to in order to buy or sell products. Some financial markets are like a street market; they have physical locations and trade is carried on within set working hours. Nowadays, however, these markets are more the exception than the rule. Most financial markets do not have any physical location and many operate internationally and around the clock. If a financial market has no tangible presence, what then is it? In its widest sense, a financial market could be defined as consisting of any exchanges of funds in the process of channelling money from economic units with a financial surplus to those with a financial deficit. If an individual made a deposit with a bank, for example, the bank and the individual could be considered to be participating in 'the market for bank deposits'. In this text, however, we will consider a rather narrower definition of financial markets.

> A financial market is considered to be a forum for the exchange of
> financial products, represented in some cases by a physical location,
> but in others by a common information system sharing data on prices
> and volumes transacted, and where a number of professionals take an
> active part in the processes of the market.

The making of a bank deposit by an individual would not come within this definition because it is a private transaction between the bank and the financial institution; there is no common information system which would make the transaction known to other deposit takers and makers. The London Stock Exchange, which permits individuals and institutions to trade shares and other securities, would, however, be termed a market under this definition as, although it has no physical location, it does have a system for reporting security transactions and includes a number of professionals who are active as dealers within the market.

Financial markets exist in the UK and most capitalist economies for the trade of company shares and long- or short-term borrowing securities. These markets enable funds to be channelled from units in the economy with surplus funds to units with a funding deficit, by enabling bodies needing funds to sell financial products to those with funds available; the sale of financial products provides money for the issuing body and so performs a similar function to borrowing directly. Some financial markets are not primarily involved in the raising of funds, however. The market for foreign currency permits one currency to be exchanged for another and may be wholly unconnected with the channelling of funds around an economy. Many countries also have markets in 'derivative products', which are financial assets such as 'futures' and 'options', which again are not primarily to do with fund raising but are instead concerned with the management of risk. The nature of all these products is discussed further below.

We have established, then, that the financial sector is made up of a number of financial institutions, some primarily involved in direct lending and borrowing and others in investing in financial products, and a number of financial markets, as narrowly defined above. How do the institutions and markets mesh together to provide the channelling of funds that the sector, overall, provides? This is illustrated in Figure 2.1, which is a more detailed representation of the financial system, building on Figure 1.1.

In the case of the direct lending institutions, shown on the left-hand side within the

Figure 2.1   The channelling of funds in different ways via the financial sector

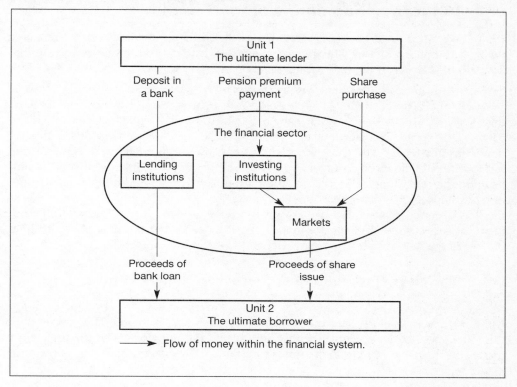

financial sector in Figure 2.1, these act outside markets, and by taking deposits from lenders and making loans to borrowers, achieve on their own the channelling of funds within the economy. In Figure 2.1, Unit 1, which has a financial surplus, is shown making a deposit in a bank, which is a typical direct lending institution. The bank uses the deposit to make a loan to Unit 2, which has a financial deficit and needs funds to finance it. The financial markets, then, stand alongside the direct lending institutions and provide an alternative means of transferring funds as required. The markets are not, however, totally separate from financial institutions, in that institutions are major participants within the markets. Investing institutions act only through financial markets. Direct lending institutions, such as banks, operate outside markets in some of their transactions, but as we have noted above, may also have sections of their business concerned with market trading. Figure 2.1 shows funds being channelled through markets in two alternative ways. In the centre, Unit 1 is shown using its financial surplus to make a payment into a pension fund. The pension fund, which is an investing institution, then uses the money to invest in financial markets; shares or other financial securities might be purchased. On the right-hand side, Unit 1 is shown using its surplus to invest in markets directly. Shares are bought through a market for shares. The shares issued, whether bought by an investing institution or by a person or company with savings directly, provide funds to Unit 2, and this finances its funding deficit.

Brokerage and financial intermediation

We have noted above that the role of the different elements of the financial sector is to come between ultimate borrowers and lenders and somehow to ease the flow of funds between them. What does the financial sector do to achieve this?

Some institutions and markets within the financial sector ease the funds transfer process simply by providing a brokerage service, bringing borrowers and lenders together who otherwise might not have been aware of each other's existence. Other parts of the financial sector, however, help to channel funds between different economic groups by actually changing the nature of the funds exchanged. Without the interposition of financial institutions and markets between ultimate borrowers and lenders, the requirements of each of these groups of economic units in exchanging funds would tend to be opposed in a number of respects. The financial sector eases the flow of funds between the two groups by creating financial products and offering financial services which reconcile these opposing needs. This process of reconciling the needs of savers and borrowers is termed 'financial intermediation'.

The divergent requirements of savers and borrowers

In what ways do the needs of ultimate savers and borrowers tend to differ without the benefit of the services offered by the financial sector? Differences tend to arise in respect of the size of the funds transferred, the time for which the transfer is made and the risk attaching to the funds transferred. We will consider each of these in turn.

Size or volume

Savings are typically made in small individual amounts. This is particularly true of savings produced by the personal sector, which, as we noted in Chapter 1, is the economic sector which most often has an overall funds surplus within an economy. Borrowing, on the other hand, tends to be undertaken less frequently but in larger amounts. This applies to much borrowing undertaken by individuals but is particularly relevant to corporate and government borrowing. The difference in the size characteristics of typical savings and borrowings would cause considerable difficulty in an economy without a financial sector. A borrower would need to negotiate tranfers of funds with several different savers in order to amass the volume of money needed to undertake a particular investment.

Time or maturity

Savers prefer, other things being equal, to preserve the liquidity of their investment, as discussed in Chapter 1. What this means in practice is that savers prefer to lend money for short periods of time, so that if an unexpected need for money should arise, the need can be met by 'liquidating' the saving, or in other words turning it back into money. Borrowers generally need to have funds available for longer periods of time. This enables capital projects to start producing cash in time for repayment or gives a borrower an opportunity to build funds gradually to pay off a larger loan.

Risk

The concept of risk was also discussed in Chapter 1. Risk arises in the context of saving and borrowing whenever the amount that a saver will receive in return for transferring funds to a borrower is not certain.

Savers prefer to take on low risk when they lend surplus funds, particularly where funds are being accumulated for a known event, e.g. retirement. Funds borrowed are normally used to acquire assets which unavoidably have risk attaching to them, and this in turn introduces some uncertainty into the amount that a borrower will pay back to a lender.

Although in the aspects outlined above the wants of savers and borrowers differ, both groups have one requirement of the funds transfer process in common. It is in all parties' interests if funds can be exchanged by the different groups with the least administrative costs incurred. These administrative costs might come in the form of search costs, in respect of finding units with the opposite funding requirements from yourself, and legal costs, in respect of drawing up documents to evidence a transfer of funds having taken place.

There is of course one final aspect of funds transfer in which the requirements of lenders and borrowers are diametrically opposed. Assuming that for most people involved in an economy more money is always better than less, someone lending funds will wish to have the highest possible return on the funds transferred. A borrower, on the other hand, will want to obtain funds at the lowest possible cost, just as with any other good acquired. As the return on funds to one party is the cost of funds to the other, borrowers and lenders have opposite requirements as far as return on the funds transfer is concerned.

Activity 1

Consider your current and likely future personal requirements as a saver and borrower. How do your savings arise, in what form are they held and what is their ultimate purpose? Overall, how do your saving requirements measure up in terms of the normal size, maturity and risk profile attributed to savings above? Why have you needed/might you need to borrow? What can you say about your borrowings in terms of size, maturity and risk?

SIZE

Most individuals make regular savings at some time in their lives, by putting money into a bank or building society, having deductions made from their income from work for a pension or making premium payments for different types of insurance. More wealthy individuals might make savings in quite sizeable 'chunks', but on average the amounts saved are small because most of a person's income is consumed by day-to-day expenditure, leaving only small amounts available for saving.

Borrowing may come in the form of an overdraft just to meet short-term shortages of income; this borrowing might be relatively small and thus be similar in proportion to saving. Some individual borrowing is likely to be much more bulky, however, e.g. a loan to buy a car or a mortgage on a house.

Maturity

Considering the maturity of saving versus borrowing, some savings, e.g. for pensions or life assurance, are actually made with a very long time horizon. Other savings will need to be easily realized if their purpose is to help with a 'rainy day', i.e. to fund someone if unexpectedly difficult circumstances arise. Thus the maturity of personal savings might be said to depend on their ultimate purpose. Borrowings of larger amounts for a car or house purchase will probably have to be relatively long term to give an individual time to pay them off.

Risk

Considering risk and your savings, you will probably not seek to take on risk for its own sake in respect of most of your savings. You may be prepared to take a big risk with a small amount of your wealth which you feel you can afford to lose. An example of this sort of attitude is shown when people are prepared to bet relatively small sums on lotteries. The risk of this 'saving' is huge and even the possibly massive pay-outs should not, in theory, counterbalance this risk. People seem, however, to be prepared to take part in such enterprises because the amount they can lose is insignificant to them. Most people would not have the same attitude to investment of their pension!

On the borrowing side, loans for a house mortgage are relatively low risk, because the assets you buy are security for the loans. However, there are undoubtedly still risks there, e.g. the reduction in asset prices which can come about in weak markets or on a forced sale if a borrower cannot keep up with loan repayments.

The process of intermediation

How does the financial sector reconcile the differing needs of savers and borrowers, thereby easing the funds transfer process? The reconciliation is achieved by funds being 'transformed' by the financial sector so that the needs of both the ultimate providers and users of funds are met.

Funds transformation is probably most easily considered in the context of financial institutions, and indeed many textbooks define financial intermediation only in connection with such bodies. However, as discussed below, financial markets achieve many of the same results for savers and borrowers, and can therefore be considered to offer financial intermediation in a wider sense as well.

What does the transformation of funds consist of? In terms of a financial institution acting as an intermediary, the institution will take in funds from savers, entering legal agreements with them that accommodate as far as possible their requirements for volume, maturity and risk. At the same time, the institution will use the funds so acquired to offer money to borrowers, entering legal agreements with the borrowers that satisfy their needs in respect of volume, maturity and risk. An example of this overall process might be a bank entering into an agreement to make a ten-year loan of £5 million available to a corporate borrower to be used to expand the borrower's business. This loan has come indirectly from many small deposits made by individuals with the bank, which are repayable on demand and which will not, in general terms, be considered significantly risky investments. The loan to the corporate borrower exhibits the normal characteristics of borrowing, in being relatively large in amount, long term in maturity and bringing with it some notable risk. The money provided by savers is, however, small in individual amount, highly liquid and carrying low risk. How has the bank achieved this transformation feat?

Volume transformation

Financial institutions transform volume for savers and borrowers by acting as a collection point for the relatively small amounts that tend to be saved and then aggregating these to provide a sizeable amount that can be lent. Some financial institutions are particularly well set up to manage small savings. The high street banks, for instance, are well known, have points of contact (their branches and, increasingly, telephone exchanges and Internet sites) which are easily accessible by the public and have standard agreements in place to govern the taking in of funds from savers. Compare this with the situation of a borrower trying to deal directly with many small savers. The savings in terms of search and legal costs will be considerable.

Maturity transformation

Some financial institutions, notably banks and building societies, achieve a transformation of maturity as well as size. As with the banking transactions outlined at the start of this section, the institutions take in savings from people which they commit to repay at short notice or even without notice, but in turn lend effectively the same money to other people for much longer terms. How can the institutions do this without putting themselves in an impossible position, where savers might demand their money back at any moment but borrowers could rely on legal agreements not to repay funds for a number of years?

Maturity transformation relies on a financial institution being large. Where there are large numbers of depositors, the managers of an institution can be reasonably certain that only a proportion of funds will be withdrawn on any one day. Although some depositors may want their money in cash, others will be depositing more funds as some counterbalance, and still others will simply leave their deposits unchanged. Having a reasonable number of borrowers will also help; whereas one borrower may take somewhat longer than expected to repay a loan, another may repay early. From experience, the institution will know how much money it needs to have available to meet depositors' requirements for withdrawals on any day, and this is likely to be considerably less than the total volume of deposits technically exchangeable for cash. Thus an institution with a large number of small depositors and a reasonable number of borrowers can transform both volume and maturity, providing savers with the small and liquid savings they require, and borrowers with the large and longer-term funds to suit their needs.

Risk transformation

The risk transformation that financial institutions can offer has two aspects.

First, in some instances, a financial institution places itself legally between the ultimate borrower and lender. In doing this the institution substitutes its own ability to repay the lender for that of the ultimate borrower. Take the example of a commercial bank. If you put your money on deposit with the bank and the bank then lends to a company, your only risk of not getting your money back is if the bank collapses. If the bank's loan to the company proves bad and it does not get repaid, your deposit is still good provided that any losses of the institution can be absorbed in its shareholders' funds and/or reserves.

The substitution of a financial institution's security as a borrower, referred to as the institution's 'covenant', for that of the ultimate user of funds does not happen with all financial intermediation. If, for instance, you have a personal pension, a financial institution may invest it on your behalf, but you may lose money if financial assets fall in price, because in this case the financial institution is not legally placing its covenant in place of that of the financial assets; in other words, it is not insuring the value of your investment.

The second transformation is diversification. This just means investing your wealth in a number of assets rather than putting it into a single or very few assets. The benefits of diversification are that you can get rid of some risks while not compromising return. The idea is that you get the benefits of an average result rather than all or nothing, and most people prefer that. To take an example, suppose you had £10,000 to invest and had no other financial assets to your name. Suppose too that you had the choice of lending the whole £10,000 to a single company, or alternatively lending £1,000 to each of ten companies. Spreading the investment over ten companies is likely to be preferable, because if one runs into financial difficulties and is unable to repay, at least this only affects 10 per cent of your total funds rather than 100 per cent. In a large group of financial assets, called a 'portfolio', problems experienced with a single asset will have little effect on the results of the whole.

Transaction costs make diversification for small-scale investors difficult and/or uneconomic. Thinking back to the example of diversification above, it would be impractical for an individual with a small saving to enter into ten loan agreements with different borrowers. The only people to benefit from that arrangement would be lawyers! It makes much more sense for the individual to make one deposit, with its associated standardized legal agreement, with a bank, and for the bank then to enter loan agreements covering much larger amounts with many borrowers.

Similar diversification opportunities exist for shares. Buying a single share will expose a saver to risks not only of shares in general doing well or badly, but also of the particular company invested in having its own specific problems, such as losing certain contracts or key members of staff. Investing in a wider range of shares should protect the saver from some of these risks. In a diversified share portfolio the company-specific problems which lead some shares to perform badly should be balanced by unexpected advantages being experienced by other companies. The return on such a portfolio should be less variable than on a single share as a result. In order to achieve diversification in shares and some other financial assets, individuals can invest in unit and investment trusts (called mutual funds in the USA), which then make large investments in a portfolio of shares on their part. The transactions costs of acquiring shares in large volume are significantly lower, as a proportion of funds invested, than when shares are acquired in small amounts.

Activity 2

What effect do you think, in theory, the presence of financial intermediation should have on the level of activity in an economy as a whole?

Efficient financial intermediation should have an effect on the cost of funds, i.e. on the interest rate charged on loans and the overall return required on shares through dividends and capital gains. If the requirements of savers for liquid, low-risk funds are met as far as possible, then savers will be satisfied to provide funds for a relatively small return. As a result of funds being available at a relatively low rate to borrowers and on terms suiting their requirements, i.e. for longer-term sums which can be invested in projects that might have high individual risks, corporate and government investment should be stimulated. Overall, the amount of activity in the economy should be higher than without intermediation.

So far we have considered only one part of the financial sector – financial institutions – performing the intermediation process. How do financial markets bring about the same sort of results as financial institutions?

Activity 3

Consider the UK market for shares, which consists largely of the London Stock Exchange, or, if you are unfamiliar with this exchange, consider the stock market you know best. To what extent does the existence of a formal stock exchange resolve the conflict of requirements of borrowers and lenders in terms of maturity, volume and risk?

VOLUME
The UK stock market is characterized by the typical differences between the needs of borrowers and lenders: the 'lenders' in many cases are individuals who want to put relatively small amounts of money into shares; 'borrowers', who are companies, tend to need to raise large amounts of money, e.g. for takeovers or business expansion. The market acts as a gathering point for the small amounts of money savers want to put into shares and thus enables companies to raise the large amounts they require.

MATURITY
Again, in the market for shares we see the divergent maturity needs of lenders and borrowers. Lenders want to be able to turn their investment into cash if needs be, while borrowers raising share capital usually need the money long term or even indefinitely. The market reconciles these differences by providing a forum where savers can sell shares to each other. Companies who raise share capital in the UK have no obligation to repay it – effectively they have the money they need indefinitely. However, a saver putting money into shares of major companies can realize his or her investment within a few days by selling shares to someone else. One notable difference, however, between this and putting money into, say, a bank, is that there is no certainty precisely how much money will be realized from the investment, as the value of shares is in no way guaranteed.

RISK
The share capital raised by companies in the stock market is used to fund risky

ventures. Does the market remove this risk for lenders? The answer is no, not in the way that the interposition of a bank removes the risk from depositors of loans going bad. People who put their money into shares are exposed to the risk that borrowing enterprises will not do well and that the value of their investment will fall. The market does, however, at least make diversification for savers reasonably easy to organize and cheap to carry out. Shares are denominated in small amounts and the costs of buying and selling shares are relatively low. It is thus possible for savers to spread their money over a number of securities reasonably cheaply and thus to get the benefits of diversification.

Thus markets and institutions are in many ways competitors in offering the benefits of intermediation to consumers. Over the past 10–20 years we have seen markets in many ways winning through in this competition, with an ever greater transfer of funds being channelled through markets rather than through direct lending by institutions. Some authors refer to this increased flow of funds through markets as 'disintermediation', because the traditional lending institutions have been considered the primary providers of intermediation in the past.

There are a number of possible reasons why funds are being increasingly channelled through markets rather than direct lending institutions:

1. Markets have developed in their ability to channel funds, particularly as a result of advances in information technology, and so offer increasing competition to traditional intermediaries.
2. Restrictions placed on financial institutions at some times in the past have encouraged borrowers and lenders to look for other ways to do business. Thus alternative channels for funds have grown up, circumventing the traditional intermediaries. An example of this in the UK was when, in the 1970s, restrictions were placed on bank lending for monetary policy reasons. To get round the restrictions, companies with surplus funds started lending directly to companies with a need for cash, and the inter-company money market was born. The market has continued operating even after the original banking restrictions have been removed.
3. As commercial companies get ever larger and more international through merger, some companies are now more secure as borrowers than even the largest banks. In such circumstances, it is pointless having a financial intermediary interposed between borrower and lender for risk reasons.

We should note that the increased flow of funds through markets is not all bad news for institutions like banks, because they have not stood still. As well as offering their traditional direct lending services, they have also become involved, as noted above, as participants in markets, so to the extent that they have lost out in one area of their business they have gained in another.

The role of financial markets

So far, we have considered both the financial institutions and the financial markets which comprise the financial sector. From here on, however, we are going to focus principally on the financial products used by the financial sector and on the financial markets in which a number of those products are traded. We are not going to study the role of the different institutions which participate in the markets or which lend directly in any detail. This is because such a study is a huge topic in its own right and because the focus of this text is principally on the use of the financial sector by ultimate savers and borrowers, rather than on the internal workings and structure of the sector itself. We will begin by considering a number of aspects common to all financial markets.

Primary and secondary markets

The activities of markets are often divided into two segments. The primary market is that part of the market through which new financial products are issued and thus, in the case of most financial markets, through which new funds for ultimate borrowers are raised. Considering the market for shares, for example, any new issue of shares by a company is a primary market activity. The secondary segment of a financial market is the forum through which holders of existing financial products can sell their assets. If an individual owning existing shares sells them on to someone else, this activity would entail using the secondary market for shares. Figure 2.2 illustrates the primary and secondary functions of financial markets, with an ultimate borrower issuing securities to an investor (Investor 1) through the primary market. Investor 1 then sells its financial assets to Investor 2 through the secondary market. When the time comes for the original borrower to pay back the funds originally raised, which is called 'redeeming' the securities, repayment is made to the then holder of the securities, i.e. to Investor 2.

Figure 2.2   Transactions via the primary and secondary segments of a financial market

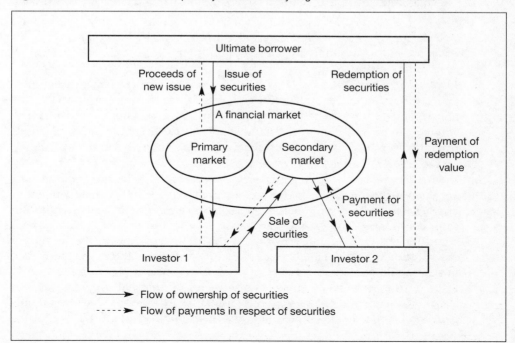

Normally the level of secondary market trading is much greater than the level of primary market activity. This is certainly true of the market for shares. In the UK, new issues of UK company shares in 1997 amounted to £11.8 billion. The turnover of existing shares was £1,012 billion (LSE Fact File, 1998). Not all financial products for which there is a primary market, however, have an associated secondary market. Some loans that are made on a large scale can be said to be issued through a financial market – for instance, the inter-bank money market in the UK. Such loans are not 'negotiable'; that is, they cannot be sold to someone else by the original provider of the loan. There is therefore no secondary market for inter-bank loans.

It should be noted that the division of market activities between primary and secondary segments is an analytical device rather than a physical separation. Often the same market professionals are involved in issues of new financial products and the exchange of existing ones. It is generally useful, however, to distinguish between primary and secondary activities in considering the importance to the overall economy of different markets.

Qualities required from financial markets

What qualities would characterize a 'good' financial market? We need to remember here that the main purpose of most financial markets, like all financial intermediaries, is to ease the transfer of funds from sectors in the economy with a financial surplus to those with a financial deficit. Markets need to be structured in such a way as to fulfil this function as efficiently as possible.

Primary markets

In order to encourage the issue of new products, primary markets need to have:

1. *Low costs of transactions.* Costs may be in the form of documenting a new issue, advertising it and then actually carrying it through. The lower the costs of an issue, the more both ultimate lenders and ultimate borrowers will be encouraged to use a primary market.
2. *Freely available information.* This helps borrowers and lenders to price new issues with confidence. One useful potential source of information to the primary market is the associated secondary market. For example, shares of a new company to be issued on a market for shares for the first time might be priced by comparing them with existing shares of similar companies already trading on the secondary market.
3. *A secondary market, if applicable, which is active and large in relation to the primary market.* An active secondary market will encourage ultimate lenders to buy new issues because potential subsequent sales of their new assets in the secondary market will provide them with liquidity. In order to give investors confidence in the liquidity provision of the secondary market, the secondary market should also be large in relation to the primary market. This difference in size should prevent new issues in the primary market affecting the level of prices in the secondary market. If new issues of financial products were so large as to depress secondary market prices, investors would have less confidence in being able to sell their new assets without loss in future.

It is important for an economy as a whole for a primary market, as well as encouraging issues of new financial products in general, to operate in such a way as to direct any financial surpluses that are available to the most productive enterprises. Channelling funds in this manner is one element of the efficiency of markets, which is discussed further below.

Secondary markets

In order to support primary markets and to provide efficient intermediation services generally, secondary markets need to:

1. *Be active.* As discussed above, an active secondary market provides liquidity to investors in the financial products traded in the market. This will encourage someone with surplus funds to acquire even the longest-term financial products, knowing that the investment can be realized at short notice should funds be required.

2. *Offer freely available information.* If information is freely available, and participants in the market are thus able to take a view on the importance of the information and to factor it into the prices of assets traded, market prices are more likely to be trusted by investors. For instance, in the London Stock Exchange, information on the prices at which shares are being traded is reported on daily in financial newspapers and by the second through the exchange's own electronic information service. In addition, news on company fortunes is reported on widely and is observed in minute detail by professionals working in the share market. An investor wishing to buy or sell a share therefore does not have to search hard to find the appropriate price of a share and may also be confident that other participants in the market are not trading with the benefit of far superior information to his or her own. Of course, there are also rules and regulations backing up the London Stock Exchange information network which are intended to reassure investors about the reliability of market prices. In particular, rules prohibit market participants from trading shares on the basis of 'inside information', i.e. on the basis of private information about a company obtained by someone particularly close to the company, such as an employee or professional adviser.

3. *Not be too volatile.* A financial market in which prices fluctuate wildly is likely to lead to a loss of investor confidence in the liquidity provided by the market. To an extent, price movements are only to be expected in a market with freely available information, because as new information is received by the market, prices should adjust rapidly to reflect it. However, a market where price changes are not only frequent but also large in percentage terms may be a disincentive to investors.

4. *Be low cost in terms of transactions.* As with primary markets, it is desirable if market participants can exchange financial products at relatively low cost. This assists the liquidity service provided by the market and should encourage market trade in response to information.

Efficiency of markets

The extent to which a particular financial market exhibits the advantageous characteristics of markets outlined above will determine that market's 'efficiency', i.e. how well the market does its job of acting as a broker and intermediary in the economy. Efficiency itself can be broken down into three elements: operational efficiency, pricing efficiency and allocational efficiency.

Operational efficiency is concerned with the costs of trading in a market. A market is said to be operationally efficient if the difference between what you can buy a financial product for and what you can sell it for, at the same time and net of all costs, is small.

Pricing efficiency is affected by the completeness of market information and the speed with which it is reflected in market prices. Different levels of market pricing efficiency have been defined according to the different types of information which may be considered to be incorporated into market prices at any time (Fama, 1970). For instance, a market is said to be 'weak form price efficient' if market prices reflect all historical information relevant to the particular security being traded. It would then be pointless for an investor to study past information about, say, a company in deciding whether or not to buy that company's shares if those shares were being traded in a stock exchange that was at least weak form price efficient. The reason it would be pointless is that the market price of the share would already reflect all the past information about the company and the investor would discover nothing the market did not already know by studying past records. To take pricing efficiency further, a market can be said to be 'semi-strong form efficient', which means that prices reflect not only historic information relevant to products traded but also current public information. Returning to the share example, there would be no benefit to an investor in studying company profit reports the moment they came out in order to decide whether or not to buy a share in a semi-strong form efficient market, because, by the time any buy or sell order was placed, market prices would already reflect the newly available public information. Finally, markets can be said to be 'strong form price efficient', which means that market prices reflect all information relevant to financial products traded, whether historic or current and whether generally available or known only to a limited number of people. Evidence has generally shown the main financial markets to be at least weak and probably semi-strong form price efficient, but not strong form efficient – hence the need for rules to prevent insider trading.

The final element of market efficiency, allocational efficiency, is about whether funds coming to the market are channelled to the most economically productive uses of those funds. For the good of the economy as a whole, we would want investors' funds in, say, the market for shares to be allocated to companies which had the most promising capital projects first, then to the next best company projects and so on. We would not want funds to be drawn to companies with poor projects which could not cover their costs and offer an appropriate return to investors. Allocating funds efficiently should then lead to the greatest possible growth being generated within the economy.

Activity 4

Is it likely that there will be a link between the different elements of efficiency of a market, and if so what will be the nature of that link? For instance, is an operationally efficient market more likely to be pricing efficient than an operationally inefficient market? How will pricing efficiency affect allocational efficiency?

The three elements of market efficiency, though separately defined, are linked. Operational efficiency should assist pricing efficiency, because low transactions costs will encourage market participants to trade market products in response to information in the hope of making a financial gain. All the trades in response to information should ensure that market prices adjust to reflect the new information.

Pricing efficiency should, in turn, encourage allocational efficiency. To take the example again of shares, a company with good capital projects should be able to sell its shares for a high price in a price efficient market, and should therefore be able to raise the funds needed to get the projects off the ground. The high price of the company shares will reflect the information about the projects available to the market; this obviously relies on good market communication by the company. The shares of a company with poor projects, on the other hand, should be lowly valued in a price efficient market, because the poor prospects of the projects should be reflected fully in the share price. It will thus be more difficult for the company to raise enough funds to be able to start the projects. In reality, markets for shares can let company managements know the wider view of projects they intend to undertake even when the managements are not actually seeking to raise new capital in order to fund those projects. Share prices in secondary markets will adjust to news about new projects being proposed, be they acquisitions of companies or new ventures undertaken internally. If a share price falls on the announcement of a new project, other things being equal, the management is being made aware that the stock market does not think that the project is a good idea.

Although price efficiency in markets will encourage allocational efficiency, it will not automatically bring it about. A market could be price efficient but still not allocate funds to the most profitable uses. For example, some investors may be subject to regulation or operate according to some bias, so that price information is not the sole determinant of where funds are invested. Pension funds in the UK tend to avoid investing in small companies because they prefer fewer, larger investments to manage and because they show a natural conservatism and have tended to view large company investments as easier to justify than smaller ones. Consequently, some studies (e.g. Dimson and Marsh, 1986) have shown that the shares of small companies are undervalued, and that small companies may not get the funds that their underlying profitability warrants.

Ways of trading in financial markets

Different participants in financial markets are going to use the markets for different purposes. The most obvious distinction in most financial markets is between ultimate users of funds, ultimate providers of funds and professionals involved in the market, smoothing the process of channelling funds between the two other parties.

Setting aside participants looking to raise funds in markets for the moment, providers of funds and market intermediaries may trade in the market following any one of three overall strategies: investment/speculation, hedging and arbitrage.

Someone investing in financial products may buy them with a view to holding them to earn income and/or to make a profit through the price of the assets increasing over time. With most financial assets, there is an element of risk inherent in undertaking investment, because the price of assets in future is uncertain and in some cases the income which will be produced is uncertain too. Speculation is in essence just another word for investment. It often has connotations in a financial context, though, of an investment being made for a quick gain and of significant risks being run in pursuit of that. Investment/speculation can be undertaken in any of the financial markets we examine in this book.

Financial products are not, however, always acquired because of the potential profits they can offer in isolation. In some instances financial assets are bought because of the way they fit together with other assets, both financial and commercial. A hedging transaction is an example of this. Hedging can be defined as the avoidance or reduction of risk by the acquisition of a financial asset, let's call it the 'hedging asset', such that the risk of the hedging asset is opposite to, and thus counteracts, the risks to which someone would otherwise be exposed through his or her normal business or financial arrangements. To take an example, imagine a company with some borrowing in US dollars which is due to be repaid in three months' time. The risk that the company is exposed to is that the US dollars will appreciate against its domestic currency and make the loan repayment more expensive. The hedging contract the company can enter into to get rid of this risk is to arrange now to buy US dollars in three months' time to satisfy the debt. A contract to buy foreign currency in future is a financial asset in its own right, called a 'currency forward contract' or 'currency future'. On its own, buying the currency future would be risky for the company, the risk being that the US dollar might depreciate against the company's currency over the three-month term of the future. However, taken in conjunction with the company's loan commitment, the risk on the two contracts cancels out, which is exactly the idea of constructing a hedge. Hedging can be undertaken by buying and selling financial assets in a number of markets, but is particularly relevant in currency and derivative markets.

Arbitrage is another trading strategy which is not much concerned with the profits an asset can offer in isolation. Arbitrage is trading undertaken to exploit price discrepancies between financial markets. Price discrepancies might arise between markets in different locations for the same financial assets or between markets for different financial assets but where there should logically be a connection between some asset prices. Logically, we would expect any discrepancies in financial market prices to be small and short-lived, bearing in mind the pricing efficiency which financial markets have been shown to exhibit, as discussed above.

The idea behind arbitrage is to buy assets in markets in which the assets are underpriced and then to resell them in markets in which the prices are higher. If the acquisition and resale are undertaken simultaneously, there should be little or no risk for the trader concerned. The arbitrage undertaken should then act as a force to eliminate price discrepancies. The financial market which was underpricing assets and in which arbitrageurs were buying products will have an upward pressure on prices because of demand to buy, whereas the market which was pricing assets higher and in which arbitrageurs were selling products will have a downward pressure on prices because of demand to sell. Overall, a pricing equilibrium should be restored between the markets concerned because of the arbitrage trading. Arbitrage, like investment/speculation, might be undertaken in any of the financial markets discussed in this text. It will be particularly relevant where the same financial assets are traded in more than one market around the world, e.g. currency and some shares and bonds. Arbitrage between markets for different products arises especially in connection with derivative products, where there is a logical connection between the value of these assets and other assets, such as shares, on which they are based. Derivatives are outlined more generally below.

Activity 5

The US$/£ exchange rate is US$1.70/£1 in New York but US$1.69/£1 in London. What arbitraging strategy would you undertake to make a profit out of the discrepancy between the two markets?

You would want to buy pounds for dollars in London and sell them back for dollars in New York. You would make a profit of a cent on every pound transacted in this way. An alternative transaction would be to buy dollars for pounds in New York and sell them back into pounds in London.

An overview of financial products

In Chapters 4 to 8 of this book we are going to study individually the main types of financial products which may be used by different sectors in an economy to balance their financial needs. Below is a brief overview of those products to give you a preliminary idea of what is available and of the main differences between alternative types of finance. The overview includes both financial products issued by institutions, such as banks, and financial products sold through markets. The latter products are often referred to as 'financial securities'. This means they are saleable financial products which are normally evidenced by some form of certificate or by an entry on a register of holders of the products.

Shares

Shares are the longest-term financial securities available, in that they are generally irredeemable, i.e. they are issued without a repayment date. An investor earns part of his or her return on shares through receiving a dividend from the issuing company. Although dividends are generally paid once or twice a year, companies have no legal obligation to pay dividends, and indeed, if they have cumulative losses, may be legally prevented from doing so. A share is thus quite a risky investment, in that dividends may be low or even non-existent if a company does badly; on the other hand, dividends can rise without limit if a company does particularly well.

Although an investor in shares cannot expect a repayment of his or her investment from the issuing company because most shares are irredeemable, shares can often be sold to other investors through a recognized stock exchange. In recent years, companies have also bought back their own shares on occasion. When an investor sells on shares, there is the possibility of a 'capital gain' or 'capital loss', these being the difference between the investor's selling price and his or her original buying price. The capital gain/loss is the other part of the investor's return on shares and, like dividends, is risky because it is not known in advance.

Another aspect of share capital is that in most cases it confers ownership of the enterprise that issues the shares. Thus, if you buy a share in a company, you become part owner of the company and will often get the right to vote on the company's affairs through annual meetings.

Share capital and the stock markets through which it is traded are discussed in more detail in Chapter 4.

Medium- to long-term debt

This is borrowing which is originally arranged to last for more than a year. It can take several forms, from loans, hire purchase or lease finance arranged through an institution, such as a bank, to bonds, which are market traded debt securities. In all cases a stream of payments to be made by the borrower will be agreed upon in advance, and these will incorporate repayment of the original amount lent plus some return to the lender. As the payments by the borrower are agreed in advance and as the lender can sue for these payments should they not be made, lending to supply funds to someone is generally less risky than providing the finance as share capital in the way described above.

You will probably be familiar with loans. They come in a variety of forms, but normally involve the payment of interest on the outstanding debt and the repayment of the amount lent, called 'the capital' or 'the principal', either in a lump sum at the end of the loan period or in instalments over the life of the loan.

Lease and hire purchase finance are types of funding normally reserved for financing equipment. The borrower pays a series of rentals which repay the amount lent to acquire the equipment and provide a return to the lender.

Bonds are long-term borrowing securities. They are effectively pieces of paper certifying that a long-term loan has been made and setting out the main terms of the loan, such as the rate of interest and the timing and amount of loan repayment. The difference between, say, a long-term bank loan and a bond is that the bond is tradable, whereas the bank loan is not. Thus an investor who buys a bond on issue from a company can sell the bond on to another investor before the bond comes up for repayment. As with shares, the value of the bond on early sale is uncertain and so the investor may make a capital gain or a capital loss.

Medium- to long-term debt capital and the markets in which debt securities can be traded are discussed in more detail in Chapter 5.

Short-term debt

This debt includes institutional funding in the form of overdrafts and short-term loans (less than a year) and also market based short-term debt, which is in the form of inter-bank loans, bills, corporate paper and certificates of deposit.

Overdafts are loans, normally from banks, which are technically repayable on demand. In practice, many overdraft facilities are continually renewed, and so this form of finance takes on the character of rather longer-term debt. Loans are also available from institutions for a defined term of less than a year. As with longer-term loans, short-term loans will have provisions agreed in advance for the amount of interest to be paid and the date for the loan principal to be repaid.

Some short-term debt products are provided through markets rather than financial institutions. The markets are 'wholesale' rather than 'retail'; that is, they are aimed at larger borrowers and lenders, with amounts transacted normally being in large amounts, in excess of £0.5 million in the UK. Some products issued through markets are tradable. Examples of these are bills; these are rather like IOUs, in that they are pieces of paper, which can be sold, promising a repayment from a borrower of a certain amount on a certain date. Other market products are not saleable, such as bank deposits arranged between banks.

The markets in which short-term borrowing securities are traded are called 'money markets'. This is rather a misleading term, in that the uninitiated might think that it was a description similar to 'financial markets', i.e. covering all markets for funds. Money markets do strictly refer to short-term borrowing, however, and we will look at them and short-term debt products in general in Chapter 6.

Derivatives

'Derivatives' are financial assets which can be traded in their own right but whose value depends on the current or future value of another financial asset, such as a share or bond. Derivatives can thus be said to derive their value from other financial assets, and hence their name. Derivatives include options, futures, forward contracts and swaps.

Derivatives do not, in most cases, raise money for borrowers; their purpose instead is to enable investors to adjust their risk. To give an example, let us consider one type of derivative, an option. A share option might give an investor a right to sell a particular share in the secondary share market at a set price on a set future date. The option may be created and sold by an options trader in the options market; it is not created and sold by the company to whose share it relates and does not raise money for that company for, say, capital projects. The purpose of the option may be to protect the purchasing investor from risk. In the example above, an investor who held a share in a company might also want to buy an option to sell it in future for a particular price to protect himself or herself from the possibility of the share price falling. This is in fact an example of a hedge, as discussed above.

Derivatives are thus rather different in their function from shares and debt products, both of which on their issue raise funds for the issuer and thus solve the problem of a funding deficit, as discussed in Chapter 1. The risk management function of derivatives, their other uses and the markets in which they are traded are studied in detail in Chapter 7.

Currencies

Currencies and currency markets are again not about fund raising. A currency is simply the denomination of money used in a geographical area. Markets which trade foreign currency, normally referred to as 'foreign exchange' or 'forex' markets, are, however, treated as financial markets both in finance textbooks and by individuals and institutions managing their affairs in the real world.

The role of the forex markets is to facilitate the exchange of one currency for another, whether the exchange be made in connection with commercial transactions, other financial transactions, such as the raising of a loan, or speculation on how the values of one currency may change against others in future.

Foreign exchange markets and related issues are discussed in Chapter 8.

Activity 6

Refer back to Chapter 1, where different sectors of the economy were identified and discussed. Note for each sector which of the financial products outlined above might be used to finance expenditure deficits.

THE PERSONAL SECTOR

In Activity 1 of this chapter, you thought about your different requirements for funds and the forms your funding might take. Which products have been relevant to you?

The first thing to note is that financial securities, i.e. saleable financial products traded through financial markets, are almost wholly irrelevant as a source of funds to individuals. Individuals cannot issue shares because they cannot sell off ownership of themselves. Any funding they undertake must therefore be in the form of borrowing. Borrowing that individuals undertake is invariably in the form of arrangements with financial institutions rather than securities issued through markets. Thus, if an individual wanted to borrow short term, he or she might get an overdraft from a bank. For longer-term borrowing to buy, say, a car, the individual could arrange hire purchase or leasing, also from a bank, and for longer-term borrowing still, he or she could get a 15–25-year mortgage from a bank or building society.

Why don't individuals borrow by issuing securities in a market? The costs would be too high in terms of advertising the credit worthiness of the individual, administering the issue etc. If we think about it further, it thus only makes sense to use markets rather than institutions if you are a sizeable user of funds who can justify the market costs which will be incurred.

THE CORPORATE SECTOR

The corporate sector has probably the widest range of funding possibilities open to it. A company can issue shares to raise long-term capital, because in this case ownership of the entity can be sold off. As an alternative, a company can use debt markets to issue long-term bonds or raise short-term money by selling bills. Companies don't have to look just to markets, however, for their funds. Institutional lending is available through overdrafts, hire purchase, leasing and longer-term bank loans. For smaller companies, institutional lending might, however, be the only source of funding available; like individuals, these companies may not be able to justify the cost of selling their securities through markets.

THE GOVERNMENT SECTOR

Share funding is not available to governments because ownership of countries, like individuals, cannot be sold. Government funding is thus confined to borrowing. For longer-term borrowing, governments sell bonds, which in the UK are called 'gilt edged securities' or 'gilts', and for shorter-term funding, governments sell bills, which in the UK are called 'Treasury bills'. Governments tend to use markets exclusively for raising funds, rather than borrowing from financial institutions. This is to minimize the effect on the country's money supply of government funding. This is discussed in more detail in Chapter 3.

Summary

The financial sector consists of financial institutions and financial markets. Some financial institutions operate outside formal financial markets and lend funds directly to ultimate borrowers. Other institutions, the investing institutions, attract funds directly from ultimate savers but channel funds to ultimate borrowers via financial markets.

A financial market is a forum through which financial products can be exchanged. It will have an information system providing data on prices and volumes transacted and a number of professionals active in the processes of the market.

The financial sector eases the flow of funds between different sectors of the economy by providing brokerage and transformation services. Funds are transformed to meet the requirements of both savers and borrowers in terms of volume, maturity and risk. Financial institutions have traditionally been considered to be the main providers of transformation services, but markets also achieve similar results and so are in many senses in competition with financial institutions.

Financial markets can be divided into primary and secondary segments. The primary segment of a market is used for issuing new securities, which raise funds for ultimate borrowers. The secondary segment of the market allows the exchange of existing securities between investors.

There are three different aspects of market efficiency. Operational efficiency is concerned with the costs involved in operating in the market, pricing efficiency with how quickly and accurately information is reflected in market prices and allocational efficiency with how closely funds coming into the market are matched with profitable enterprises requiring funds. Operational and pricing efficiency should encourage allocational efficiency, which is important for the overall performance of an economy.

Three different strategies which could be followed when trading financial securities are investment/speculation, hedging and arbitrage. Investment/speculation is acquiring financial assets with a view to making a profit through income or gains generated, and will almost always involve risk. Hedging is acquiring financial assets in order to reduce risk in an investor's overall financial or commercial holdings. Arbitrage is trading financial assets in order to exploit pricing discrepancies within or between markets. Hedging and arbitrage are low risk or risk-reducing activities.

The principal financial products to be considered are shares, medium- to long-term debt, short-term debt, derivatives and currencies. The first three categories raise funds for ultimate borrowers on their issue. Derivatives are products which enable people to adjust risk, although they can be used for investment in a way similar to assets such as shares and debt. Foreign exchange markets are also not primarily concerned with fund raising, but instead enable one currency to be exchanged for another. The financial products which can be used by the personal and government sectors for raising money are various types of short- and longer-term debt. The corporate sector also uses debt but has the option of issuing shares.

Notes

1. Building societies are called 'thrifts' in the USA.
2. Unit and investment trusts are called mutual funds in the USA and some other countries.

References

Fama, E. F. (1970) Efficient capital markets: a review of theory and empirical work. *Journal of Finance*, May.

Dimson, E. and Marsh, P. (1986) Event study methodologies and the size effect: the case of UK press recommendations. *Journal of Financial Economics*, 17.

Questions

Note: suggested solutions are provided for questions marked *

1. Explain the divergence that we typically see in the requirements of savers and borrowers. How do different types of financial institution bring about some reconciliation of these different needs?

*2. What is the overall function of a financial market? What characteristics do financial markets need to exhibit in order to carry out this function well?

3. Explain what is meant by the operational, pricing and allocational efficiency of a financial market.

*4. What type of financial transaction is being carried out, i.e. arbitrage, hedging or speculation/investment?:
    a) Alexandra buys French francs in New York, where they are quoted at French francs 6.25 per US$1, and sells them in Paris where the rate is Franch francs 6.15 per US$1.
    b) Bob buys shares in Microsoft because he thinks that the Internet is going to have an even greater impact on business than market prices reflect and because he believes that this company is going to be one of the best placed to exploit the phenomenon.
    c) Carol holds shares in a variety of UK companies. She buys a derivative product, the value of which goes up if share prices in general go down.

5. Douglas Brown plc has a forecast deficit of funds in the next financial period of £30m; the deficit arises because of planned capital expenditure which exceeds the internal funds the company is expected to generate. What are the alternative types of funding products that Douglas Brown could use to fill its funding gap?

3

The role of the financial authorities in financial markets

YOU CANNOT STUDY FINANCIAL PRODUCTS and markets properly without considering the role of a number of financial authorities. This is because the financial authorities have a huge influence on the financial sector as a whole, acting as major fund users or providers alongside other participants in the sector, but also having special roles as sector supervisors or bodies seeking to influence financial rates or volumes.

Before we go on to consider the role of financial authorities in more detail, we should first specify exactly what is meant by 'financial authorities'. The authorities consist of national or regional central banks (for example, the Bank of England in the UK, or the European Central Bank in that part of the European Union participating in the euro), and, where these are separate institutions, national bodies set up to supervise, or regulate, the operations of the financial sector (for example, the Financial Services Authority in the UK). Behind all these institutions are national or regional governments under whose auspices the institutions operate and to whom many of them are accountable. In some cases, indeed, governments act in part as financial authorities themselves, with governmental departments having direct responsibility for some of the aspects of the financial authorities' functions which we examine below. In the UK, the governmental department which has most influence on the financial sector is the Treasury, headed by the Chancellor of the Exchequer.

There are also a number of supranational bodies which have a role, through the systems they operate or the rules they impose, in domestic and international financial markets. Examples of these are the International Monetary Fund (IMF), which has responsibility particularly for exchange rate stability around the world, and the Bank for International Settlements (BIS), which is concerned with regulation of financial institutions, again on a worldwide basis.

In this chapter, we will consider the different ways in which financial authorities can influence financial products and markets, whether that be through the conduct of monetary policy, in the course of financial regulation or simply as large-scale fund users or providers. Domestic financial authorities will be considered first and supranational authorities at the end of the chapter.

Learning objectives

The purpose of the chapter is to make plain the impact of financial authorities on financial products and markets as far as other users of those markets and products are concerned. What is not intended is to provide a detailed analysis of the financial authorities themselves or a complete coverage of some of their activities, such as the rationale for and results of different forms of monetary policy. These matters cannot be studied in depth because they are complex subjects in their own right and as such are beyond the scope of this book.

Important points to get out of the chapter are:

- the overall purpose of monetary policy and the effects on financial markets and products of the conduct of such policy;
- the reasons for the financial sector being regulated and the results of regulation for end users and providers of funds;
- the objectives of different supranational financial authorities and their influence on domestic and international financial sectors.

An overview of the role of financial authorities

If we start by considering financial authorities in the widest context, i.e. including the financial arm of government, central banks and supervisory authorities, the influence of the authorities on the financial sector results from activity in four main areas:

- fund raising and investment;
- the conduct of economic policy;
- sector regulation;
- taxation.

Fund raising and investment

The financial authorities, and more particularly governments, are traditionally significant borrowers from the financial sector. This was evident from our examination of sector surpluses and deficits in Chapter 1, where we noted that the public and corporate sectors are often in the position of running funding deficits while the private sector acts as a provider of funds, having a financial surplus. Governments raise funds to meet their financial deficits by issuing debt products. In the UK, government debt products consist of long-term tradable debt products, called 'gilt edged securities', and short-term debt products, 'Treasury bills'. Governments do not raise share capital, because, as discussed in Chapter 2, selling shares involves selling part ownership of an organization and this is not appropriate for a government. Government fund raising is also concentrated on financial markets rather than institutions; institutional lending is not sought because it is likely that this would lead to inflation, as discussed in more detail below. Occasionally governments are in the position of running funding surpluses (for instance, in the UK in 1998 and 1999, as shown in Table 3.1). Surpluses are used to retire outstanding government debt issued in previous deficit periods.

The overall influence of government borrowing, if it is substantial, on the financial sector as a whole is likely to be to push up returns for savers and generally to make it

Table 3.1 UK public sector net cash requirement (£ million)[a]

Year	Requirement
1994	39,342
1995	35,446
1996	24,778
1997	11,773
1998	−6,654
1999 (quarter 1)	−12,339

Source: Financial Statistics, March 1999.

[a]Formerly the public sector borrowing requirement (PSBR).

more difficult for other parties to raise their funds. This phenomenon has been labelled the 'crowding out' effect of government borrowing. The difficulty experienced by companies at some times (the 1970s in the UK particularly) in borrowing funds long term has, for instance, been blamed on high government borrowing. Savers are likely, other things being equal, to prefer to lend to a government rather than to a company, because the former will probably be the more secure borrower. Companies competing against governments to attract funds therefore have to offer higher rates of return to overcome their less attractive security status.

The conduct of economic policy

Governments in most countries pursue economic policies in order to try to enhance their country's economic preformance. Particular goals they set out to achieve are growth in the amount of goods produced and consumed by the members of the economy, a high level of employment and economic stability.

There are two broad aspects of economic policy: fiscal policy, which has to do with managing the level of demand in an economy through adjusting the overall level of taxation and the amount of government expenditure; and monetary policy, which is concerned with controlling the monetary side of the economy and through this influencing inflation. Fiscal policy will have some impact on the financial sector through its effect on the financial surpluses and deficits of different economic sectors and through its influence on the level of economic activity overall. The conduct of monetary policy is likely to have a more direct effect, however, as the tools used to carry it out are within the sector itself. In order to try to control inflation and in turn influence positively the ultimate economic goals of growth and employment, monetary authorities seek to manage short-term interest rates or parts of the money supply created by financial institutions.

Regulation

Regulation concerns measures taken by financial authorities to protect participants in the financial markets and to maintain overall financial market or sector stability. Thus rules might be imposed on the amount of information that must be made available to customers before they are sold financial products. The purpose of this would be to ensure that the customer, who might be inexperienced in financial matters, is not sold an unsuitable financial product for lack of knowledge about the product and/or alternatives. At the same time, rules might also be in place regulating the amount of its assets that a bank could lend to a single client. The purpose of this would be to prevent the bank becoming too exposed to a single customer, which could threaten the bank's stability.

The regulation of the financial sector comprises a mixture of specific regulatory laws, codes of practice applicable to different parts of the financial sector, and often administered by the professionals active in that part of the sector themselves, and more informal supervision, where a regulatory authority maintains a regular contact with an institution and keeps up to date with developments in its business.

Taxation

The influence of fiscal policy, of which the overall level of taxation is part, has already been mentioned above. The way in which tax is raised and, perhaps more importantly, the nature of any tax incentives which might be included in the tax system can, however, have a significant additional impact on the financial sector.

The overall structure of tax in an economy – tax rates, the income or capital to which it is applied, etc. – is unlikely to be designed primarily with its impact on the financial sector in mind. Of far greater importance is likely to be its impact on the wider economy and political fortunes. Some tax measures are specifically aimed at the financial sector, however. Examples of these are incentives introduced to try to encourage individual share ownership, such as the Business Expansion and Enterprise Investment Schemes in the UK, both of which encouraged investment in small companies, and the more widely applicable Personal Equity Plans, which allowed individuals to invest in shares generally without suffering tax on their returns. Other tax incentives, while not being primarily aimed at bringing about a particular change in the nature of investment undertaken in the financial sector, have nevertheless had a huge sector impact. Tax relief allowed for investment in pension funds has resulted in a dramatic growth in such institutions, such that by the 1990s in the UK these were the largest group of institutional investors.

In the following two sections we will take a closer look at two of the aspects of financial authority influence on the financial sector, namely monetary policy and regulation. The funds raised by governments are discussed in more detail in subsequent chapters, which deal specifically with long- and short-term debt. The influence of taxation, while no doubt important, is not studied further because, as noted above, its impact on the financial sector is generally incidental to other government aims.

Monetary policy

The overall purpose of monetary policy is to exert some control over the monetary variables in an economy – interest rates and/or the money supply – in order to get closer to the ultimate goals of the economy, i.e. high growth and employment. Different theories of how best to do this have dominated economic thinking at different times, but the prevailing belief in most capitalist economies at present is that monetary policy ought to be directed towards controlling inflation, since low inflation is likely ultimately to produce high growth and employment. This correlation between low inflation and high growth is not undisputed, and in particular it can be questioned whether, once inflation is relatively low and stable, it is desirable to try to bring it lower still. There is, though, at least some consensus that high and escalating inflation is damaging to an economy's prospects (*The Economist*, 7 November 1992).

A diagrammatic representation of economic policy is represented in Figure 3.1, with particular emphasis being given to monetary policy. This diagram will be referred to further in the discussion below. It should be noted that Figure 3.1 gives a simplified picture of how economic policy works, with interrelationships between fiscal and monetary policy, for example, not being represented.

Figure 3.1   The influence of government on ultimate economic goals through fiscal and monetary policy

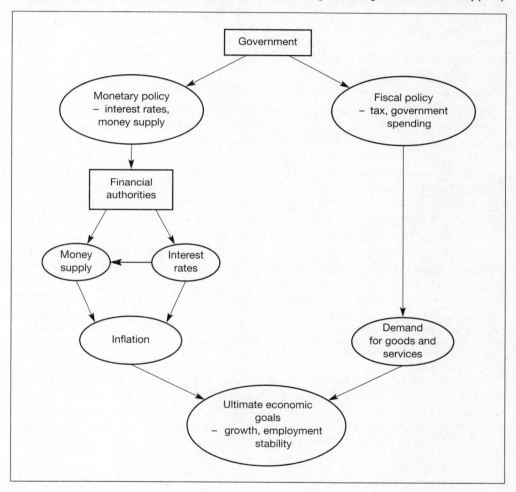

Accepting that the aim of monetary policy will be to control inflation, how will the monetary authorities seek to bring this about? There are broadly two ways that the authorities can try to influence inflation through monetary variables:

- by directly controlling parts of the money supply;
- by controlling interest rates.

These alternative approaches to controlling inflation are shown on the left-hand side of Figure 3.1.

Controlling parts of the money supply

The components of the money supply were discussed in Chapter 1. We noted that money in a modern economy includes not only notes and coin but also bank and other deposits which can be used to purchase items in the same way as cash.

If the money supply in an economy grows too fast, this is likely to lead to inflation, since there will be an excess of money being spent on a given amount of goods. One way of seeking to control inflation is thus to try to limit the growth of the money supply so that the amount of money available will be consistent with a stable price level. Certain elements of the money supply, such as the amount of cash, in the form of notes and coin, are wholly within the control of the financial authorities. Other elements, however, are decided upon by other institutions, and it is these elements which at times the authorities have sought at least to have an impact upon.

The part of the money supply that financial authorities have sought to control are deposits created by banks. How do these deposits arise as a part of the money supply separate from cash? We have in fact touched on their foundation in Chapter 2, where we considered maturity transformation by financial institutions, such as banks, noting that, at any time, banks need to keep only a relatively small amount of cash compared to the total deposits of customers. The institutions can afford to keep only a small amount of cash to back deposits because they are large in scale and because deposits made by some customers will offset withdrawals made by others. What we are going to consider in this section is the money supply implications of this.

Banks and the money supply

How do the managers of banks decide how much cash they need to support deposits? From experience, they will have a good idea how much cash will be demanded; in an emergency, if their estimates are wrong, they can seek short-term funds from other institutions or from the financial authorities in a way discussed further below.

To see how money is created by banks in carrying out maturity transformation, let us take the example of a country in which there is a single commercial bank. Let us assume too that the managers of the bank, taking into account past experience, want to keep 10 per cent of customers' deposits in cash. The bank initially has the desired cash ratio of 10 per cent and its balance sheet is as shown below:

Liabilities (£bn)		*Assets (£bn)*	
Deposits	100	Cash	10
		Loans	90
Total	100		100

Let us now assume that the central bank of this country creates a further £10 billion of bank notes which finds its way into the commercial bank by way of deposits by the bank's customers. For instance, the government might print an extra £10 billion of notes and use these to pay higher benefits to individuals. The individuals receiving this extra money deposit it in their bank accounts. The bank's balance sheet then looks like this:

Liabilities (£bn)		Assets (£bn)	
Deposits	110	Cash	20
		Loans	90
Total	110		110

Deposits have increased by £10 billion and so has the cash held by the bank, since this is the form in which new deposits were made. The bank now has more cash than it needs to support customers' deposits. It only needs £11 billion cash to support £110 billion deposits (i.e. 10 per cent), and so can lend out the surplus £9 billion cash in the form of extra loans to customers. The balance sheet then becomes:

Liabilities (£bn)		Assets (£bn)	
Deposits	110	Cash	11
		Loans	99
Total	110		110

However, the £9 billion lent out gets used to buy goods and services, and then gets deposited back into the bank. For example, say part of the money was used to buy goods from a shop. The shopkeeper would pay the cash into his or her account at the bank, thereby restoring the sum of cash in the bank. This leads to the following balance sheet:

Liabilities (£bn)		Assets (£bn)	
Deposits	119	Cash	20
		Loans	99
Total	119		119

The bank now needs £11.9 billion in cash to have a 10 per cent base for deposits and can lend out £8.1 billion. So the process goes on until loans and deposits reach the following position:

Liabilities (£bn)		Assets (£bn)	
Deposits	200	Cash	20
		Loans	180
Total	200		200

Cash is now the desired 10 per cent of deposits and credit creation stops.

The point of all this is to appreciate how much the money supply consists of money created by banks and how little it consists of cash. In the example above, £100 billion of money has been created from the relatively small original increase of £10 billion in cash. The factor by which the total money supply grows as compared to an initial increase in cash is called 'the money multiplier', and in the example above was 10 (£100 billion/£10 billion).

What the example above demonstrates is that financial authorities wishing to control money supply are likely only to have a significant impact if they can influence its major component – bank deposits. The example also shows how inflationary the creation of extra cash by a government can be. At some times in the past some governments have been tempted to finance expenditure by printing money; Germany was an example of this with reference to the First World War, and hyperinflation was the result. It also shows why governments normally raise money through markets rather than borrowing from institutions. Government borrowing from banks would be treated by banks as an asset similar to cash and could thus be used as a base to create further deposits, with a resultant much multiplied effect on total money supply.

Activity 1

Consider a bank wishing to hold 5 per cent of cash against deposits. Suppose the bank starts off with £1 billion of cash and £20 billion of deposits, but that there is then an injection of a further £0.5 billion of additional cash. Show the initial loans that will be made by the bank to adjust its cash holding and the amount of money created at the end of the adjustment process.

OPENING POSITION

	Liabilities (£bn)		Assets (£bn)
Deposits	20	Cash	1
		Loans	19
	___		___
Total	20		20

INJECTION OF CASH

	Liabilities (£bn)		Assets (£bn)
Deposits	20.5	Cash	1.5
		Loans	19
	___		___
Total	20.5		20.5

FIRST ROUND OF ADDITIONAL LOANS

	Liabilities (£bn)		Assets (£bn)
Deposits	20.5	Cash	$1.025 = 0.05 \times 20.5$
		Loans	19.475
	___		___
Total	20.5		20.5

FINAL EQUILIBRIUM POSITION

Liabilities (£bn)		Assets (£bn)	
Deposits	30	Cash	1.5
		Loans	28.5
Total	30		30

Thus £10bn of additional bank deposits have been created from the injection of £0.5bn of cash.

If the portion of the money supply created by institutions such as banks is so significant, how can the financial authorities seek to control it? Authorities in the past have tried to limit the creation of bank deposits directly either by imposing financial penalties on institutions creating deposits over a given level or by restricting the rates of interest that could be offered on deposits.

The Bank of England took such action through its Special Deposits and Supplementary Special Deposits Schemes, which were operated from 1960 and 1973 respectively. The Special Deposits Scheme allowed the Bank of England to call for commercial banks to make deposits with it over and above the deposits those banks held for normal operational purposes. The special deposits earned interest but deprived the banks of part of their cash reserve on which to create deposits for other customers. The Supplementary Special Deposits Scheme was a harsher regime, as this time deposits could be required by the Bank of England which carried no interest at all. The deposits were required if the deposits created by a bank grew by more than a stated percentage. Both schemes were intended to give the Bank of England some direct control on the volume of deposits created by commercial banks. In the USA, a similar direct control of credit creation was attempted through legislation known as Regulation Q. This operated in the 1950s and 1960s and placed a ceiling on interest rates which could be offered to attract depositors.

Such attempts directly to control monetary supply are not undertaken now, however. The attempts to restrict deposit growth on the most part were unsuccessful because other institutions which were not subject to the regulations tended to be set up to get round them. In addition, the focus of monetary policy shifted away from trying to define and control money supply directly. Controlling money supply was abandoned because money supply targets had proved to be too difficult to achieve and because their relationship with inflation and the level of activity in the economy was increasingly in doubt.

Controlling interest rates

The idea behind financial authorities seeking to control interest rates is that through this action they will influence the amount of money companies and individuals will have available and will wish to spend on goods and services and that this will thus have an impact on inflation.

Activity 2

Consider how an increase in interest rates can reduce the demand for goods and services in an economy. You might start by thinking how such an event influences your own spending, but then also go on to consider companies, both domestic and international.

If the financial authorities take action to raise interest rates, this can affect demand for goods and services in the following ways:

- People with current borrowing outstanding find themselves with less money to spend because of the higher cost of servicing their current debt.
- Individuals and companies will be less keen to take on new borrowing to finance expenditure because this now has a higher cost.
- The price of assets owned by individuals and companies might fall because of the interest rate rise, giving a lesser feeling of wealth and therefore discouraging high current expenditure. Examples of asset values which might be sensitive to interest rate increases are houses and shares.
- The value of the country's currency might increase *vis-à-vis* other currencies. The price of imported goods should decrease and the price of exports increase. This should have a downward pressure on domestic prices, since within the country there might be a switch of spending away from home produced goods towards imports as a result.

Individuals and companies in different countries are likely to have varying levels of sensitivity to interest rate changes. For example, with reference to the first point above, individuals in the UK are considered to be particularly sensitive to the reduced income effect of an increase in interest rates because there is a high level of home ownership, house prices are high relative to incomes and mortgages are traditionally arranged with variable interest rates. In other countries, the level of personal indebtedness is lower and more borrowing is on a fixed rate basis.

Controlling inflation through interest rate management is the prevailing theme of monetary policy in most developed countries at present. The policy can be oriented towards achieving a given inflation target directly or can be considered as a tool to bring about a particular money supply target, which will then have its associated impact on inflation.[1] In the UK, for example, there is a published inflation target (currently 2.5 per cent) but no money supply target. Interest rates are set specifically to ensure that the inflation target is met, with a wide variety of statistics used to inform the interest rate decision; the statistics include the growth of different measures of the money supply but also other factors, such as recent wage inflation and asset price levels. In Germany, where the success of financial authorities in meeting money supply targets in recent years has been greater than in the UK, money supply targets were still used up until monetary policy was taken over by the European Central Bank in 1999. Figure 3.1 illustrates the way interest rates can be used either as a tool to meet a money supply target (hence the arrow from interest rates towards money supply in the diagram) or as a direct means of targeting inflation.

Monetary policy conducted through interest rate management can be said to be achieving some success. In the latter part of the 1990s, inflation in the largest capitalist economies is at historic lows and growth is being maintained at relatively high levels for long periods. The curse of previous economic policies – economies experiencing booms followed by severe recessions – appears, for the moment, to be being avoided in many countries. A particularly notable success was the action taken in autumn 1998 by financial authorities around the world, but led by Alan Greenspan, Chairman of the Federal Reserve in the USA, to prevent a world economic slump in the wake of the Asian financial crisis. Interest rates were reduced at an unprecedentedly fast rate to boost economic confidence and to encourage spending. Certainly for the moment, this seems to have averted the most feared consquences of the Asian problems, and financial markets and economies as a whole have recovered and gone on to produce further growth in value.

The conduct of interest rate management

In trying to control inflation, financial authorities do not seek to control all interest rates in an economy. Instead, their activity is focused on only the shortest-term interest rates and only on borrowing undertaken by financial institutions. The idea is that the rates on this type of borrowing will then have a knock-on effect on borrowing undertaken by other parties and on borrowing arranged for longer periods. Through their action in a limited area, the authorities thus hope to influence demand and inflation in a much wider sense.

Financial authorities could try to control short-term interest rates in a number of ways, and these are illustrated in Figure 3.2.

Figure 3.2 Alternative methods used by financial authorities to control interest rates

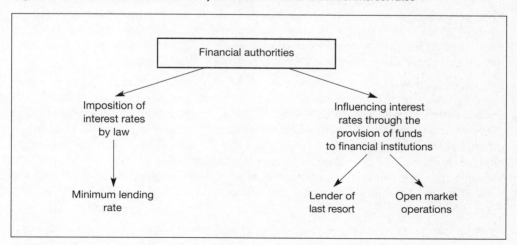

In many countries, legislation is in place which allows the authorities to impose a given short-term interest rate. In the UK, such a rate is called 'the minimum lending rate' and the authorities have used their power to impose it only once in recent years. This was in September 1992, when the government was trying to keep sterling in the European Exchange Rate Mechanism and was forced to raise interest rates more than once in a day in order to do so.

Another way financial authorities can bring about a particular short-term interest rate is by creating a need for short-term funds among financial institutions and then meeting this need by lending to the institutions at the rate of interest the authorities wish to see in place. How can the authorities create a cash need among institutions? Remember that, as we saw from examples above, institutions such as banks hold only a relatively small percentage of their assets as 'cash'. Many of their assets will be in the form of longer-term loans, but even their shorter-term assets will be invested to earn a return if possible rather than being held literally as notes and coin. Short-term assets that institutions will be particularly keen to hold will be government borrowing securities, because financial authorities in most countries will be prepared to lend against these or buy them back if institutions find they need actual cash. On any particular day, there will be a volume of short-term loans from the financial authorities to institutions maturing and needing to be replaced, and the authorities might also be issuing new government borrowing securities which the financial institutions will be required to purchase. There will thus in general be a need for a certain amount of finance to be provided by the financial authorities every day.

Financial authorities can provide funds to institutions which are short of cash either by making them a traditional-style loan or by buying back financial securities from them. If a financial authority lends directly to a financial institution it is said to be acting as 'lender of last resort'. More normally, financial authorities lend money to institutions by participating in the 'repo' market. This is described more fully in Chapter 6, but in principle involves the authority buying a financial security from the institution needing funds but with an associated agreement for the institution to buy the security back at some time in the future. The arrangement has the same consequences as a short-term loan, in that the institution obtains funds on the original sale of its security but then has to pay those funds back when it buys the security again some time later. In the UK, the Bank of England formerly provided funds to institutions by buying back government debt securities, particularly Treasury bills, but with no agreement then to sell them again later. In line with other European countries, the Bank now brings about interest rate changes predominantly through action in the gilt repo market.

When financial authorities undertake the buying and selling of securities in order to bring about an interest rate change, they are said to be performing 'open market operations'. You might ask, and with some justification, whether this process isn't somewhat convoluted and why they do not use the apparently simpler methods of imposing a minimum lending rate or acting as lender of last resort. The ultimate result of all methods is the same, but in the free market culture prevailing in the 1980s and 1990s, influencing interest rates through open market operations perhaps seems less heavy handed and interventionist than using other methods.

The final question we need to ask ourselves in respect of conducting monetary policy by way of interest rate management is how the authorities' action with regard to short-term and wholesale interest rates is intended to feed through to interest rates in the rest of the economy.

Let us think first about how institutional borrowing rates influence interest rates charged to other people. The institutions which end up borrowing from the financial authorities cannot afford to make a loss on lending money on to other people. If the rate at which they borrow from the authorities goes up, this is thus likely to have an upward pressure on the rates at which the institutions lend to their customers. Generally, the short-term rates at which the major high street banks offer loans tend, in the UK, to move directly in line with rates of interest charged by the financial authorities. Rates charged and offered by other institutions, such as building societies, tend to follow a slightly more independent course, but over the longer term again tend to follow official rates.

How do changes in short-term interest rates in turn affect longer-term interest rates? One factor in this is that many longer-term lending arrangements have interest rates set to be a certain percentage above short-term interest rates. Thus a five-year loan from a bank to a company might have the interest rate set as, say, 2 per cent above that bank's short-term base rate. Longer-term interest rates will also be influenced by short-term rates because savers and borrowers will have some flexibility over the term of debt they choose. If, for instance, short-term interest rates increased but longer-term rates remained unchanged, savers would be attracted towards the shorter-term end of the debt market and borrowers towards the longer-term end, other things being equal. The extra demand from borrowers for longer-term debt and the lesser supply of savings would tend to push up longer-term interest rates. Overall, medium- and longer-term interest rates tend to be influenced by, but not move directly with, shorter-term rates. The movement of longer-term rates with changes in short-term ones is not proportional because other factors come into play, such as any further changes in short-term interest rates that people expect in future. The relationship between long-term interest rates and expectations is discussed further in Chapter 5.

Regulation

The financial sector is, in many countries, the most highly regulated of all sectors in the economy. Why should this be? There are a number of reasons put forward for regulating the financial sector in terms of ensuring its stability and preventing consumers from being given bad value.

The purpose of regulation

From our consideration of the maturity transformation role of many financial institutions it should be evident that maintaining confidence in the banking system is vital. Institutions which keep only a small proportion of their assets in cash or near cash assets and lend the remainder out on a longer-term basis ('fractional reserve banking') rely wholly on all customers not wanting to withdraw their deposits at the same time. One aim of regulation is thus to ensure that institutions involved in deposit-taking are stable, secure bodies, so that the whole banking system retains the confidence of its customers.

The stability of the financial sector is important not only because of the particular way it is organized but also because of the sector's central role in the rest of the economy. We saw in Chapter 1, where we considered funds flow, that all sectors in the economy are likley to need to deal with the financial sector in order to make transactions and to save and invest over time. Any crisis in the financial sector would thus probably have a knock on effect on other sectors; probably no other sector in the economy would have quite such a wide effect if it ran into trouble.

What about the need to regulate the financial markets so as to protect customers from being sold inappropriate products? The need for regulation here is a less clear-cut case. It is argued that financial investments – for instance, pension purchases – are usually among the largest investments individuals make and that therefore protection from disasters is important to avoid personal misery. It is also argued that because financial assets are intangible, i.e. not physical, it is relatively difficult for non-experts to appraise their worth, and therefore more easy for professionals to get away with offering poor value for money.

Activity 3

Are there other sectors in an economy which would appear particularly to warrant a high level of regulation, and if there are, how does the actual regulation in place compare to that in the financial sector?

Two other sectors which might appear to warrant special regulation are the car and housing markets. Both cars and housing represent particularly significant investments in individuals' lives; both are quite difficult to assess in terms of quality if you are not an expert. One argument in favour of strict regulation of these markets which does not apply to the finance market is that both have safety implications – poor cars and housing could lead to personal injury as well as financial loss. A final argument for housing market regulation is that the market, certainly in the UK, does have a wider economic impact than most sectors, in that the wealth effect it produces when prices are rising can influence the general spending pattern of home owners.

The manufacturers of cars and the builders of houses are regulated, e.g. houses have to satisfy planning permission and building regulations before they can be supplied to new owners. Older cars also have to pass safety tests (MOT tests in the UK), but older houses, interestingly, are not supervised for their soundness at all. Unlike the position on financial products, there are no special rules protecting buyers of houses or cars from poor value buys.

Considering the wider economic impact of the housing market, government influence is exerted mostly through the tax system, with adjustments being made to tax subsidies on mortgage interest, for example, to try to influence demand; government does not seek directly to regulate the supply of new houses, for instance, to meet wider financial goals.

In summary, car and housing markets are probably regulated more than markets for other goods and services but not as much as the financial sector.

Although a case can certainly be made out for applying particular regulations to the financial sector, there are costs associated with doing so. Institutions and markets incur actual costs, 'compliance costs', in meeting regulations. The costs might be in the form of staff needing to be employed to ensure that institutions act in a way consistent with regulations. Often such costs end up being passed on to customers and thus a higher cost of financial services and products results. Other problems are that regulations can deter new businesses wishing to set up in the financial sector because of their complexity, and this limits competition and thus again tends to put up prices. A balance needs to be struck, therefore, between the advantages of regulation in promoting stability and preventing poor service to customers, and the disadvantages of it in generally putting up prices and discouraging competition.

Regulatory measures

As has been noted above, the principal aims of financial regulation are to ensure financial sector stability and to protect sector customers from being sold inappropriate or poor value products. There are different types of regulation which may be used to bring about these two goals, and these are illustrated in Figure 3.3.

Figure 3.3   The purpose and practice of financial regulation

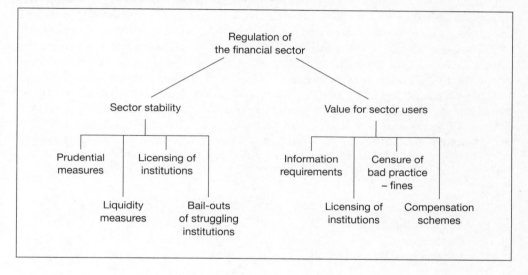

Measures to bring about sector stability

The main concern here is to ensure that financial institutions (and, to a lesser extent, markets) do not put themselves into a position of incurring such huge losses or running so short of liquid funds that they cannot carry on their business in an orderly manner. The risk if an institution, such as a bank, were to get itself into such a poor financial position would be not only that individuals and companies who had deposits with the institution would lose money but also that other financial institutions which had lent wholesale to the struggling bank might suffer losses too. The latter position could lead to other institutions getting into financial difficulties and that in turn could threaten the whole financial system. The risk of one institution's difficulties leading to problems in other institutions is termed 'systemic risk', and is particularly significant in a fractional reserve banking system.

Regulation to ensure financial sector stability consists of measures designed to prevent overwhelming losses being incurred ('prudential measures') and measures designed to ensure that institutions maintain sufficient liquid funds ('liquidity measures').

One of the most important prudential measures and one applying increasingly to financial businesses all over the world is the requirement for 'capital adequacy'. The idea is that financial institutions should have sufficient capital of their own, mainly in the form of their own shareholders' funds, such that any losses they incur on their lending or security dealing will be absorbed in their own capital rather than impinging on their ability to repay depositors or other customers. The more risky an institution's lending or market dealing, the more capital it is required to have to support it. In line with this thinking, different business activities are given different risk weights. Investing in government securities, for example, has been considered a lower risk business than lending to companies, and banks have needed to have less capital to support the former than the latter. Overall, banks are required under international regulations operated by the Bank for International Settlements (BIS) to have capital which is at least 8 per cent of their risk-adjusted assets.

Let us look at an example of how the BIS capital adequacy rules work in relation to a hypothetical bank. The rules as they currently stand categorize loans into three broad categories. Loans to Organization for Economic Development and Cooperation (OECD) governments – for example, in the form of government bonds – require no capital to be set against them, i.e. they have a zero risk weighting. Loans to banks centred in OECD countries are looked on as somewhat more risky and have a 20 per cent risk weighting, requiring a capital backing of 1.6 per cent (20 per cent of the capital asset ratio of 8 per cent). Loans to other borrowers, including all commercial firms, are given a 100 per cent risk weighting and thus require a full 8 per cent capital backing. Supposing that our hypothetical bank had holdings of £10 billion UK government debt, £10 billion UK interbank loans and £20 billion loans to commercial companies, capital would be required to back this calculated as follows:

	£bn	% risk weighting	capital required (£bn) *
UK government debt	10	0	0
Bank loans	10	20	0.16
Commercial loans	20	100	1.6
Total capital required			1.76

*Capital required = loans × risk weighting × 8 per cent

It should be noted that the BIS capital adequacy rules have represented a minimum standard with which banks in different countries have had to comply. Financial authorities in individual countries have in some cases imposed stricter requirements. The Bank of England, for instance, has required UK banks to have 10 per cent capital to support their lending rather than the BIS level of 8 per cent.

The BIS capital adequacy rules have been criticized for not reflecting accurately enough the real risk of different types of loans. For example, some OECD governments, South Korea could be one, may be relatively risky borrowers, while some commercial companies, such as Microsoft, might present no recognizable default risk at all. Proposals were announced in August 1999 to revise the regulations. It is suggested that the credit rating of different sovereign and commercial borrowers should be used to set the amount of capital needed to back loans. Credit ratings are provided by a number of agencies, as discussed further in Chapter 5.

Other prudential rules in place in some countries or in relation to some institutions limit the amount of its total assets that an institution can lend to one customer or invest in one market. These measures are designed to ensure that financial institutions are sufficiently diversified to withstand financial losses from the failure of particular customers or the drop in value of particular markets.

Liquidity, or solvency, measures regulate the amount of liquid funds institutions have to have available to ensure that any demands for withdrawal of funds by customers can be met. In the UK there are no hard and fast rules, as there are with capital adequacy, on the amount of liquid funds an institution must maintain. Instead, regulators agree with individual institutions what level of liquid assets is reasonable.

A further measure which is designed to support the stability of the financial sector is that in most countries there is a system of licensing institutions which wish to participate in different financial activities. Before a licence is granted the authorities will check that the people running the institution are suitably qualified and honest and that the institution is thus likely to be run on a reliable basis.

Should a financial institution, despite all the measures in place designed to bring about stability in the system, find itself in financial difficulties, the financial authorities will on occasion arrange a syndicate of other institutions to provide funds to the ailing body. This happened in America in 1998, when an investment institution, Long Term Capital Management (LTCM), found itself in financial difficulties as a result of the collapse of some asset prices during the Asian market crisis. The American central bank, the Federal Reserve, arranged a $3.5 billion injection of funds and LTCM was saved from collapse. The reasoning behind the bail-out appears to have been that market confidence at the time was so fragile that the collapse of such an institution could lead to general panic, and that could have had much more far reaching effects. In general, arrangements are only put in place to save institutions which have the widest sphere of influence; it would be unlikely, for instance, that a retail deposit-taking bank would ever be allowed to fail, because the knock-on effects on the wider economy would be too great. The collapse of Barings Bank in 1995 illustrates this principle. The Bank of England did not arrange a rescue of Barings, because the bank was too small to pose a serious systemic risk.

Most of the comments so far on regulation to ensure stability have related to institutions rather than markets. Markets as bodies themselves are unlikely to incur losses or to have liquidity problems, since their primary role is to bring different participants in a financial area together and to provide a system for them to trade with each other rather than using their own capital to participate in lending and borrowing directly. It is, however, important that a market has systems in place to ensure that its operation is not disrupted because of the financial problems of some of its participants. Many markets thus require certain levels of capital to be evidenced by anyone wishing to trade in the market. Other markets operate clearing houses so that participants are isolated from the financial risks of other participants. Such systems are operated in the derivatives markets, and Chapter 7 provides a more detailed discussion of them.

Measures to protect users of financial products

Measures taken to ensure financial sector stability, discussed above, are one form of protection for users of financial products, in that they should prevent, for example, institutions going bankrupt and investments thus being lost. Other measures are in place in many countries, however, aimed at protecting participants in the financial sector in their individual financial dealings rather than bolstering the sector itself.

The sorts of measures that are put in place in this context concern information made available to users of financial products, compensation schemes in case of financial losses being incurred and complaints systems, backed up by penalties, in case of rules being contravened. In the UK, under the Financial Services Act 1986 (FSA 1986), institutions selling financial products are required to make given levels of information available to customers and must also ensure that professional advisers find out enough about a customer's circumstances to give suitable advice. Table 3.2 gives a summary of the principles which firms in the financial services sector in the UK have to observe under the FSA 1986. Institutions contravening the rules are subject to fines and may have their licences to operate in the sector withdrawn in extreme cases.

Table 3.2   Some of the principles applied to firms in the financial services sector in the UK, under the FSA 1986, designed to protect customers of the financial sector

1. Integrity, skill, care and diligence	A firm should exhibit all these in the conduct of its business and in dealings with its customers.
2. Information	A firm should seek such information from its customers concerning their personal circumstances and investment objectives so as to be able to advise them or select suitable investments for them. A firm should also provide sufficient information to its customers in order for them to make balanced decisions about the advice or products offered.
3. Conflicts of interest	A firm should avoid conflicts of interest with its customers, but where these arise, should ensure that customers' interests are not prejudiced by declining to act or otherwise.
4. Customers' assets	Where a firm has control or is otherwise responsible for a customer's assets, these should be segregated from the firm's own assets and safeguarded in a proper manner.
5. Financial resources and internal organization	A firm should have sufficient financial resources to be able to conduct its business in an orderly manner and to be able to withstand risks to which its business is exposed. The firm should organize itself in a responsible way, keeping adequate records and training staff so as to be able to offer a reliable service to customers.

Source: The Financial Services Authority.

The division of responsibility between different financial authorities

How is it best to organize the different roles of financial authorities, and in particular the functions of fund raising for government, monetary policy and financial sector regulation? This has been a question very much at the forefront of financial sector debate in recent years.

Monetary policy

Debate has particularly surrounded the question of which authority should be responsible for monetary policy. In many countries, the UK included, government has traditionally controlled monetary policy, just as it has fiscal policy. Decisions to change taxation or government spending were made on specific occasions during the year, notably the annual Budget in the UK in March, but the Chancellor of the Exchequer made decisions to change interest rates whenever he felt it appropriate to achieve his monetary objectives.

This system has been criticized, however, in that it is argued that politicians, of whom the Chancellor of the Exchequer is one, might be tempted to raise or lower interest rates in order to achieve political goals instead of considering the long-term monetary stability of the country. For example, a government just about to face an election might be encouraged to lower interest rates to give voters a feeling of wealth and well-being and thus, it might be hoped, an inclination to vote for the governing party. This type of action would be likely to be damaging to the long-term economic prospects of the country, because it is believed that monetary policy needs to be conducted with the long-term goal of price stability in mind. It has thus been argued by economists that it is better for monetary policy to be taken out of the hands of politicians and to be run instead by independent central banks. The leaders of independent central banks should be able to take decisions on monetary policy without the temptation to manipulate interest rates or other monetary variables to secure popularity with electors. The counter-argument to this, however, is that while politicians are directly accountable to the electorate for their policy, independent central bankers might pursue policies of which the people of a country did not approve. For now, the benefits of central bankers not suffering political temptations seem to be outweighing the disadvantage of less direct accountability, and monetary policy is increasingly being conducted by independent central banks.

In the UK, responsibility for monetary policy was transferred from the Treasury to the Bank of England in May 1997 as one of the first acts of the newly elected Labour government. The transfer followed a gradual heightening of the monetary policy role of the Bank in prior years. Originally the Chancellor of the Exchequer decided at what level interest rates ought to be set and when to introduce any changes. He then simply instructed the Bank of England to carry out his policy. From 1993, however, the Bank was given responsibility for the timing of interest rate changes and also commented publicly on the monetary actions of the government in the light of information on inflation.

The current monetary policy role of the Bank of England under the 1998 Bank of England Act falls short of full independence, in that the UK government still decides what inflation target is to be the goal of monetary policy; currently it is 2.5 per cent. Once this inflationary target has been established, however, it is up to the Bank of England, through a Monetary Policy Committee (MPC), to decide at what level interest rates need to be to achieve it. The inflation target is the primary goal of the Bank, but subject to achieving that, the Bank is instructed to support the wider economic goals of the government. The MPC is responsible to Parliament for its performance and there are provisions for the Treasury to retake control of monetary policy in extreme economic circumstances. The MPC is made up of the Governor of the Bank of England, two Deputy Governors and six further members, who are drawn from the academic world, industry and finance.

While the independence of a central bank is a relatively new phonomenon in the UK, it is a well established idea in some other countries. Germany has had an independent central bank, the Bundesbank, since 1987. Its sole purpose has been to protect the stability of the Deutschmark and to operate monetary policy to that end. The Bundesbank has had complete control in setting inflation targets and designing policy to meet them. The European Central Bank (ECB), established in Frankfurt in 1998, has been modelled on the Bundesbank and has a similar level of independence. Price stability is the ECB's sole objective. Central bank independence has also become the norm among European Union members because it is a prerequisite of a country participating in European Monetary Union. Countries such as France and Italy, which once had central banks subordinate to government, have therefore introduced independence in recent years. One of the longest standing independent central banks and in many ways the blueprint for most others is the Federal Reserve of America (also known as the Fed). The Federal Reserve has control over interest rate policy in a similar way to the ECB. The Federal Reserve is on paper, however, not as powerful as the ECB because the governors who run it are appointed by the US President, whereas the board of the ECB is appointed by a wider group of people and has an eight-year term of office. In practice, the power and influence of the Fed depends on the personal standing of its Chairman. The current Chairman, Alan Greenspan, is currently in his third four-year term and is widely respected the world over.

Regulation and fund raising

At the same time that the Bank of England was given responsibility for monetary policy, its role as a supervisor of part of the financial sector, the banking system, and its responsibility for raising finance for the government were taken from it. Why was it considered necessary to reduce the scope of the Bank of England's role?

Responsibility for managing the funding of the UK government has passed from the Bank of England to a new department at the Treasury (the Debt Management Office). It has been argued that a central bank with responsibility for monetary policy and debt funding could face a conflict of interest. To reduce inflationary pressures, the Bank might need to raise interest rates, but to sell off government securities, it might be tempted to keep rates low. To enable the central bank to concentrate wholly on its enhanced and vital monetary policy role, debt funding is no longer part of its remit. The argument for removing banking sector supervision to a new, wide-ranging financial sector supervisor is similar. It could be argued that a central bank with supervisory responsibilities might want to keep interest rates down – to help an ailing bank, for example. There was also a good case for bringing all regulation under a single institution, as the previous system was fragmented and confusing. Most other central banks with responsibility for monetary policy have a similar narrow role which does not include supervision or fund raising. The Bundesbank has never had a supervisory role and nor has the Federal Reserve. Financial sector supervision in the United States is carried out by a separate body, the Supervisory Exchange Commission (SEC).

Regulation of the financial sector in the UK is now largely under the auspices of the Financial Services Authority (FSA). Other bodies created under specific financial legislation – for example, the Building Societies Commission – also have responsibilities for particular parts of the sector.

The original role of the FSA (and its forerunner the Securities and Investments Board) arose from the Financial Services Act 1986. This Act was predominantly designed to protect customers of the non-bank financial sector from receiving poor value at a time when there was some deregulation of markets and institutions. Deregulation – for instance of the Stock Exchange through Big Bang (discussed further in Chapter 4) – was aimed at improving competitiveness but at the same time removed some checks in place to prevent market professionals acting in their own rather than their client's best interests. At the same time, institutions were entering wider spheres of business, and this made it more difficult for regulatory authorities to carry out informal supervision in the way they had before. As well as trying to protect consumers, the FSA 1986 did include some measures to protect the stability of the financial sector as a whole, in, for example, covering the capital requirements of securities trading business. Deposit-taking activities, however, such as those undertaken by banks and building societies, were outside the scope of the Act.

In order to carry out its function of ensuring that financial services are offered on a proper basis, the FSA delegates the supervision of different parts of the financial sector to professional bodies and markets. The structure of regulation is shown in Figure 3.4.

Figure 3.4 The regulatory structure under the Financial Services Act 1986. Source: Financial Services Authority web page.

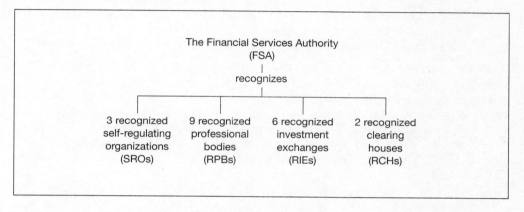

There are three self-regulating organizations (SROs) within the structure.[2] These are bodies specifically set up following the introduction of the FSA 1986 which regulate different types of financial business. As their name would suggest, the SROs are bodies run and financed by the parts of the financial sector that they monitor. The Investment Management Regulatory Authority (IMRO) oversees practitioners providing invesment management services. The Securities and Investments Authority (SFA) supervises firms trading in organized financial markets, such as the Stock Exchange and derivatives markets. The Personal Investment Authority (PIA) is in charge of firms offering advice to, or otherwise acting for, private investors, including such products as pensions and life assurance. The SROs are responsible for authorizing firms to conduct business in their particular area of authority, checking that the way business is carried out is fair and proper and imposing penalties in cases where firms do not act as they ought.

Alongside the SROs, recognized markets such as the Stock Exchange, and professional bodies, such as the Chartered Institute of Accountants, are authorized to regulate their own members in the conduct of their business. Both types of organization need to have rules and codes of practice to satisfy the FSA.

Since June 1998, the FSA has been responsible for regulating individual banks as well as other financial services firms. The FSA authorizes banks to conduct business and ensures that individual institutions then remain sound in terms of both capital adequacy and liquidity. The Bank of England retains responsibility for the overall stability of the banking system and works with the FSA to ensure this.

Supranational financial authorities

Operating alongside domestic financial authorities are a number of supranational authorities and a body of legislation and agreements covering more than one country. The purpose of these, taken together, can be summarized as follows:

- To promote stability within the international financial system. Action taken might be in the form of stabilizing exchange rates or setting worldwide capital requirements for financial institutions.
- To promote competition between financial institutions worldwide. In this area, measures are in existence to ensure recognition of the licensing of financial institutions outside their country of origin. Worldwide capital adequacy requirements also promote free competition in trying to ensure that the same capital standards have to be met by all.
- To assist poorer areas of the world through investment on preferential terms.

The International Monetary Fund was set up after the Second World War as part of the 1944 Bretton Woods Agreement. The main role of the IMF is to promote exchange rate stability around the world. It has funds at its disposal provided by its member states which allow it to offer financial assistance to countries experiencing short-term economic difficulties which would otherwise lead to exchange rate instability. Funds are generally only offered if the government of a country in difficulty agrees to an economic package to put it back on to a more stable course. Action may be required, for example, to reduce inflation through reduced government spending and higher interest rates if funds are to be provided to meet a current government borrowing requirement. The role of the IMF and in particular the importance of stable exchange rates is discussed further in Chapter 8, which deals with the foreign exchange markets.

The Bank for International Settlements is a committee of central bankers, the main function of which is to promote the stability of the global banking system. In 1988 a capital adequacy ratio applicable to all banks was announced; this has been referred to above, and requires banks to have capital of at least 8 per cent of their risk-adjusted assets. BIS has attempted to come up with regulations covering capital to back the wider activities of financial institutions; for example, their risk exposure in dealing in different securities markets rather than lending. No specific capital ratio could be agreed upon, however, and instead individual institutions' risk management procedures are vetted.

The World Bank (more properly known as the International Bank for Reconstruction and Development) was set up at the same time as the IMF under the post-war Bretton Woods Agreement. The purpose of the World Bank is to invest in projects in less well developed parts of the world in order to alleviate poverty and promote economic growth. In some cases money is lent interest free. More usually sums are invested in projects over a longer term and at a lower interest rate than could be obtained from commercial organizations. The European Union has institutions which have a similar function to the World Bank, but focused specifically on Europe. The European Investment Bank (EIB) invests in infrastructure projects in the European Union, while the European Bank for Reconstruction and Development (EBRD) is oriented towards regeneration projects in the former communist countries of Europe.

As well as influencing financial variables in particular parts of the financial sector, such as the exchange rate of an individual country, the supranational authorities can have a wider effect on financial markets and products as significant borrowers of funds. The IMF, World Bank and EIB are particularly significant borrowers in international markets for medium- to long-term debt. As with domestic governments, their presence in such markets can push up rates of return and make it more difficult for commercial borrowers to raise the funds they need.

Summary

Financial authorities influence the financial sector through their significant fund raising and investment activities, but also as the implementers of monetary policy and sector regulation. Taxation can also affect the sector, particularly where provisions are introduced to encourage activity such as share ownership.

The overall purpose of economic policy in most countries is to stimulate growth, bring about high employment and encourage economic stability. Monetary policy is designed to control inflation, which in turn is believed to have an influence on these ultimate economic goals. Monetary policy can be aimed either at controlling parts of the money supply or at influencing interest rates, the latter being the more usual method adopted in most countries currently.

Attempts to control the money supply directly have been focused on limiting the expansion of bank deposits, since these are one of the largest constituents of money supply. If there is an injection of cash into an economy, this leads to a much greater increase in money supply, since banks will create deposits with only a percentage backing of cash. The money multiplier calculates how much a country's total money supply increases for a given increase in the cash base. Attempts to limit the expansion of the money supply directly have included the corset measures in the UK and Regulation Q in America; both were somewhat unsuccessful because institutions grew up outside the controls and so avoided them.

Financial authorities seek to control only the shortest-term interest rates paid by financial institutions. There is then a knock-on effect to longer-term and more widely applied rates through institutional lending to other borrowers. Short-term interest rates can be controlled through the imposition of a minimum lending rate or through the financial authorities acting as lender of last resort or participating in open market operations. The latter method of influencing rates is the one most commonly used today.

The purpose of regulation is to ensure the stability of the financial system and to protect users of the system from receiving bad value. Sector stability is brought about through prudential and liquidity measures. International prudential measures are in place in the form of capital adequacy ratios, while liquidity measures are often agreed on a case-by-case basis. Users of the financial sector are protected by a combination of laws and self-regulatory practices which deal with information that has to be provided to anyone buying financial products and provide compensation in case things go wrong.

The trend is for authorities which control monetary policy to be separate from elected governments. This structure is intended to enable authorities to pursue a single-minded inflation control policy. Regulation of the entire financial sector in the UK is under the control of the Financial Services Authority, while fund raising for the government is undertaken by a department of the Treasury.

There are a number of supranational authorities which influence the international financial sector. The IMF is concerned with supporting a stable world financial system, and in particular with reducing exchange rate fluctuations. The BIS has a role of standardizing regulation of financial institutions worldwide, while the World Bank has the task of lending and investing funds so as to relieve poverty. The EU has its own institutions carrying out similar functions, but on a Europe-wide rather than worldwide basis.

Notes

1. In some cases interest rate management is used to achieve a particular exchange rate target rather than to achieve an inflation or money supply goal. An example of this was the UK during its membership of the ERM from October 1990 to September 1992. The purpose of maintaining a particular exchange rate in this instance was, however, to apply the monetary policy of another country – in this case Germany. By keeping the value of sterling stable against the Deutschmark, the UK government was requiring the UK economy to keep to inflation levels in Germany.
2. Two other SROs, FINBRA and LAUTRO, are in the process of being phased out, their activities having been merged with those of other bodies.

Questions

Note: suggested solutions are provided for questions marked *

1. Explain the overall aims of the finanancial authorities in
    a) conducting monetary policy and
    b) imposing financial sector regulation.

2. Identify and discuss different methods of conducting monetary policy open to the financial authorities. In your discussion, note particularly how the activities of the authorities affect different parts of the financial sector.

*3. A bank has the following financial assets:

	£bn
Cash	5
UK Government gilts	20
UK Government Treasury Bills	10
Corporate bonds	30
Loans to UK and US banks	40
	105

Under the BIS capital adequacy rules, what is the minimum capital the bank should have in order to support these assets?

4. Explain how the functions of monetary policy, financial sector regulation and government funding have been shared among different financial authorities in the UK since May 1997.

4

The market for shares

THE FINANCIAL MARKET that probably most hits the headlines is the market for shares. Typical headlines might be:

> Footsie falls 100 points in a day!

> Biggest banking takeover ever announced!

> New shares reach 30p premium on issue price!

All the above represent news about the markets for shares and all could be newsworthy enough to command a prominent place in the pages of our daily newspapers.

Why does the market for shares get so much attention? As we noted in Chapter 2, shares are just one way for companies to raise the funds they need and are not relevant at all for governments and individuals with funding deficits. Other forms of funding are also more significant than shares in terms of their total market turnover.

The happenings in markets for shares probably get more coverage than those in markets for other financial assets because shares, which are more risky than most alternative products, are subject to more notable changes in value, and because the indirect effect of what happens to shares can be very widespread. The ownership of ordinary shares, as is discussed further below, normally brings with it part ownership of a company and with that control of what the company does. If the share capital of a company changes hands – for instance, in the course of a takeover – that can have a profound effect on the lives of all the people involved in the company, such as employees, suppliers, customers and people living in the community where the company operates. Shares also act as an important store of wealth for millions of people, both as individual investors and as contributors to company or personal pension schemes. Any significant change in the value of shares can thus have an effect on the general feeling of well-being and spending power within an economy. Within companies which issue shares, share capital too has an importance beyond its direct contribution to funding needs. As we shall see below, while share capital is an important direct source of company funding, it also acts as a base for other types of funds that companies raise.

Most shares issued by companies and then traded on stock exchanges are 'ordinary shares'. These shares give the holder part ownership of the issuing company and a right to participate in the profits the company makes after paying all other obligations, such as wages, interest on debt and tax. A less common form of share capital is a 'preference share', which does not usually entitle the holder to the same control over company affairs but does give a prior right to company income. In this chapter, we will look at both types of share capital and at the markets in which they are issued and traded.

Learning objectives

This chapter will make clear the nature of share capital as an investment and funding product, the meaning of information provided on shares for investors and the principal operations of a stock exchange. A number of topics covered in particular are:

- how share capital compares with debt in terms of its risk and return;
- how to interpret data provided on shares in the financial press;
- why share prices go up and down;
- the different ways that shares can be issued and traded.

The main characteristics of share capital

Shares are a type of financial product that can only be issued by 'joint stock companies'. These are organizations which are set up in accordance with a particular body of law in a country (in the UK, company law) in order to achieve given objectives. Shares are, effectively, a right to part ownership of a joint stock company, and are issued by the company in exchange for money that the shareholders 'subscribe', i.e. pay in to the company. Not all private sector commercial organizations are in the form of joint stock companies; many enterprises operate as a sole trader or partnership, and indeed these are probably the oldest forms of commercial venture in most countries. The first joint stock companies were formed in the sixteenth and seventeenth centuries, mostly in connection with foreign trade. Some of the best known of these original share-issuing companies were the East India Company, formed in 1600 in order to trade in Asia, and the Hudson Bay Company, established in 1668 to carry out business in Canada.

It is useful always to keep in mind that shares represent *the owners' stake* in the company when we consider these assets' main characteristics. In particular, *vis-à-vis* all other participants in a company, shares always rank last for payment of income or repayment of capital. This position of shareholders is represented in Figure 4.1, which shows the allocation of money in a company with an ongoing business.

As shown in Figure 4.1, money received by a company is used to pay all other claimants on the company – suppliers, employees, providers of debt capital and the taxman – before shareholders get anything. The position of shareholders were the company to be 'wound up', i.e. its business terminated and capital repaid, is similar; all other claimants would be paid money outstanding to them before any capital was repaid to shareholders.

Against this low ranking in terms of income or capital entitlement, shares do give their owners the right to any extra wealth that the company might generate, after all other participants have received the normal return to which they are entitled. This is typical of the position of owners of most other commercial enterprises. There is though one major difference between being an owner via shares and being a business owner in other circumstances. Most joint stock companies today are formed with 'limited liability'. This means that the shareholders are not liable for the debts of the company beyond the amount they actually subscribe for their shares. Thus if a company undertakes trading or other actions that result in the loss not only of its shareholders' capital but also of

Figure 4.1 The allocation of money generated by an ongoing business

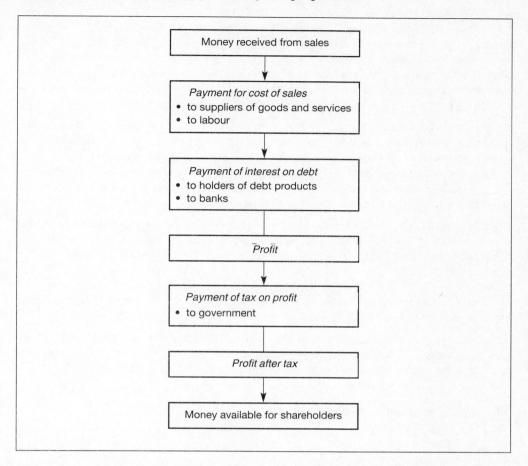

money that it has borrowed or owes to other parties, such as suppliers or employees, the shareholders will lose all the money they put into the company but cannot be asked also to meet the losses of anyone else. This compares with the position of most sole traders or partners who have 'unlimited liability', which means that any losses incurred by their business can be sought from them personally.

Ordinary shares

As mentioned in the introduction to this chapter, there are two principal types of share capital: ordinary share capital and preference share capital. Ordinary share capital is also often referred to as 'equity', and both types of shares may be termed 'stock', notably in the USA. We will begin by considering the main characteristics of ordinary share capital, which can be summarized as follows.

Income from an ordinary share

If you invest in shares, the share may provide an income in the form of a dividend. A dividend is not the same as the total money available to shareholders and shown in

Figure 4.1. The directors of a company can choose to keep some of the profits earned for shareholders to reinvest in the business, and these funds are represented in company accounts as 'retained earnings'. Dividends are the element of profits available to shareholders that the directors of a company choose to pay out in cash rather than keeping within the business as retained earnings. The shareholders' profits that the directors retain in the business to invest should produce higher dividends in future. If funds are invested wisely, an attractive return should be earned on them by the company and this should lead to higher profits and dividends for shareholders in future.

Both the total profits earned for shareholders and the dividend paid out of them are uncertain. The directors of a company have no legal obligation to declare a dividend. If a company makes low profits or a loss, the directors may pay a reduced dividend or no dividend at all. Indeed, in the UK it is against the law for a dividend to be paid unless the company concerned has a store of shareholders' profits from the current or past years in the form of accumulated retained earnings.

If a company's operations are funded by a mixture of borrowing and share capital, the very existence of borrowing makes the shareholders' income position more uncertain. This is because any profits the company does earn, after allowing for sums due to suppliers and employees, is used to pay lenders an income before shareholders; this is illustrated in Figure 4.1, where debt interest is shown as being paid, and then tax, before any money is allocated to shareholders. Lenders are paid before shareholders because interest on debt has to be paid by law.

The comments above emphasize how low or non-existent dividends can be. The other side of the dividend story is that there is no upper limit on dividends; if the company does well, the return to shareholders may be unexpectedly high in consequence.

The capital value of an ordinary share

There are two forms of capital value of a share: the 'par value', which is the value recorded in the accounts of the issuing company and which is formally repayable on a winding up; and the market value, which is the value the share can be sold for in a secondary share market. Generally, the second measure of value will be the far more relevant one for investors, because winding up will not be anticipated and because otherwise most ordinary shares carry no other provision for repayment by the issuing company. In order to realize their investment, shareholders will thus have to sell their shares to someone else in the secondary market and market value is crucially important.

The determinants of the market value of a share are discussed in more detail below. Value will essentially depend on what income people expect the share to generate in the form of dividends in future and on what price they expect the share to command if sold again in the secondary share market. Both these factors are uncertain and thus the value of a share is uncertain too.

Although the capital value of a share will be uncertain, one thing we can say is that shares will never have a negative value. This is because shareholders enjoy limited liability, as explained above, and in financial terms the worst that can happen to a shareholding investment is that it becomes worthless. Although shareholders do have the protection of limited liability, their stake in the company is likely to have little or no value should the company incur sufficient losses to be wound up. This is because, as noted above, shareholders rank after all other parties in being repaid their capital. In most liquidation cases, shareholders get nothing, while other parties may get fully, or at least partly, repaid.

Ownership rights conferred by ordinary share ownership

Shareholders, as part owners of a company, have the right to vote on certain matters concerning the company which are considered at annual general or certain other meetings. Notably, if enough shareholders vote together, they can get rid of the board of directors who run the company and replace these individuals by a board more to their satisfaction. In practice, where shares are 'widely held', i.e. where there are many shareholders in a company, all with a relatively small stake, action is rarely taken to remove or even modify the composition of a board of directors. The shareholders are likely to be too geographically and organizationally widespread to take effective action together. Shareholder control may be more of a reality where one or two organizations, such as pension funds, hold significant stakes. The importance of larger shareholders run by full-time professionals has been recognized in the Cadbury Report (Report of the Committee on the Financial Aspects of Corporate Governance 1992).

Preference shares

Preference shares differ from ordinary shares in entitling their holders to only a limited dividend, but against this offer preferential rights to the payment of that income and to capital on a winding up. Preference shares do not generally have voting rights attached and may or may not include planned repayment.

The limited dividend on a preference share is normally set as a fixed percentage of the par value of the share. An example of a preference share dividend might be 10 per cent cumulative on the basis of a £1 par value. This means that the preference shareholder is entitled to a dividend of 10p per share per year (10 per cent of the £1 par value), but if there are insufficient profits to pay the dividend in one year, it will be cumulated and paid out in the following year. The dividend is 'preferential' in that profits must be used to pay it before ordinary shareholders get any dividend themselves. In the nature of share capital in general, though, the dividend is still paid after all other parties have been satisfied, such as employees, lenders and the tax authority. If we were going to include preference shares in Figure 4.1, we would thus show preference share dividends coming out of the 'Money available for shareholders' at the bottom of the diagram, with the remainder of these funds then being the amount available for ordinary shareholders.

The claims of preference shareholders are also ranked before those of ordinary shareholders in a winding up. Preference shareholders will be repaid the par value of their shares before ordinary shareholders receive anything, but only after the claims of all other parties have been satisfied. Thus, preference shares have a lower risk for investors than ordinary shares, but the other side of this is that they have limited return in terms of dividends.

Share capital and debt

It is the position of shareholders ranking *behind* other parties involved in a company in terms of receiving income and capital repayment which makes share capital such an important base for other forms of company funding. A bank lending to a company will derive some reassurance from the existence of a significant amount of share capital in making its loan; this is because the money paid in as share capital is like a 'cushion' for the bank loan. Any shortage of income or capital will be borne by the shareholders first, the bank's interest and debt repayment being made before the shareholders receive any income or capital repayment themselves.

From the point of view of an investor, though, the ranking of share capital behind all other forms of finance makes investment in shares relatively risky. Why would anyone buy shares when he or she only gets paid out once everyone else involved in the company is satisfied? The inducement must be that people expect to make more money on shares than on other investments to compensate for their risk. For an investor, a share is a high-risk, high-return investment. For a company it is the other way round. Issuing shares is low-risk because the company does not *have* to pay dividends if times are hard and does not have to put money aside for capital repayment; having shares also helps the company to raise other types of funding. The *quid pro quo* is that share capital is a high-cost form of funding. The company will have to pay out attractive dividends in the longer term and/or see that its share price keeps rising to keep shareholders happy.

The relative riskiness of shares as an investment is illustrated by a study of returns and risks on shares as compared to those on government bonds (gilts) in the UK over the period from 1946 to 1995 (BZW Equity Gilt Study, 1996, cited by Arnold, 1998). The study showed that the average real annual return on shares (i.e. the return after allowing for inflation) was 9.44 per cent, which compared to a real annual return on UK Government bonds ('gilts') of only 0.77 per cent. The risk of the two types of assets is represented by a statistic called 'standard deviation'; this statistic shows how variable returns are over time, with a higher standard deviation indicating a more volatile picture of return over the period. The standard deviation for the real return on shares was 24.62, while for gilts it was considerably lower, at 13.65. In the period studied, shares thus exhibited a higher real return than gilts but a higher risk associated with that return, and this is what we would expect from our analysis above.

The importance of share capital in company funding

How important is share capital in the overall funding of companies? Table 4.1 provides a breakdown of UK company financing in the 1990s; figures from one year in the 1980s are also included for comparison. The conclusions that can be drawn from Table 4.1 are:

1. Typically the largest source of company funds (in most years at least 50 per cent of the total) is cash generated by a business itself, i.e. retained profits.
2. The second most significant source of finance, in terms of size, has traditionally been bank borrowing (20–30 per cent). This was not the case in the early 1990s, though, when issues of share capital actually led to net repayments of bank borrowing.
3. Ordinary share issues represent typically only around 10 per cent of funds raised, though shares were more important in the early 1990s, as mentioned above.

New share issues represent, therefore, a surprisingly small proportion of company funds. The largest source of funds, retained earnings, does represent shareholders'

Table 4.1   Sources of funds to UK companies (£ million)

	Total sources	Internal funds	Shares	Bank[a] borrowing	Debentures and pref. shares	Other[b]
1989	108,292	35,603	1,882	44,497	6,164	20,146
1992	53,542	36,530	7,400	−2,845	3,310	9,147
1993	77,643	49,958	13,954	−7,491	5,452	15,770
1994	82,469	60,099	11,435	−1,929	7,796	5,068
1995	106,711	56,925	12,574	16,802	12,345	8,065
1996	117,792	58,124	12,758	22,645	5,113	19,152

Source: Financial Statistics.

[a]Bank borrowing includes other loans and mortgages.
[b]Other funds included capital transfers, such as grants, overseas funds and other capital issues, such as employee share schemes.

funds, however, in that these are profits earned for shareholders but kept by companies to make further investments. As we have noted too, the existence of share capital supports the raising of other types of funds, such as bank loans. Indirectly, equity is thus involved in all the types of funds noted in Table 4.1 as having been raised by companies.

Data on shares in the financial press

Figure 4.2 shows the information typically provided to investors on shares in the financial press. The data are from the *Financial Times* of Thursday 7 October 1999 and show the general retailers sector.

The first column of the table in Figure 4.2 gives the name of the relevant company, followed often by symbols which give further general information on the shares. For instance, Allders, the second company listed, is a company operating general stores; the club sign after the company's name indicates that a free company report is available from the *Financial Times* on request. The column headed 'Price' then gives the market price of the shares in pence at the end of trading on the previous day and the column to the right of that shows whether and by how much the price rose or fell compared to the day before. The price given for a share is in fact an average of the closing buying and selling prices of the share at the end of the previous day's trading. There will be a difference between the price at which shares are sold and bought in the market to provide a dealing return to market intermediaries. The difference between buying and selling prices is called 'the spread'.

You may notice that some prices in Figure 4.2 have an 'xd' after them (see, for instance, the tenth share down, Bentalls). This stands for 'ex-dividend'. There is always a gap between dividends being announced by a company's directors and the dividend actually being paid to shareholders. If shares during this gap period change hands, the question arises of who should get the dividend – the original shareholder who owned the share at the time the dividend was announced, or the new shareholder who will own the share at the time the dividend payment is actually made. This really boils down to administration. If the share is sold soon after the dividend announcement, it is practical for the new owner to get the dividend, because there will be time for the dividend-paying company to amend the details of its shareholders and make the

Figure 4.2   Data provided on shares in the financial press. Source: *Financial Times*, 7 October 1999.

GENERAL RETAILERS

	Notes	Price	+ or -	52 week high	low	Volume '000s	Yield	P/e
Alexon		$183\frac{1}{2}$	-1	230	$167\frac{1}{2}$	8	-	8.6
Allders	♦	$145\frac{1}{2}$	....	$167\frac{1}{2}$	$92\frac{1}{2}$	24	5.8	9.7
Allied Carpets	♦‡	$92\frac{1}{2}$	$+\frac{1}{2}$	$95\frac{1}{2}$	$25\frac{1}{2}$	12	0.5	
Arcadia Group		$188\frac{1}{2}$	$+3\frac{1}{2}$	$302\frac{1}{2}$	$133\frac{1}{2}$	1,358	6.2	8.6
Arnotts IE	♦	$458\frac{1}{4}$	....	$553\frac{1}{4}$	$435\frac{1}{4}$	-	3.3	15.3
Ashley (Laura)		$15\frac{1}{4}$	....	$22\frac{1}{4}$	$11\frac{1}{2}$	171	-	-
Austin Reed	♦	$97\frac{1}{2}$	....	$123\frac{1}{2}$	$73\frac{1}{2}$	62	7.7	8.4
Beale	♦	$118\frac{1}{2}$	....	145	$90\frac{1}{2}$	6	4.1	10.1
Beattie (J)	♦†	$174\times d$	....	$184\frac{1}{2}$	$145\frac{1}{2}$	4	6.3	10.3
Bentalls		$70\frac{1}{2}\times d$	....	$88\frac{1}{2}$	$63\frac{1}{2}$	2	5.6	-
Blacks Leisure	♦	$261\frac{1}{2}$	$+7$	$299\frac{1}{2}$	180	36	2.3	9.3
Body Shop		116	....	$119\frac{1}{2}$	$64\frac{1}{2}$	20	4.9	53.1
Boots		681	$-4\frac{1}{2}$	1067	$621\frac{3}{4}$	2,220	3.6	17.6
Brown & Jcksn		211	$+\frac{1}{2}$	211	53	138	1.2	16.7
Brown (N)		326	....	385	210	127	2.5	18.8
Cadoro		$0\frac{3}{4}$ #	....	$2\frac{1}{4}$	$0\frac{1}{2}$	-	-	-
Carpetright	♦	419	$+\frac{1}{2}$	472	168	40	5.3	19.1
Cash Converters Units		5	....	$8\frac{1}{2}$	$4\frac{1}{2}$	-	6.0	24.5
Church	♦♦	$1005\times d$	....	1010	261	4	1.8	34.3
Clinton Cards	†	281	$+2\frac{1}{2}$	319	$123\frac{1}{2}$	46	1.7	14.4
Country Gardens	♦†	$248\frac{1}{2}$	-3	$305\frac{1}{2}$	$150\frac{1}{2}$	3	0.9	19.2
Courts		$385\times d$	-15	$442\frac{1}{2}$	$207\frac{1}{2}$	-	1.2	18.6
DFS Furniture		291	$-1\frac{1}{2}$	339	152	1	4.9	16.2
Debenhams	†	$303\frac{1}{4}$	$-3\frac{3}{4}$	$502\frac{1}{2}$	290	157	3.3	12.1
Dixons	s	1000	-41	1578	516	4,166	1.5	25.9
(Net) Dv Cv Pf		270	$-7\frac{1}{2}$	$413\frac{1}{2}$	142	-	1.9	-
Electronics Boutique		$97\frac{1}{2}$	$+2\frac{1}{2}$	114	$66\frac{3}{4}$	3,655	1.1	22.1
Era		$11\frac{1}{2}$	....	14	$3\frac{3}{4}$	1,018	-	-
Falkland Islands		$89\frac{1}{2}\times d$	....	116	50	-	4.5	6.3
Fine Art Devlpts		145	....	$159\frac{1}{2}$	$76\frac{1}{2}$	35	6.9	10.4
Flying Flowrs Uts	♦	$163\frac{1}{2}\times d$	$-2\frac{1}{2}$	246	$141\frac{1}{2}$	19	4.5	11.6
Forminster		$49\frac{1}{2}$	....	$86\frac{1}{2}$	$42\frac{1}{2}$	-	6.9	6.2
French Connect	†	786xd	$+10$	$787\frac{1}{2}$	285	-	0.6	18.2
Gleves & Hawkes		$37\frac{1}{2}$	....	$43\frac{1}{2}$	$27\frac{1}{2}$	-	2.3	8.5
Grampian	♦†	$107\frac{1}{2}$	$-2\frac{1}{2}$	$122\frac{1}{2}$	70	18	7.3	9.1
Great Universal		$482\frac{1}{2}$	$-20\frac{1}{2}$	857	450	5,945	4.3	11.9
Hamleys	†	130	-12	$192\frac{1}{2}$	$97\frac{1}{2}$	36	7.7	9.4
Hampden	♦♦	$112\frac{1}{2}\times d$	....	$112\frac{1}{2}$	$35\frac{1}{2}$	-	2.6	16.1
Harvey Nichols Group		$210\frac{1}{2}$	....	223	$111\frac{1}{2}$	11	3.3	12.1
Harveys Furnishing	♦	148	....	$205\frac{1}{2}$	$61\frac{1}{2}$	4	6.4	12.1
Heal's		178	....	193	$87\frac{1}{2}$	-	3.3	8.8
House of Fraser	♦	$77\frac{1}{2}$	....	111	$50\frac{1}{2}$	216	7.3	13.4
Hughes TJ		316½	$+1\frac{1}{2}$	386	$123\frac{1}{2}$	30	1.3	21.2
JJB Sports		370	$+7\frac{1}{2}$	$452\frac{1}{2}$	180	50	2.3	13.6
Jacques Vert		21	....	$27\frac{1}{2}$	$12\frac{1}{2}$	2	-	6.7
John David Sports	♦	140	....	$152\frac{1}{2}$	$44\frac{1}{2}$	5	4.0	9.7
Kingfisher		618xd	$-16\frac{1}{2}$	$946\frac{1}{2}$	505	4,315	2.1	20.6
Liberty		130	$+5$	185	105	-	-	-
Limelight	♦‡	$54\frac{1}{2}\times d$	....	71	24	128	0.9	8.0
MFI Furniture		44	....	50	$24\frac{3}{4}$	1,582	1.6	-
Marks & Spncr		318	$-6\frac{1}{2}$	$472\frac{1}{2}$	300	9,924	4.5	21.2
Mallett		120xd	$+1$	$123\frac{1}{2}$	$80\frac{1}{2}$	-	5.2	5.2
Marchpole		$11\frac{1}{2}$	$+\frac{1}{4}$	$17\frac{1}{2}$	$6\frac{3}{4}$	2,154	11.3	6.9
Matalan		1040xd	$+2\frac{1}{2}$	$1319\frac{1}{2}$	$247\frac{1}{2}$	68	1.0	34.6
Merchant Retl		$65\frac{1}{2}$	....	$67\frac{3}{4}$	$30\frac{1}{4}$	38	1.0	20.6
Monsoon		$68\frac{1}{2}\times d$	....	101	$43\frac{1}{2}$	86	6.6	8.7
Moss Bros		116	$-1\frac{1}{2}$	$198\frac{1}{2}$	109	12	5.5	12.4
New Look Group	♦	$199\frac{1}{2}$	-3	$245\frac{1}{2}$	$122\frac{1}{2}$	304	2.8	13.6
Next		618	-1	860	400	1,289	3.2	15.8
Novara	†‡	52xd	....	$70\frac{1}{2}$	$35\frac{1}{2}$	5	9.9	15.5
Oasis Stores	♦†	$223\frac{1}{2}$	$-\frac{1}{2}$	278	115	94	3.9	12.6
Oliver Grp		$15\frac{1}{2}$	....	$25\frac{1}{2}$	12	-	-	64.2
Ottakar's	♦†	159xd	....	$243\frac{1}{2}$	$156\frac{1}{2}$	-	1.6	20.2
Partners	†	$29\frac{1}{2}$	$+1\frac{1}{2}$	$32\frac{1}{2}$	$17\frac{1}{2}$	-	1.7	-
Partridge Fine	†	$57\frac{1}{2}$	....	$75\frac{1}{2}$	$52\frac{1}{2}$	-	5.1	12.2
QS Grp	†	37	....	$47\frac{1}{2}$	$15\frac{1}{2}$	-	2.0	13.9
Rosebys	♦a	$238\frac{1}{2}$	$+5\frac{1}{2}$	290	55	357	4.3	23.5
SCS Upholstery	♦†	$94\frac{1}{2}$	....	$100\frac{1}{2}$	$55\frac{1}{4}$	-	3.8	10.3
Save Grp		34	....	$80\frac{1}{2}$	33	125	9.7	13.3
Selfridges	†	$253\frac{1}{2}$	....	$288\frac{1}{2}$	207	251	2.0	19.8
Signet		$53\frac{1}{2}$	$+\frac{3}{4}$	$61\frac{1}{4}$	$24\frac{1}{4}$	1,685	2.3	12.3
Smith (WH)	†a	$480\frac{1}{2}$	$-18\frac{1}{2}$	$792\frac{1}{2}$	$468\frac{1}{2}$	706	3.6	19.5
Sothebys A $		$1777\frac{1}{2}$	....	$2762\frac{1}{2}$	950	-	1.4	-
Storehouse		$87\frac{3}{4}$	-1	183	83	907	10.4	5.4
Style Holdings	♦♦	$182\frac{1}{2}$	....	$192\frac{1}{2}$	$114\frac{1}{2}$	-	1.2	20.5
Stylo		$34\frac{1}{2}$	....	47	$29\frac{1}{2}$	-	-	-
Ted Baker	♦	214	....	$228\frac{1}{2}$	$91\frac{1}{2}$	23	2.5	16.7
Topps Tiles	♦	$232\frac{1}{2}$	-2	$267\frac{1}{2}$	70	69	1.4	24.5
UNO		47	-1	87	$27\frac{1}{2}$	73	2.6	23.1
Upton & Sthn		$2\frac{1}{4}$	$+\frac{1}{4}$	$3\frac{1}{4}$	$1\frac{1}{4}$	290	-	-
Wickes	†	$356\frac{1}{2}$	....	$418\frac{1}{2}$	$165\frac{1}{2}$	4	1.8	12.0
Wyevale GC	†	460xd	$+2\frac{1}{2}$	$470\frac{1}{2}$	$256\frac{1}{2}$	1	1.8	23.3

payment to the new owner; in these circumstances the share is said to be sold 'cum-dividend'. If a share is sold, however, only shortly before the dividend is to be paid, the dividend-paying company may not be able to amend its records of shareholders in time. The dividend will then be paid to the previous shareholder and the sale of the share is 'ex-dividend'. The dividend status of the share is noted in the table, because the entitlement or otherwise to a forthcoming dividend payment affects the value of the share.

The two columns to the right of the most recent price and daily movement headed '52 week' show the highest and lowest value that the share has achieved in the 52 weeks before the day reported. This information is provided to give investors an idea of where the share is trading within its recent price range. The column headed 'Volume £000s' then gives the total value of the company's shares traded on the previous day. This gives an investor an idea of how liquid a share might be. A share which is infrequently traded or traded in small volumes may be more difficult to sell in future than a more actively traded alternative. The final two columns in the table give, respectively, a measure of the income return an investor can expect to earn on the share (the dividend yield) and a rating of how the current market value of the share compares with the total return earned on the share (the price/earnings or P/E ratio).

Dividend yields and P/E ratios

The dividend yield, ignoring the complications of taxation on dividends, is calculated as:

$$\frac{\text{dividend per share from the most recent set of accounts}}{\text{market price per share}}$$

The P/E ratio is calculated as:

$$\frac{\text{market price per share}}{\text{earnings per share from the most recent set of accounts}}$$

Activity 1

The following is a summary of the profit and loss account of ABC plc:

Year to 31 December 200X

	£000s
Trading profit	94,000
Interest	−6,000
Profit before interest	88,000
Tax	−20,000
Profit after interest and tax	68,000
Dividends	−30,000
Retained profit for the year	38,000

The company has 80 million ordinary shares in issue and the current share price is £10.20.

Calculate the dividend and earnings per share from the above accounts, and using these, the dividend yield and P/E ratio on the basis of the current share price.

You find the dividend and earnings per share as follows:

$$\text{Dividend per share} = \frac{\text{total dividend per accounts}}{\text{number of shares}}$$

$$= \frac{£30,000,000}{80,000,000} = £0.376 \text{ or } 37.6\text{p per share}$$

$$\text{Earnings per share} = \frac{\text{profits after interest and tax}}{\text{number of shares}}$$

$$= \frac{£68,000,000}{80,000,000} = £0.85 \text{ or } 85\text{p per share}$$

Note that the earnings per share (EPS) represents the total profits available per share. It includes dividends and the proportion of shareholders' profits retained in the business.

We can then find the dividend yield and P/E ratio using the definitions above:

$$\text{Dividend yield} = \frac{\text{dividend per share}}{\text{price per share}}$$

$$= \frac{£0.376}{10.2} = £0.036 \text{ or } 3.6 \text{ per cent}$$

Shareholders in this example are seeing under a 4 per cent return on their share value in the form of dividends, and this is not untypical. How does this square with our recognition earlier that shares are a very risky form of investment and that shareholders need a high return in order to be persuaded to buy them? The remainder of the shareholders' expected return – say, 10 per cent plus – will come in the form of share price rises (they hope!). The premiss behind the expected share price rise is that dividends and share value will go up in future as the company earns increased profits on the shareholders' funds it is retaining now and has retained in the past.

The dividend yield, while not being a comprehensive indicator of the overall return expected on a share, is helpful to investors in showing the annual income which can be expected on the investment. Regular income can be important to some investors; for example, pension funds with regular payment commitments or individual investors borrowing to invest in shares and therefore having to fund their borrowing as they go.

Now let us turn to the P/E ratio.

$$\text{P/E ratio} = \frac{\text{price per share}}{\text{earnings per share}}$$

$$= \frac{10.2}{0.85} = 12$$

The P/E ratio shows how many years of current earnings are reflected in the current share price of a company. It is probably the most important statistic on shares produced for investors. What dictates the level of a company's P/E? One of the most significant factors behind a company's P/E will be its potential for growth in profits in future. A company with good growth prospects will tend to have a high P/E, because investors will be prepared to pay a relatively high price for the share now on the expectation that earnings will grow rapidly in future. Indeed, some companies with current *negative* earnings still attract a high share price. Amazon, the Internet book company, for example, was valued in share markets at one point in 1998 at $30 billion. This value was higher than all other US book stores and, indeed, higher than Texaco, one of the USA's largest and most well established oil companies. Yet Amazon is a loss-making company. Why were investors prepared to pay so much for the shares of a company which lost money? The reason was that Amazon exhibited impressive growth in turnover and investors believed that current losses could be turned into impressive profits in future. Other examples of loss-making companies being sold on share markets for high values are the Internet company Yahoo, the mobile phone company Orange and the satellite communications company BSkyB.

P/E ratios and dividend yields are used by investors to select particular shares within industry sectors and/or to structure a portfolio to produce certain required characteristics. Some investors may try to select shares for which the P/E ratio looks low compared to what they judge it should be; the investor would then believe the share to be undervalued. Other investors may choose shares with a high dividend yield but drawn from a wide range of industry sectors; the resulting portfolio would have a broad coverage of market sectors and would offer a relatively high income each year.

Activity 2

Look in your financial press for data on quoted shares. Try to find, particularly, information on P/Es and dividend yields for a range of companies. Note which companies or sectors have particularly high or low P/Es and see if you can rationalize the figures given. Note also whether there are any sector patterns on dividend yields – do some industrial or commercial sectors tend to pay out higher dividends than others and, if so, can you think why?

You will expect to see the highest P/Es relating to companies and sectors which have the best growth prospects, as per the discussion above. Mature sectors, perhaps heavy engineering, should have lower P/Es on average than high-technology sectors, such as computing, leisure and communications. Obviously the measure is not perfect, however. There are difficulties in any comparison of P/Es because, for example, earnings relate to accounting periods, and the figures for different companies can be substantially affected by whether their accounting period has just ended or is just starting. The amount of borrowing in different companies also affects P/Es because the risk of shareholders is affected by borrowing. The amount of a company's borrowing affects the risk of its shares because of shares' ranking behind borrowing, as explained above, and risk in turn affects the price investors are prepared to pay for shares.

Dividend yields tend to follow less obvious patterns. You might see low payouts in sectors with high growth potential, because companies may want to retain earnings in order to finance new investment. In other cases, companies may design a dividend policy specifically to suit certain types of investors. For instance, institutions with regular payment commitments, such as pension funds, may be attracted to companies with high and stable dividend payments. Other institutions wishing to avoid taxes on income may prefer investing in companies with low dividend payouts but good prospects for share price increases. You may thus see quite different dividend yields from companies within the same market sector.

Share indices

As well as providing information on individual share prices, financial information sources often also report on the movement of the value of shares as a whole by recording and commenting on share indices. A share index records the change in the aggregate value of a particular group of shares from a base period. For instance, the Financial Times-Stock Exchange 100 index, otherwise known as the 'Footsie', was started in 1984 and records the total value of the hundred largest UK firms by market capitalization. The index started at a value of 1000 and stands at just below 6000 at the time of writing (September 1999). What this means is that the top hundred firms in the UK are worth six times more in autumn 1999 than they were in 1984.

The Footsie is one of the most important share indices in the UK, though there are other broader indices too, notably the FTSE All Share index, which includes around 850 UK quoted companies. Indices of European shares are also produced by the *Financial Times* in conjunction with the Stock Exchange. The FTSE Eurotop 100 index records the value of the hundred most actively traded shares in Europe, while the Eurotop 300 is more similar to the Footsie in being based on the 300 largest European companies by market capitalization. Other important indices from around the world are the Dow-Jones 30 share index and Standard and Poor's 500 index, which are based on American shares, and the Nikkei 225 index, which reports movements in the Japanese market.

The market value of shares and share price movements

We noted above when we first considered the capital value of a share that the most important type of value for most shareholders will be market value, and that this will depend on what income investors expect the share to generate over the time they hold it and on what price they expect the share to fetch if sold again at some time in the future. What, though, will determine the value of the share at the time of any future sale?

In theory, the future price of a share should depend on what dividends the share is generating at the time of that sale and on what expectations there then are for future dividend growth. This is because, with the lack of any likely repayment of capital by the issuing company, the only cash flow that the share itself can be expected to offer to a buyer is a future stream of dividends; the value of the share should be the current value of this future cash flow. The valuation of a share on this basis is represented in Figure 4.3.

Someone who buys a share now will be entitled to dividends from the share both in the next immediate period (period 1 in Figure 4.3) and in all future periods. The share will produce dividends indefinitely: the period *n* shown in Figure 4.3 could be interpreted as being infinity or the furthest period ahead that investors think worth considering.

Figure 4.3   The relationship between share values and dividends

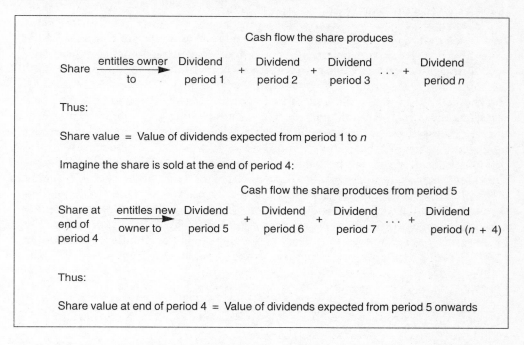

The current market value of the share is the value in today's money terms of all dividends expected from period 1 to n. What happens, though, if an investor buys a share now but intends only to hold it for a limited time, say up to the end of period 4? The second part of Figure 4.3 deals with this situation. Someone buying the share at the end of period 4 is buying the entitlement to the share's cash flow from period 5 onwards. The price the new owner should logically be prepared to pay will be the value of dividends expected from period 5 to infinity or the end of his or her investment horizon, say period $n + 4$. What this example shows is that the value of a share should in theory depend fundamentally on dividends, both as the source of current income and as the basis for future value of the share on a resale.

The comments so far have related to the pricing of shares 'in theory'. Is share pricing theory reflected in fact? There is some concern (see below) that share prices at the time of writing (autumn 1999) do not reflect their underlying current and expected future income. How could this be? When you think about the valuation of any asset, one undeniable measure of what it will ultimately be worth is what someone else will be prepared to pay for it. If people are prepared to pay prices for shares unrelated to the shares' underlying cash flow, or at least if people *believe* now that others will be prepared to pay such prices in the future, then share prices can become divorced from dividends. This sort of environment can lead to share price 'bubbles'; that is, escalating share prices that have no obvious rationale behind them. Is this sort of pricing sustainable? The problem with bubbles is that they tend to pop!

Share prices and news

The value of shares changes in response to news about the companies which issue them and also in connection with the economy in general. Sometimes the changes produced can be dramatic. For instance, the value of shares around the world fell by £2,100 billion between July and October 1998, when news of a financial crisis in Asia and the default by Russia on debt caused concern that there would be a worldwide recession; the fall was equivalent to two and a half times the gross domestic product of the UK. In less than a year the ground lost was recovered, however. Interest rate reductions, led by the USA but echoed around the world, helped, together with growing confidence, as some of the problems which brought about the crisis were tackled. Individual shares can experience dramatic price changes too. At the end of September 1999, the Bank of Scotland announced a totally unexpected £22 billion bid for National Westminster Bank. The shares of NatWest jumped 29 per cent on the announcement of the bid. They rose to a level 3 per cent higher than the actual price bid by the Bank of Scotland on the expectation that there might be a battle for NatWest, the Royal Bank of Scotland being another potential bidder. An example of individual company shares going down significantly in value in response to bad news is Glaxo at the beginning of October 1999. A flu treatment produced by the company, Ralenza, was not recommended by an advisory body for use by the National Health Service in the UK. This adverse decision from Glaxo's viewpoint lead to a fall in its share price of 2 per cent.

Does it make sense that share prices changes in response to news, and in some cases are altered dramatically by it? It does if the news items have an effect on likely current and future dividends, because these, we know, are what should rationally underlie share values. If the world is hit by recession, for example, it is likely that companies will sell lower volumes of goods or services, make lower profits and thus have less to distribute to shareholders in the way of dividends in future. Remember too that shareholders, as the party last in line to be paid anything by a company, are likely to bear more of the brunt of any change in company fortunes than other participants, such as employees or lenders. A relatively small reduction in overall company profitability due to recession can thus be expected to cause a much larger fall in the percentage return earned by shareholders. A cut in interest rates, in turn, should boost the value of shares, both by lowering the amount companies have to pay out on money they borrow and by stimulating demand generally in the economy. Lower interest rates will also make any dividends that are paid out on shares seem relatively more attractive to investors when compared with the lower rates of return earned on money invested in debt products, e.g. on money put on deposit with a bank. The relative attraction of dividends again boosts share prices.

It is thus not surprising that share prices react to news and that the percentage change in value can be large. There is considerable debate, however, about how quickly and how accurately news is incorporated into share values. This is the subject area of the pricing efficiency of share markets.[1] The level of price efficiency exhibited by share markets is important for investors, because if share prices are sluggish in responding to news, there will be opportunities for investors to make money by buying or selling shares when news stories break and then waiting for the markets to adjust to the news items over time. If market prices adjust to news too quickly for investors to make money in this way, then the markets are said to be 'price efficient', and investors and companies can have confidence that market prices accurately reflect the true value of shares. Most, but not all, academic studies have concluded that the largest markets for shares, such as those in the USA, Japan and the UK, exhibit at least 'weak form pricing efficiency'; that is, that prices fully reflect all historic price-sensitive information. Some studies have shown the markets to be semi-strong form efficient, with prices also reflecting new items of news made publicly available almost instantaneously. The conclusion that can be drawn from this is that it is extremely difficult or even impossible to outperform a large share market by trying to select shares on the basis of information about the past or by trading as new items of news become available.

Activity 3

Look in the financial pages of a newspaper or review other forms of financial media and try to find coverage of changes in share price indices and of the value of shares of particular companies. What caused the change in the share index and individual share prices? Was the direction of change in index and price what you would expect?

Share indices will change in response to general economic factors, such as the growth rate of the economy and interest and exchange rates. The political climate can in turn affect these factors, so the strength or weakness of government and prospects of conflict with other countries can also cause changes in share prices.

Individual shares will be affected by company-specific factors, such as the winning of new contracts, the development of new products, changes in personnel and the chances of takeovers or mergers. Industry matters, such as new regulation or the development of new technologies, will also have an impact.

Note that it is the *expectation* of changes in any of the above factors which normally underlies share price movements, because investors are concerned not just about the income that shares can generate today but also about prospects for the future. Thus a set of inflation figures which show prices rising more quickly than had been anticipated can lead to a share price fall because the market will anticipate that these figures may cause interest rates to be raised. As and when interest rates are actually increased, there may be little reaction in the stock market, because the rate rise has already been reflected in market prices. Similarly, you sometimes find a 'bad' piece of company-specific news being released – for example, lower profits being earned than the previous year – and the company's share price actually going up at the same time. This is probably because the news had already been indicated to the market before the formal announcement and the actual result turned out to be better than at first thought.

Share issues

The issuing of shares is the primary market activity of the market for equity. Share issues can come about for a number of reasons. 'New issues' arise when shares of a company which has formerly been in private hands are sold to the general public for the first time (a 'flotation'). Smaller companies are continually coming to the market in this way, but in the past ten or so years we have also seen the flotation of former building societies converting into banks and of subsidiaries of large corporate groups being demerged to be owned directly by shareholders. Sales by the government of shares it holds in national companies are also new issues; these are specifically termed 'privatizations' and there have been several in the UK in the 1980s and 1990s, including British Telecom, British Gas and British Rail. In all cases new issues are made in order to raise money for the former owners of the companies sold off and perhaps also to put the new companies in a stronger position to raise more capital in future.

Share issues also arise when companies which are already quoted need to raise more equity capital. Companies tend to raise new capital relatively infrequently, because, as we shall see below, the costs of arranging share issues can be high and because a company can increase its share capital in any case by earning profits for shareholders and then retaining some of these to reinvest in the business. New issues may, however, need to be made if a company is going through a substantial change which requires a bigger injection of shareholders' funds than could otherwise be achieved through normal generation of profit. In 1997, £4.1 billion was raised by existing UK companies by issuing shares on the London Stock Exchange (LSE Primary Market Fact Sheet, 1998).

There are a number of different ways in which shares can be issued, and the method chosen will depend in part on the circumstances in which money is being raised. The possible methods are:

1. New issues
    (a) public offer for sale, or
    (b) placing.
2. Issues of more shares by a company already quoted on a stock exchange
    (a) rights issue, or
    (b) placing or bought deal.

The different methods have different levels of cost associated with them, such as advertising the issue and paying underwriters, as discussed below. Arnold (1998) estimates the costs as being between 5 and 12 per cent of the amount raised, with small issues costing more than larger issues in percentage terms, and offers for sale costing more than placings.

Public offer for sale

With a public offer for sale, shares can be offered to the public either at a fixed price or by tender. Technically, all the shares will be acquired by a lead investment bank which will then offer to sell the shares to investors. A prospectus will be drawn up giving details of the company's recent performance and setting out some forecasts for the future. Advertisements will also be taken out in the financial press to publicize the issue. Under an offer for sale at a fixed price, the price at which shares will be sold will be agreed in advance by the issuing company and its lead investment bank. Investors can then apply for the quantity of shares they wish at the fixed price. With a sale by tender, investors are invited to submit their chosen offer for the shares, though a minimum acceptable price might be indicated. Once all tenders are received, they will be ranked from the highest downwards and a 'striking price' established, which is the price of the last tender which just clears the issue. In the case of most tenders, even though many offers will have been submitted at above the striking price, shares will be allocated from the highest downwards but all applicants will be charged only the striking price. Occasionally, tenders are arranged where each applicant pays the actual price tendered.

Underwriting

Inevitably there is some time lapse between new issues being organized and fixed or minimum prices being agreed upon, and offers actually being received from investors. There is thus always a risk that in the interval the market for shares will fall and the prices established will prove to be unattractive. To ensure that the issuing company does raise the money it requires, particularly taking into account the expense of embarking on a share issue, new issues are 'underwritten'. The underwriting of an issue involves the lead investment bank guaranteeing to buy any shares at the fixed or minimum price should insufficient offers be received from the public. In order to avoid taking on too much risk itself, the lead bank will then probably organize a syndicate of sub-underwriting institutions, which in turn promise to acquire some unwanted shares from the lead bank should the underwriting facility be called upon. In return for agreeing to underwrite the issue, the lead bank will be paid an underwriting fee, tradi- tionally in the order of 2 per cent of the total capital to be raised. Sub-underwriters will take a smaller fee, often in the order of 1 to 1.25 per cent. The risk, however, of the lead or sub-underwriters actually having to take on any of the shares in an issue is relatively low because new issues, as an added insurance of success, are normally priced below the value the new shares are expected to command in the market. It has long been argued by academics and companies that the cost of underwriting is too high taking into account its low risk, and that the high pricing must represent some sort of pricing club in financial centres. This point has now been officially recognized in the UK and an inquiry undertaken into underwriting costs (study by Paul Marsh of the London Business School, commissioned by the Office of Fair Trading). Perhaps cheaper share issues will result.

Placings

Instead of organizing an offer for sale, new shares can be sold by means of a 'placing'. With a placing, shares are offered to clients or other contacts of the investment bank leading the issue, rather than to the general public. The benefits of the method are that costs of advertising the shares and producing documentation are reduced, which makes it particularly relevant for smaller companies. The possible disadvantages are that the shares end up being held by a smaller number of more powerful investors and that often the discount on the issue (i.e. the difference between the price at which the shares are first sold and the price at which they are subsequently traded in the market) is greater than with public offers.

Rights issues and bought deals

In the UK and most of Europe, the majority of issues organized by companies with an existing quotation in order to raise new share capital are in the form of 'rights issues'. A rights issue is an issue of new shares where existing shareholders have rights (pre-emption rights) to subscribe for the shares before other investors. The form a rights issue might take would be, say, an issue of 'one for five'. What this means is that for every five shares an investor holds, he or she has the right to invest in one new share. The rights to buy the new shares issued are normally valuable, since typically the new shares are priced at a significant discount (on average 15 per cent) to the current share price. An existing shareholder can choose either to exercise his or her rights and buy the new shares offered or to sell the rights in the market place. In the latter case, the acquirer of the rights will then be entitled to subscribe for the new shares at the attractive rights issue price.

Why do many countries have laws entitling existing shareholders to subscribe for new capital before outside investors? The purpose of such laws is to protect the position of shareholders as part owners of a company. As long as a shareholder keeps investing in rights issues made by a company, his or her ownership of the company cannot be eroded by, or more technically 'diluted' by, more shares being issued. Pre-emption rights are, however, gradually being eroded themselves as companies are increasingly permitted to make placings. In the UK, up to 1986, existing quoted companies could not use placings for an issue above £3 million; the £3 million was then changed to £15 million and then in 1991 to £50 million. Now there is no limit on the amount that can be raised through placing. As the costs of rights issues are high, particularly in terms of communicating with individual shareholders and getting the issue underwritten, placements are often a cheaper alternative, particularly if the amount raised is relatively small.

In the USA, existing shareholders have never had pre-emptive rights and the method often used to issue shares is the 'bought deal'. Under this method, a company invites a number of investment banks to bid for the whole of the block of shares it wishes to issue. The company then chooses the offer it considers most attractive, bearing in mind the price it will get for its shares and probably also the likely make-up of its new shareholders. The investment bank that wins the issue then trades it on to its institutional or individual clients. Obviously, there is a risk for the investment bank if it prices the issue incorrectly and gets left with a block of shares it cannot sell. Bought deals differ from traditional European placings in that in the latter a company will normally ask the investment bank that regularly acts for it to place the shares on the company's behalf. The investment bank does not take risk itself, as the company just gets paid whatever price the bank can achieve from its investing clients. Bought deals are now becoming increasingly common in Europe, and this form of issue may well be one of the most important in future.

Before we leave the subject of rights issues, there is one aspect of this activity which often leads to confusion and even misleading media comment. It was noted above that typically rights issues are priced significantly below the current market value of a company's shares. This factor often gives rise to comment that the rights issue shares are a bargain; however, if the discount offered is considered too large, the company might be viewed as somehow undervaluing its shares. Rights issues need to be priced at or below current market price, or no shareholder would subscribe for new shares at all. It also makes sense to build in some kind of discount in case market prices fall in the time it takes for a rights issue to be announced and applications for new shares to be received; the possible problems with this time interval have been discussed above in relation to offers for sale. How large or small the discount is, however, has no bearing whatever on whether the new shares are a good or bad investment. It may seem surprising that the pricing of rights issues 'does not matter', in that shareholders do not benefit or lose in wealth terms from the issue price being set 'high' or 'low'. The basic idea behind the irrelevance of rights issue pricing is that if lots of shares are issued at a low price to raise a certain sum of money for a company, shareholders end up with a high number of shares but with a low individual price. If, alternatively, the company issues fewer shares at a higher price to raise the money needed, the shareholders end up with fewer shares but with a higher individual price. The net wealth effect, in terms of number of shares multiplied by price, for shareholders under the two alternatives is the same.

The amount of primary share market activity varies considerably from one year to another and in a way not wholly explained by theory. There tend to be share issue waves, mostly at times when the secondary market for shares is popularly considered high. Financial theory would suggest that share prices are never 'high' or 'low' but simply reflect all the latest information about company prospects. According to this theory, there should be no 'good' or 'bad' time to issue shares, but company directors do not seem to act in this way, presumably issuing shares at particular times because this is when they feel they will get the most for their company's shares. Table 4.2 provides data on UK capital issues in the 1990s.

Table 4.2   Total funds raised by UK companies through capital issues[a] (£ million)

Year	Funds raised
1993	24,389
1994	25,462
1995	12,807
1996	19,531
1997	13,569

Source: Fact File 1998, The London Stock Exchange.
[a] Includes issues of UK registered fixed interest securities. In 1997, such securities represented £2.4 billion of the issue total.

The secondary market for shares

As with most markets for financial securities, particularly those of a longer-term nature, the turnover in the secondary market for shares dwarfs the volume of funds raised in the primary market. The total turnover of UK shares in the London Stock Exchange in 1998, for example, was £1,037 billion – 250 times the total sum raised by new equity issues in the same year (LSE Primary and Secondary Market Fact Sheets, 1998).

Any exchange of existing shares could be said to constitute a transaction in the secondary market for shares. Shares of unquoted companies may be exchanged between individuals or venture capital institutions without the participation of any intermediaries or market trading mechanisms. In other cases informal 'markets', 'over the counter markets', may be used, where brokers organize the sale of shares either by phone or, increasingly, the Internet. However, most sales of the shares of larger companies are transacted through more formal exchanges. In the UK there are two recognized share exchanges, the London Stock Exchange and Tradepoint; these two exchanges are discussed in more detail below.

Sales of shares through an exchange may be organized in person with a broker, over the phone or via the Internet. Internet trading appears to be an increasing phonomenon. In spring 1999, one in four US share transactions was reported to be taking place on the Internet. In March 1999, Barclays Bank launched a service in the UK enabling individuals and professional traders to obtain stock market information and to trade shares via the Internet.

Internet trading may be seen as offering advantages over trading via a stock broker in a more traditional way. An investor should be able to respond more quickly to news or price changes than would be the case were a broker to need to be contacted. The price of transactions also tends to be lower, because fewer people are employed giving advice and actually carrying out transactions. Against this, some investors may value the personal service provided by a traditional broker and be prepared to pay the probable higher price for it.

Secondary market systems

One of the main functions of any formal security market is to operate systems which permit investors to exchange financial products quickly, cheaply and in a secure manner. The systems encompass trading mechanisms, by which investors can establish prices and agree a trade, and then the administration of the trade entered into to achieve the legal transfer of ownership of the relevant financial securities; the latter systems are referred to as 'settlement systems'.

Trading systems

There are two different types of share trading systems that markets can adopt:

1. *Order-driven systems.* These operate rather like auctions. If you want to sell your shares, you ask a broker/dealer to do this for you and you may also specify a reserve price below which you are not prepared to deal. The broker/dealer then goes into the market and achieves the best price possible for you, the exchange information system acting as a means of matching buyers and sellers. The broker/dealer is not taking a risk with his or her own money in this, but is acting more as an agent on a client's behalf in finding the best price available in the market.

2. *Quote-driven systems.* These operate with a system of professional dealers in a market. In this instance, if you wished to sell your shares, you, or an agent, could look at the different quotes available from dealers in the market and then choose the most attractive price. If you chose to sell to a dealer, he or she would buy the shares using his or her own capital and hold them in stock ready to trade on. The dealer takes a risk here in buying the shares in on his or her own account with a view to dealing on at a profit.

From an investor's point of view, the two trading systems offer advantages and disadvantages. The choice between the two is rather similar to owning an antique and having the option of selling it either through an antiques auction or through an antique dealer. If you use the auction method, you might expect the professional costs to be kept low because the auctioneers are not putting their own money at risk in selling your asset. However, you have the worry of not knowing from the outset what you will receive for your asset. If you use an antique dealer, you will be offered a firm price straight away, but the costs may be higher because the dealer is taking the risk of getting that price wrong. Whatever the arguments in favour of either system, order-driven trading systems do seem to be winning out against quote-driven ones. The overriding factor seems to be the cost advantage of the former, and more and more markets are switching in that direction in order to remain competitive.

Settlement systems

While the quality and cost of trading systems will have a significant influence on how much trade a stock exchange attracts, the efficiency of its systems to administer share transactions will also be important. Traditionally, the payments for shares and the exchange of share documentation have taken place some days after a share transaction has been agreed. Often, all the share transactions in a certain period would be settled at one go on a day some time after a specified accounting period; presumably the delay was to allow book keeping to be completed in an age without computers. The problem with this method is that it does present opportunities for short-term speculation, in that it is possible to buy and sell within an accounting period without ever having to put up any capital to back your trades. Such a system can, on the other hand, prohibit trade in different accounting periods because of the delay in getting full documentation for a share purchase. Exchanges have attempted to move to a rolling settlement system, which is where transactions are carried through a set time after each transaction as opposed to a set time after the end of a period of transactions. In the interests of minimizing costs, saving time and improving security for transactions, they have also tried to eliminate paper in the administration process, and replace it by electronic transactions. Many exchanges now have paperless settlement systems, with paper evidence of the transfer of a financial asset only being supplied on the particular request of an investor.

Stock exchanges

Stock exchanges are markets for shares, and in some cases also for fixed interest securities such as government bonds. According to Arnold, in 1998 over 80 countries had officially recognized stock exchanges. The biggest and most influential are in the USA, Japan and the UK, as shown by Table 4.3, which gives an indication of relative quarterly turnover.

Table 4.3 Quarterly equity turnover[a] of different stock exchanges

	$billion
New York	900
NASDAQ[b]	800
London	300
Tokyo	200
Germany	200
Paris	less than 100

Source: Bank of England Quarterly Bulletin, February 1997.
[a]Turnover is reported for the third quarter of 1996 and includes domestic and foreign shares. Relative turnover figures are difficult to calculate precisely because different exchanges report trades in different ways. The figures above are indicative only and are rounded to the nearest $100 billion.
[b]NASDAQ, the National Association of Securities Dealers Automated Quotations, is an American exchange specializing in new technology and smaller company shares.

In the UK, there are two share exchanges recognized by the Financial Services Authority: the London Stock Exchange, which is the country's traditional stock exchange and which has operated for centuries; and Tradepoint, which is an electronic share market which only gained its officially recognized status in 1995.

The London Stock Exchange

The LSE, while principally being thought of popularly as a share exchange, is in fact an exchange for all long-term securities. Around 65 per cent of the turnover on the LSE is represented by sales of bonds, probably more than that if intra-market trading was taken into account (LSE Secondary Market Fact Sheet, 1998). The systems for trading bonds, however, differ from those relating to shares, so we will concern ourselves primarily here with the operations of the LSE in connection with shares and then refer back to this chapter where necessary when we come to look later at bonds.

The LSE until 1986 was a physical market, i.e. it consisted of a trading floor within a dedicated building in the City of London. When the market was deregulated (of which more below), it was generally expected that the old trading floor would still be used, and several million pounds were spent modernizing it. However, in the event, the traders 'voted with their feet' (in a physically passive way) and stayed at their desks within bank dealing rooms, using their new computer system. Hence the market has become a non-physical entity, consisting of dealing rooms linked by a common computer network giving information on prices, etc., and a common set of operational rules. Most other stock markets around the world are now computerized rather than physical. One exception is the New York Stock Exchange, which still has a physical presence on Wall Street. The main problem with a physical trading location is cost, both of the market location itself and of member firms organizing a presence at it. The benefits are perhaps a more human interaction between market participants, and, some dealers would claim, the potential for the market to act more quickly to a change in circumstance than a computerized market could.

The LSE has two main market tiers or segments: the Official List, which is intended for larger and longer established companies; and the Alternative Investment Market (AIM), set up to accommodate smaller companies.

Activity 4

Most stock markets have a separate section for smaller companies. What do you think are the reasons behind setting up such a market?

In many countries, smaller companies experience difficulty in raising finance, particularly equity finance. The vast majority of equity investment (over 80 per cent in the UK) is through large institutions, and these institutions tend to favour investment in large rather than small companies. The reason is that larger companies can absorb larger investments and their shares are considered more marketable and less risky than their smaller versions. The fact that small companies can experience difficulty in raising funds is normally of concern to governments, because small companies are big employers in total and may also offer better growth prospects in future than larger, more mature companies. There is often pressure, therefore, on financial markets to ensure that funds are provided for small companies as well as larger ones.

One of the factors that has often deterred smaller companies from obtaining a quotation on a formal stock exchange is cost. Achieving and maintaining a full quotation can be costly, generally over £100,000 per annum; extensive information has to be supplied to investors, and events such as share issues have to be widely publicized to ensure that all shareholders are informed. Special 'second markets' (not to be confused with secondary markets in the sense of markets trading existing securities) tend to be formed by most share exchanges, and these have less onerous entry and information requirements than the market for full listings. In the UK, AIM was set up in 1996, succeeding two previous second markets, the Unlisted Securities Market and the Third Market. By the end of 1997, 308 companies were listed on AIM and a total of £1.6 billion had been raised in new issues (LSE Factfile, 1998).

LSE trading and settlement systems

In 1986, when computerized trading systems were first introduced at the LSE, it was decided to operate a quote-driven system incorporating intermediaries who would buy and hold stocks of shares; these intermediaries were called 'market makers'. A computer pricing system was modelled on one used by the over-the-counter American stock exchange, NASDAQ; the pricing system was called the Stock Exchange Automated Quotation system (SEAQ). Under the SEAQ system, traders could view different quotations from market-makers in respect of particular shares. Deals were then conducted over the phone. Most other European markets and the New York Stock Exchange operated order-driven systems, or hybrid systems which incorporated order-driven transactions with some market-making activity.

London's quote-driven system was generally considered to have performed better than New York's order-driven one during the crash of stock markets worldwide in 1987. New York had to be closed because the market fell so sharply that matching orders fairly became impossible. The London market, on the other hand, remained open throughout because of the market-makers' commitment to provide continuous prices; you could say, therefore, that in these circumstances the London market did a better job of maintaining liquidity for investors. (Some investors did comment rather wryly that while market-makers may technically have kept open for business throughout the crash in London, it was so hard to get them on the phone that their willingness to trade was more apparent than real.)

Despite London's success in maintaining services in the crash, its quote-driven system did threaten the competitiveness of the LSE because of its cost. In the London market, the quote-driven system was at first dropped in the second market – at that time the USM. It was found that there was not enough trade in small company shares to justify market-making activity, and so a cheaper order-driven system was introduced, called SEATS Plus. Then, in October 1997, an order-driven system was introduced for trading of shares of the top hundred companies which form the FTSE 100. The new order-driven system, which is called the Stock Exchange Electronic Trading Service (SETS), was intended to reduce trading costs in respect of the most frequently traded shares and thus maintain competitiveness with other stock exchanges, particularly those in Europe, and electronic exchanges such as Tradepoint in the UK. Costs have reduced (LSE Factfile, 1998), though there have been some problems in establishing the level of share prices at the start and finish of trading, when the volumes of transactions tend to be small.

The LSE has had a recent history of severe problems in creating and establishing a paperless settlement system. After some aborted attempts, CREST was introduced in London in 1996. Trades are now settled on a rolling basis five days after a trade is agreed, and institutional trades do not involve any exchange of paper; individual buyers can still receive a share certificate if they require.

Deregulation and subsequent changes in the structure of the LSE

Stock exchanges in many parts of the developed world have undergone considerable structural change in the 1980s and 1990s. The changes were prompted by commercial and financial companies becoming larger and more global and thus requiring stock exchanges that could offer share issuing and trading facilities to accommodate this. Advances in information and computer technology also allowed an operation of exchanges quite unlike that possible in decades previously.

A series of major changes to the UK stock market took place in 1986 and were termed collectively 'Big Bang'. Prior to Big Bang, the LSE was a relatively small, high-cost exchange. There was a system of fixed commissions in operation, whereby set amounts had to be charged on any trading of shares, which limited competition. Firms operating in the exchange also had to be organized as partnerships and to be UK owned. This structure resulted in LSE firms being relatively small because of the limitations of capital needing to come from partners' own resources. A further restriction was that members working in the Exchange had to act in a single capacity, either as a dealer in shares, called a 'jobber', or as a 'stock broker' in direct contact with clients, taking their trading orders and advising them on what shares to buy or sell. The purpose of single capacity was to avoid potential conflicts of interest. If jobbers dealt directly with investors, conflicts could potentially arise where a jobber held a stock of particular shares and might be tempted to suggest that the client purchase those shares as against others of which he had no stocks. A broker, on the other hand, who held no shares on his own account, should be in a position to give unbiased advice on shares to his client.

Change was somewhat forced on the London Stock Exchange by the Office of Fair Trading commencing proceedings against it because of the system of fixed commissions. Rather than face a full case, the Exchange agreed to reform itself voluntarily. Another commercial spur for reorganization was that the relatively high costs of the exchange and lack of membership capital meant that it was losing business to other more efficient exchanges. In particular, the American equity markets had been deregulated about ten years before the UK one and hence were able to offer share dealing services at considerably lower prices. Just before Big Bang, 40 per cent of the trade in the shares of ICI, one of Britain's foremost companies, was said to be taking place in the USA.

The changes introduced by Big Bang were that fixed commissions were abolished, membership of the Exchange was opened up to companies and foreign ownership, and single capacity operation in the market was replaced by dual capacity. At the same time, a computerized quotation system was introduced, SEAQ, which has been outlined above.

How was dual capacity in the Stock Exchange intended to work? Following Big Bang, members trading on the stock exchange could be market-makers, dealer-brokers or just brokers. Market-makers were to be firms which were prepared to offer and deal on the basis of continuous buy/sell quotations on particular shares; they would use their own capital to acquire shares and hold them in stock to trade on to other investors at a later time. The market-makers' continuous quotations meant that there should always be a market for an investor's shares, and hence the name market-maker. In exchange for their commitment to provide constant quotations, market-makers would get certain privileges, such as exemption from some tax on share dealing and the facility to publish their prices more widely than other dealers. Market-makers could deal directly with buyers/sellers of shares from outside the exchange or from other institutions within it. Dealer-brokers were to have a similar role to market-makers in holding stocks of and dealing in some shares, but also in carrying out transactions as agents for clients; dealer-brokers would not have the same requirement to provide continuous quotations as market-makers and would not enjoy special privileges in return. Some former stock brokers also remained in their single capacity role, solely providing advice to and carrying out the trades for clients from outside the stock exchange.

How would investors be protected from the potential conflicts of interest that the single capacity system was designed to prevent? At the same time as Big Bang, an extensive law on investor protection, The Financial Services Act 1986, came into force, and this regulated how advice could be offered and products sold. Thus Big Bang was about deregulation to reduce costs and increase efficiency, but was accompanied by re-regulation to protect investors in this more free market environment.

Overall, was Big Bang a success? The answer to that is, on the whole, 'yes'. Prior to deregulation, the LSE was losing business to the USA and was increasingly doing an inadequate job in providing funds to UK business. Following Big Bang, equity turnover doubled and share issues increased. The crash of 1987 caused a break on growth, but this was a worldwide event and generally the UK market was considered to have coped reasonably well, as noted above. Costs of trading for large investors have reduced significantly, but costs for smaller traders have in some cases increased; the latter is not surprising when you bear in mind that the pre Big Bang system of fixed commissions was effectively a subsidy from large transactors in shares to smaller ones. The increase in cost-effectiveness of the UK market also allowed it to win business from other stock exchanges, particularly those in Europe. Valdez (1997) makes the point that European share exchanges were slower to deregulate than London. Hence London became a centre for trading foreign, and particularly European, shares; it was able to boast a greater turnover in Swedish shares, for instance, than Stockholm. The European exchanges have, since 1986, undergone their own forms of Big Bang, and this has enabled them to win back some of the trade in domestic shares which had migrated to London. The LSE nevertheless remains a distinctly international exchange, with 68 per cent of its turnover in 1998 being in non-UK shares (LSE Secondary Market Factfile, 1998).

Big Bang marked a significant package of reform for the LSE, which substantially altered its system of operation and commercial effectiveness. Since 1986, there have been further changes, albeit generally on a more modest scale. The introduction of an order-matching trading system in 1997, discussed above, for the top 100 shares somewhat eroded the position of market-makers. Market-making still takes place for companies below the top 100 on the Official List and for AIM companies. A more significant change was announced on 7 July 1998: the LSE announced that it was to merge with the German stock exchange located in Frankfurt, the Deutsche Borse. The aim of this merger, to which other European countries have since also become party, is to develop a Europe-wide stock exchange. Initially the intention is to harmonize regulation and settlement systems to allow shares of the largest European companies to be traded from the stock exchange of any participating country. A common electronic trading system will be developed as a second project. The German and UK exchanges agreed to merge on equal terms, with the shares of a joint venture company set up to operate the new European exchange being split equally between them. This was noteworthy, as the UK exchange had been much the larger of the two in terms of domestic market capitalization (£1,000 billion versus £400 billion in 1997) and international business. The terms of the merger indicate how much other European exchanges have fought back against London's domination in share dealing since their own deregulation in the late 1980s and 1990s.

Tradepoint

Tradepoint is an electronic share exchange which is available to professional and institutional traders of shares; it is not at present open to individuals. The exchange was set up in 1992 but formally recognized as an exchange by the UK financial authorities in 1995.

Tradepoint sets out to allow its members to trade shares at a lower cost than is possible through the LSE; the system it has used from the start is an order-driven one. It also aims to offer greater anonymity for traders and easier electronic access than is possible through the more traditional exchange. Although Tradepoint continues to build its credibility, and has had significant boosts in 1999 through being approved by the US regulatory authorities in March and receiving a substantial capital injection in May, its share of the total UK equity market remains small. Even according to Tradepoint's own figures, its turnover in most of the shares it lists is less than 5 per cent of the volume traded on the LSE; in respect of many shares it is less than 1 per cent (Tradepoint website, 7 October 1999: www.tradepoint.co.uk).

Other exchanges

As well as formally recognized share exchanges, there have existed for a number of years less regulated exchanges which allow shares of unlisted companies to be exchanged by investors. In the UK, Ofex is a market which was set up in 1995 and which allows the shares of mostly smaller companies to be traded without the expense of a full official market listing. It costs only £2,000 per year for a company to be listed on Ofex.

Another relatively new phenomenon is for larger institutional shareholders to get together to arrange their own networks for exchanging shares, mostly organized by way of the Internet. The inter-institutional networks that are being set up are termed 'electronic communications networks', or 'ECNs'. If institutions exchange shares between themselves through these networks, they tend to use prices established on more formal networks and then report the trades that have taken place to the financial authorities. The institutions avoid the costs of trading through a more formal exchange in this way. However, the use of LSE market prices in the process has led to such systems being criticized as being parasitic in relation to the established markets. One concern is that if sufficient trade starts by-passing established markets because of ECNs, then formal market prices will start to be unreliable.

Some issues concerning share markets

It was noted at the start of this chapter that the markets for shares excite more comment and interest than markets for any other financial products. Some of these, such as the difficulty of small companies in raising share capital, have been touched on above. Before closing the chapter, it is worth mentioning a few others.

Who owns shares?

Shares around the world are increasingly owned by institutions rather than individuals. In the UK, over 80 per cent of all shares are estimated to be owned by institutions such as pension funds, unit trusts and insurance companies; in 1963, the comparable figure was 46 per cent (Arnold, 1998). In the USA, there is a stronger tradition of individual share ownership, with around 50 per cent of shares still being in private hands in 1997. The trend here too, however, is for institutional share ownership to grow. The increasing dominance of institutions is in many respects a natural by-product of other social changes, in particular the growing expectation that individuals should provide for their old age by having their own funded pensions. Tax incentives, such as relief for saving through pension vehicles, also encourage investment to be through institutions.

Does it matter that institutions dominate share ownership? There would certainly appear to be some unease about it, even in government circles. In the UK, privatizations often included inducements aimed especially at individuals to encourage them to apply for shares. The total number of individual shareholders has increased in recent years, but still the proportion of shares in individual hands has fallen. One potential problem with most shares being in institutional hands is that institutions are thought to be more conscious of performance than individuals, which might lead to short-termism, discussed below. The fact that so many shares are controlled by so few people, all of whom may be conscious of each other's views and actions, might also make the market more volatile. There is a concern that investment managers will tend to think and act in the same way, reinforcing bull or bear markets, whereas individuals will tend to have a greater diversity of views. Institutional shareholding may also divorce the 'man in the street' from the workings of the financial markets, and this might lead to an ignorance of and antipathy towards the markets and their influence on the economy as a whole.

In favour of institutional holding of shares, however, are the arguments that larger shareholders can exert more influence on potentially wayward boards of directors than can smaller shareholders, and that holding shares through institutions may offer particular benefits *vis-à-vis* individual share holdings. In Chapter 2 we noted that risk can often be reduced by diversification, and it may thus be beneficial for an investor with limited funds to invest in shares via an institution, such as a unit trust, and thereby gain the benefits of diversification, rather than investing in shares directly.

However we balance the arguments outlined above, the dominance of shareholding by institutions looks set to continue, certainly if the current tax incentives for investing via institutions remain in place.

Are shareholders too short term in their views of companies?

Shareholders in Western capitalist countries have for long been compared unfavourably with their Eastern counterparts, in particular for taking too short term a view of company investments. Japanese shareholders, for example, have traditionally been prepared to take around a fifteen-year view of capital investment, whereas UK or US investors would require a return in less than five years. This short-term view was believed to discourage companies from undertaking the long-term investments required to keep companies in a world beating commercial position. The problems experienced by Asian countries in the late 1990s, in part blamed on investors who demanded insufficient return for the risks undertaken, has quieted the loudest complaints. The basic criticism remains, however, that shareholders in the USA and the UK are often too keen on short-term performance and that this can be detrimental to the profitability of companies in the longer term.

The dominance of institutional shareholders in the equity markets of many Western countries is believed to play a large part in any short-termism that does exist. Fund managers within institutions, it is argued, will be concerned with the short-term performance of the money they manage, both to advance their own careers and earn them bonuses and to attract new investors towards their organizations. Individual shareholders, on the other hand, with performance less critical and probably unjudged, may be prepared to forgo returns in the short term if they can see the logic of investment being undertaken and believe that returns will flow from it in the future. Individuals may also take a wider set of criteria into account in making their investment decisions. Employees of institutions may feel bound, by performance measures and in some cases by the rules under which their institutions operate, always to make decisions which maximize the return earned on the funds they control. Individuals may forgo some return if they dislike some implications of the decision; for instance, the likelihood of employees of companies being made redundant or the operations of a company being changed as a result of new ownership. An example of the latter was the potential acquisition of Manchester United by BSkyB, which was opposed by some fans who were also shareholders. The potential takeover in the end foundered in any case on opposition from the Monopolies and Mergers Commission.

Are stock markets too volatile?

In the past two decades there have been some swift and spectacular changes in the values of shares. For the most part, share prices tend to go up fairly steadily but can come down very sharply. Crashes have been experienced in October 1987, to a lesser extent in 1991 and again in October 1998. In some cases, double digit percentages have been knocked off the value of shares in a matter of days or even hours. Are these potential large changes in the value of markets for shares something to be concerned about?

It was noted above that share prices respond to news, and if markets are operating efficiently we would expect the effect of news to be incorporated in share prices rapidly. In many ways it is thus not surprising that share prices change and change rapidly, because the content of news changes too. What has been concerning about the crashes, in particular the one of October 1987, is that value changes sometimes appeared not to be in

Figure 4.4   The level of the FT 100 share index from October 1997 to October 1999. *Source:* Datastream.

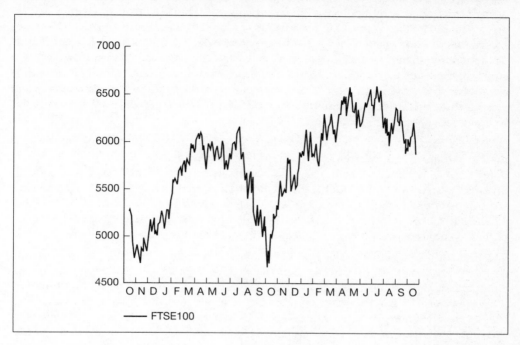

response to news. For instance, a dramatic drop in share prices would possibly be expected if a country suddenly entered a war or a period of political unrest without warning. Such events would represent news which would rationally have a significant effect on the value of shares. In 1987, however, there was no special piece of news that triggered the crash, more a market change of view on news that had been public for some time. It has also been suggested that institutional dominance of shareholding reinforced the drop in share prices. Institutions which controlled such vast blocks of shares and decided to sell influenced the market in a downwards direction just by their selling activity. Interestingly, the recovery of stock markets in late 1998 and early 1999 after the October crashes connected to the crises in Asian markets has also been attributed in some part to individual investors keeping their stock market investments, while institutions were keener to sell so as not to be left in a falling market.

Are current share prices justified?

The valuation of shares was discussed above. Even if you accept that share values are wholly logical, and will just reflect future dividends on a share, valuation is still not a cut and dried thing. Different people will have different views on how dividends will grow and how much any dividend that will be received should be valued in today's money terms. There will always be a range of opinion on the worth of shares for those reasons. Even taking this into account, there has been considerable concern and doubt, certainly in academic circles, about how current share values, particularly those in the USA, can be justified.

Traditionally there have been certain relationships which have provided a guide to the reasonableness or otherwise of share values. For a start, share prices would normally be expected to be at a level where the anticipated return on a share is greater than that on debt. This makes sense because shares are more risky investments than debt, as discussed at the start of this chapter. Various studies from the 1950s to the 1980s have shown that the extra return that shareholders were believed to look for over that offered on debt investments was in the region of 8 per cent per year. When, however, we compare current share prices to bonds, those prices appear justifiable only if the extra return for shareholders is more like 2 to 3 per cent. The only other justification for current share prices is if dividends grow in the future at an unprecedented rate, roughly by 7 per cent a year.

Is it likely that investors have become less concerned about the risk of shares and therefore require less inducement in the way of return to invest in them? The greater opportunities for international diversification of share investments may have reduced investors' sensitivity to risk, but the reduction of a risk premium from 8 to 2 per cent still looks substantial. Dividends may also be expected to grow at a rapid rate because of the exciting advances in technology which affect all aspects of commerce at present. Still, a year-on-year increase of 7 per cent *for ever* still looks ambitious.

The rise and rise of share prices may have something to do with demographic factors. In most developed countries, the population is an ageing one, with millions being encouraged, in many cases for the first time, to save personally to fund their retirement. This environment has brought about a huge current demand for shares, which are viewed as the financial asset whose value best keeps pace with wages. A niggling question is what might happen to share values when all the current savers start to cash their investments in on retirement and when there may be fewer newly ageing workers behind them looking to invest in shares.

Can share prices be said at present to be too high? If share markets are pricing efficient this should not happen, and underlying factors might be argued to have changed so that new relationships between share values and returns and those on other assets now persist. The alternative view is that what we are experiencing is something of a share price bubble; prices are becoming divorced from fundamentals and instead are being set by a belief that, simply, there will always be someone else in the market to pay a higher price in future. If this alternative view is correct, then there may be a significant realignment of share values just waiting to happen.

Summary

There are two types of share capital: ordinary share capital and preference share capital. Ordinary shares normally confer voting rights on company matters and a right to any profits left over after the fixed claims of other company participants have been satisfied; against this, ordinary shareholders rank last in line for any income on their investment or capital repayment. Preference shares provide a fixed percentage return, rather like debt, and do not generally have voting rights attached. In terms of rights to income or capital repayment, preference shareholders rank after all company participants, such as suppliers and debtholders, but before ordinary shareholders.

As a result of the ranking of share capital behind debt for income or capital repayment, an investment in shares is more risky than one in debt; the compensation for the extra risk is that shareholders will expect to receive, on average, a higher overall return on shares. From a company point of view, share capital is a low-risk but high-cost form of funding. Share capital assists a company to raise other forms of funds because its low ranking for income and capital repayment provides some security for other providers of funds.

Income on a share comes in the form of dividends. There is no legal requirement on a company to pay dividends, and this income is therefore uncertain. Most share capital has no repayment provisions attaching to it, although some companies do choose to buy in some of their own share capital from time to time. In order to realize an investment in shares, an investor will therefore have to rely on selling the shares in a secondary share market. Market value is thus the most important type of capital value of a share, and it too is uncertain.

The most important measures provided in the financial press in respect of share capital are the dividend yield and the P/E ratio. Dividend yield provides information on the cash income generated by a share. The P/E ratio relates current share price to recently reported earnings on a share. It indicates how the share markets view a company's future prospects, but is also affected by how much borrowing a company has and by how up to date the earnings figures used in its calculation might be.

In theory, the market value of a share represents the value in today's money terms of the future dividends that a share is expected to generate. It thus makes sense if share prices respond to news which affects the expected future earnings that a company will earn for shareholders. As shareholders are last in line for income in a company, any changes in the environment which affect a company's income will have a magnified effect on the return to shareholders. If share markets are efficient, any change in share income foreseen would be also expected to be reflected in share prices quickly. Share prices can thus be expected to change frequently and significantly in response to news of items which affect company earnings.

Shares of a company being sold publicly for the first time may be issued by means of a public offer for sale, either fixed price or by tender, or a placing. Placings are normally cheaper than public offers for sale because there are fewer administrative and advertising costs. Further share capital can be sold by companies whose shares are already publicly held, by means of either a rights issue or placing. Public offers for sales and rights issues are normally underwritten.

Partly as a result of the potentially infinite life of shares, secondary share markets dwarf primary markets in terms of turnover. The level of service that such secondary markets can provide is determined by their systems for trading shares and then administering the transactions afterwards. Trading systems operated by share markets are either order-driven or quote-driven; order-driven systems are becoming the more prevalent because of their cost advantages. Modern settlement systems allow paperless administration of share transactions.

The largest stock exchanges by turnover in the world are in the USA, the UK and Japan. The UK has two formally recognized exchanges, the London Stock Exchange (LSE) and Tradepoint. There are also less formal and lightly regulated markets for the exchange of shares of smaller companies, and, increasingly, networks between large institutional traders of shares which by-pass all exchanges.

The LSE has operated for centuries, and is the most international share exchange in the world. It has undergone significant change in the past two decades, moving from an exchange with a physical location to one with a computerized network, and, through

'Big Bang', widening the permitted ownership of professional members and removing restrictions on trading practices so as to lower costs. The exchange now operates a mixture of order- and quote-driven systems, and is in negotiation to merge with other European exchanges. The LSE can be accessed either through traditional means involving personal contact with a stock broker or via the Internet, using services offered by a growing number of share trading companies. Tradepoint is an electronic exchange which has only been established in the past five years. It aims to offer lower cost share transactions to professional share traders than the LSE, but has secured only a small share of the UK equity market to date.

In many countries there is a trend for shares to be increasingly held through institutional investors, partly as a result of tax incentives to boost personal saving. The dominance of institutions may cause problems in equity markets, in that institutional investors may make more similar investment decisions than individuals, which could lead to increased market volatility, and may be short term in their views. Short-termism in share markets has been argued to lead to under-investment by companies. Volatility in share markets is a concern if share price changes, particularly drops in value, are unrelated to news affecting company profits. If markets are inexplicably volatile, the confidence of investors and fund raisers in share markets may be undermined.

There is academic and market debate about the justification or otherwise for current share prices. If traditional relationships between share prices and other variables hold, current valuations appear only to be explicable if investors are considerably less concerned about share risk than they used to be or if dividends are expected to grow at an unprecedented rate in future. An alternative interpretation of current share prices is that they are not supported by fundamental factors, and may exhibit the characteristics of a price bubble.

Note

1.   Market efficiency is discussed in relation to financial markets in general in Chapter 2. Financial management textbooks such as those by Arnold (1998) and Brealey and Myers cover the subject in greater depth.

References

Arnold, G. (1998) *Corporate Financial Management.* London: Financial Times Professional Limited.

Brealey, R. A. and Myers, S. C. (1996) *Principles of Corporate Finance*, 5th edn. London: McGraw-Hill.

Valdez, S. (1997) *An Introduction to Global Financial Markets.* London: Macmillan Business.

Questions

Note: suggested solutions are provided for questions marked *

*1. Mrs Jackson has £10,000 to invest and is considering putting the money into either shares or corporate bonds. Her financial adviser informs her that in the last few years shares have yielded on average 10% per annum and corporate bonds 7%. The adviser suggests that an investment in shares is clearly preferable. Comment on this advice.

*2. BLD plc has the following accounting information in respect of the year ending 30 April 200X:

Profit and loss account for the year to 30 April 200X

	£000s
Trading profit	80,000
Interest	−4,000
Profit before interest	76,000
Tax	−20,000
Profit after interest and tax	56,000
Dividends	−10,000
Retained profit for the year	46,000

Extract from the Balance Sheet as at 30 April 200X:

	£000s
Share capital (Note 1)	12,500
Retained earnings	50,000
Shareholders' funds	62,500

Note 1: The company's share capital is in the form of shares with a 25p par value.

If the current market value of BLD shares is £16.5, find the BLD dividend yield and p/e ratio from the above accounts.

3. Stock markets have sometimes been described as being similar to huge casinos. Discuss to what extent such descriptions can be justified.

*4. How, and why, would you expect the share price of a UK house building company, Bargate plc, to change in response to the following information:

a) The Bank of England raises interest rates; this move is wholly unexpected by the financial markets.

b) The Bank of England lowers interest rates. The Governor of the Bank of England has attended a number of dinners the previous week at which he has spoken of the strong case for lowering rates.

c) The Chancellor of the Exchequer abolishes mortgage tax relief in his annual budget. The tax change induces much adverse press comment, as the party in power has always maintained that mortgage relief would not be cut.

d) The Managing Director of Bargate, Sue Littledale, announces that she is leaving Bargate to join rival house builders, Stanton Homes. Littledale's record at Bargate has been controversial and the financial results of the company disappointing under her stewardship.

5. Explain the distinction between
a) in the primary market, a public offer for sale at a fixed price and by tender;
b) in the secondary market, the trading of shares by means of an order driven and quote driven system.

5

The market for medium-
to long-term debt capital

THE RAISING OF DEBT CAPITAL IS, generally, much less newsworthy than the raising of equity capital, with any commentary on it in the financial press being confined to the small print of the 'markets' pages in most newspapers. This is in part because debt is often raised privately through financial intermediaries rather than through markets, and also because any market debt that is raised is generally the preserve of institutional investors and extremely rich individuals rather than being aimed at the mass of personal investors. This is not to say that debt capital is less important than equity capital; as we noted in Chapter 4, the amount of debt capital raised by companies is generally several times the amount raised via equity issues, and debt capital is the only form of funds available to government and public institutions.

Debt capital comes in many forms, and the way we categorize these forms in order to study them is in many ways arbitrary. In this text, debt has been categorized by its original maturity, with medium- to long-term debt being covered in this chapter and short-term debt being studied in the following chapter; both chapters look at domestic markets for debt as well as the international markets, generally referred to as the 'euro markets'.

Short-term debt is universally defined as being debt with an original maturity of less than one year. The products available in this category include bills, overdrafts and short-term loans. There is no universally accepted definition of medium-term, as opposed to long-term, debt. A debt with an original maturity of one to five years might be considered medium-term debt and anything over that maturity would then be classed as long-term debt. Products which are medium- to long-term debt include leasing and hire purchase, bonds, bank loans and mortgages.

Learning objectives

This chapter will examine the different types of debt product and their uses, as well as the value of traded debt in relation to interest rates. Particular points to note will be:

- different aspects of debt capital to weigh up when choosing between debt types;
- the information bond prices can give on future inflation, and how this is used by financial authorities;
- how bonds are traded domestically and internationally.

Factors to consider when comparing different types of debt capital

The fact that there are so many different types of debt, with their corresponding different characteristics, makes it often quite difficult for anyone looking to borrow or to invest in debt products to decipher what is the best available deal. There are three broad factors to consider when comparing debt products. These factors are:

- the cost of/return on the debt;
- the risk of the debt;
- the repayment provisions on the debt.

A fourth factor that debt raisers may need to consider is the source of the debt. These factors are considered in more detail below.

The interest of borrowers and lenders is generally opposite in respect of the above factors. We will see below, for instance, that steps can be taken to limit the risk of a debt. This will normally be in the interests of a lender, but, other things being equal, something that the borrower would rather not have to get involved in. The cost of debt to the borrower is also equivalent to the return on debt to the lender. For example, if I lend you money for a year and you agree to pay me back the money plus £100, the £100 is your cost of debt, but also my return. Lenders will obviously look for a high cost/return while borrowers will want a low cost/return. For simplicity in the following discussion, cost and return are together referred to just as 'cost of debt'.

The cost of debt

There is more to comparing the cost of different types of debt than might at first seem apparent. For a start, cost comes in many forms. The most obvious form of cost of debt is any interest paid to the lender. In comparing the interest on different types of debt, though, you need to consider whether the interest is fixed (i.e. a stated immovable percentage of the capital amount, or 'principal', lent) or floating (i.e. a variable interest rate, generally an agreed percentage above some reference lending rate, such as bank base rate). The frequency of interest payments also affects the full cost of the loan to you, and this is illustrated in the following activity.

Activity 1

Suppose two banks offered you one-year loans on identical terms, except that one bank would charge you 10 per cent interest, with the whole of the interest being payable at the end of the year, whereas the other bank would charge you 10 per cent interest, with the interest being added to your loan account on the basis of 2.5 per cent of the amount outstanding at the end of every quarter. Which loan would be the more expensive?

The second loan arrangement would be the more expensive for you, because at the end of the second quarter you would be charged interest on the principal originally lent plus the interest added at the end of the first quarter. At the end of the third quarter, you would pay interest on the principal plus two quarters' interest, and so on.

Using techniques taking into account the time value of money, you can calculate an equivalent annual rate of interest for loans of the second type, and thus can compare on equal terms such loans with others charging interest annually.

Not all forms of debt even pay interest as their main form of return. We shall see in Chapter 6 that many short-term debt products do not have any interest provisions at all, but instead offer a profit to investors, called a 'discount', in terms of the price at which such products are sold being less than the price that the borrower has to pay back to cancel, or 'redeem', the debt on maturity. Medium-term debt products such as leasing and hire purchase also do not expressly involve interest payments. In these cases periodic rental payments are set to cover repayment of the principal lent plus a return on the money to the lender.

Interest and its discount or rental equivalents are even then not the end of the cost story, however. Lenders may also charge fees for, variously, arranging a debt (an arrangement fee, up to 1 per cent of the amount raised), making debt available for a period without it being used (a commitment fee, around 0.25 per cent of the amount made available) and reviewing longer-standing debt (review fees, often a set amount per year). In order to help borrowers and investors compare all the different types of debt which might be available to them, financial institutions are often required to quote an 'APR', an annual percentage rate. This rate expresses the interest, or other return equivalents, and fees payable on the debt as a simple annual interest rate comparable with a loan that had interest only payable at the end of each year of the loan.

The comments made so far on the cost of different types of debt relate specifically to charges explicitly made by lenders. Borrowers may, however, have internal costs in raising debt, and for a fair comparison to be made between different debt types, these costs too need to be factored into the debt cost equation. As we shall see below, some debt types are sold through markets rather than financial intermediaries. Market debt may not have costs such as arrangement fees attached, but will involve selling and administrative expense in, for example, marketing the debt products to potential investors and then managing a register of debtholders afterwards.

The risk of debt

Investors putting money into debt products will be interested not only in the return they can expect to earn on their investment but also in the risk they will be running in making that investment. Debt risk arises in part because of the chance that the borrower will not make interest and principal payments as agreed (referred to as 'default risk') and also because the value of some debt products can vary over time ('capital risk'). As most investors are risk-averse and thus require a risk/return trade-off, as discussed in Chapter 1, lenders will require a higher return on debt the more default and capital risk they expect to run.

Different borrowers will represent different chances of default risk for lenders, depending on the value of assets they own and which back the debt, and the amount and stability of the borrower's income. A number of institutions, the 'credit rating agencies', exist to monitor the riskiness of the larger and more significant borrowers. Moody's and Standard and Poor's are the most well known agencies in the USA, while IBCA is an agency operating in Europe. The agencies give different borrowers credit ratings, varying from Triple A for the most secure borrowers to D for borrowers considered quite likely to default on their debt obligations.

Default risk can be reduced for lenders by security being taken against a debt. The security might be in the form of particular assets being pledged by the borrower, such that, on any debt default, the assets can be realized by the lender to satisfy any income or capital payments outstanding. If a debt is secured against particular assets, this is termed a 'fixed charge'; if assets in general are offered as security, such as debtors on a company's books at any time, this is termed a 'floating charge'. A different type of debt security from that offered by a borrower's assets is a debt guarantee from a third party. With a guarantee, if the original borrower defaults on a loan, the party guaranteeing the debt, the 'debt guarantor', will be legally bound to make up any loss to the lender. Guarantors are often company directors, in the case of small companies, or financial institutions who charge a fee for any guarantees they offer. In the UK, government-backed loan guarantees are made available through a Loan Guarantee Scheme (LGS) for a fee. LGS loans can be an indespensable part of financing for small or medium-sized companies.

Another step lenders can take to limit default risk is to impose conditions on borrowers at the time any debt agreement is entered into. Conditions built into loan agreements are termed 'restrictive covenants'. The sort of action that restrictive covenants are designed to limit are the taking on by borrowers of more debt, as this can increase the risk to the original lender, and the making of payments other than on the original debt, such as, in the case of a company, the paying of dividends to shareholders and the purchase of capital equipment. If a borrower does not keep within the bounds of the covenants imposed by debt agreements, he or she is said to be 'in breach of' debt covenants and the debt will normally become repayable immediately.

From the point of view of borrowers, offering security to lenders is likely to restrict the scope for further borrowing and perhaps also the freedom to carry out other financial actions in future. Further borrowing may be limited if a borrower's principal assets, or those of a connected debt guarantor, have all been offered to secure the current debt. Both borrowing and other financial actions may be limited by restrictive covenants. Borrowers will therefore prefer, other things being equal, to acquire debt without offering security.

Debt repayment provisions

Debt instruments provide for repayment of debt principal in a variety of ways. In some cases the principal is repaid in a single lump sum at the end of the debt period; some bank loans, bills and bonds offer repayments of this type. In other cases the principal is repaid gradually over the life of the debt; leases, hire purchase, mortgages and other bank loans are typical examples of this type of repayment.

Where repayment is over the life of the debt, the borrower may make equal loan payments in all periods, the early payments consisting mostly of interest but the proportion of capital repayment gradually increasing as the principal outstanding is reduced. Mortgages, leases and hire purchase are typically structured in this way. An alternative payment schedule is for equal capital repayments to be made over the life of the debt, the total payments being made by the borrower then being greater at the start of the debt period, when interest charged is high, and reducing towards the end of the

Table 5.1 Alternative debt repayment schedules on a ten-year loan of £20,000 with a 10 per cent interest rate

Year	Total annual payment (£)	Interest payment (£)	Capital payment (£)
a. Equal annual payments on the loan, capital payments increasing over the life of the loan			
1	3,255	2,000[a]	1,255[b]
2	3,255	1,875[c]	1,380
3	3,255	1,736	1,519
4	3,255	1,585	1,670
5	3,255	1,417	1,838
6	3,255	1,234	2,021
7	3,255	1,032	2,223
8	3,255	809	2,446
9	3,255	565	2,690
10	3,255	296	2,960
Rounding			−2
			20,000
b. Reducing annual payments on the loan, capital payments being equal over the life of the loan			
1	4,000[e]	2,000[a]	2,000[d]
2	3,800	1,800[f]	2,000
3	3,600	1,600	2,000
4	3,400	1,400	2,000
5	3,200	1,200	2,000
6	3,000	1,000	2,000
7	2,800	800	2,000
8	2,600	600	2,000
9	2,400	400	2,000
10	2,200	200	2,000
			20,000

[a] Interest payment = 10 per cent of original loan less cumulative capital payments = $0.1 \times 20,000$.
[b] Capital payment = total annual payment less interest payment = 3,255 − 2,000.
[c] Interest payment = $0.1 \times (20,000 - 1,255) = £1,874.5$.
[d] Capital payment = Loan amount divided equally over loan term = 20,000/10.
[e] Total annual payment = interest payment plus capital payment.
[f] Interest payment = $0.1 \times (20,000 - 2,000) = £1,800$.

life of the debt as interest charged reduces. Table 5.1 illustrates the two alternative ways of structuring debt repayment just discussed. There are, then, many variations on this sort of theme. Some loans, for instance, are offered with 'grace periods', which are repayment free periods, normally in the early stages of the debt.

Both borrowers and lenders will want to choose debt products which offer repayment provisions that fit in with their general cash flow. For instance, a business just starting up might find a loan offering a grace period attractive, so that trading cash flow can be established before any debt repayments have to be made. Individual borrowers will probably find cash budgeting easier when total payments on debt, covering interest and capital, are even over the life of the debt. This is as shown in the first part of Table 5.1.

Debt source

Where a debt comes from can be an important factor for some borrowers, particularly small companies. It can often be difficult, as discussed in Chapter 4, for small companies to raise equity finance, and debt thus becomes the principal source of funds for such businesses. Raising sufficient debt capital to fund a business, particularly in its early years, may also, however, not be straightforward, as lenders may view these businesses as high risk because of their small size and possibly limited track record. In such circumstances a small company may be able to raise more finance in total by arranging relatively small amounts of debt from a number of sources, each prepared to take a limited risk in lending to the business, than could otherwise be achieved by getting all finance from a single source. A small company might, for instance, choose to raise hire purchase finance from a specialist financial institution even if the cost of this finance would be greater than that of borrowing from its principal bank. The small company might consider the preservation of lending capacity with its bank well worth the slightly higher cost of funds from the alternative finance source.

A borrower or debt investor will need to take all the above factors into account in choosing between alternative debt products. Many of the factors can be included in numerical form in financial calculations which then produce an objective valuation of the different debt choices. We are not going to go into how these calculations are performed here as this is not within the scope of this book. Other factors are more subjective in nature and cannot be captured by a number to be incorporated within a calculation. There will therefore be an element of judgement and subjective choice in any selection of debt type.

Types of medium- and long-term debt

The main types of medium- and long-term debt are bank loans and mortgages, leasing, hire purchase, medium-term notes and bonds. The first four types of debt finance are arranged by a borrower with a financial intermediary. They are not tradable forms of finance as such, although financial institutions are increasingly devising ways of 'manufacturing tradability' from them. The only forms of medium- to long-term debt that are directly tradable in established markets are medium-term notes, bonds and asset-backed securities.

Bank loans and mortgages

Bank loans and mortgages (loans secured on property) are an important source of finance to companies. Small companies are particularly dependent on these types of debt because borrowing through debt markets tends to be too costly for them in terms of developing a market presence and administering a debt issue. Governments do not raise money in this form because borrowing from the banking sector would be highly inflationary, as explained in Chapter 3.

Up until the end of the 1970s, commercial banks in the UK lent to companies on a short- or, at most, medium-term basis. Long-term loans only became available following the 1979 Wilson Report, which identified lack of long-term funding as a problem, particularly for smaller companies. Loans can now be arranged with a term over ten years.

Bank loans and mortgages come with a great variety of interest and repayment profiles. Interest can be fixed or variable, or might be arranged to have elements of both; for instance, a variable interest rate but with a ceiling beyond which the rate cannot rise. Repayments may be a set amount of capital per period or an even total loan payment, with the allocation between interest and capital changing over the life of the loan, as explained above and illustrated in Table 5.1. Other aspects of loans to be considered will be the fees which will be charged on the setting up of most loans and the security which will normally be required in some form by the institutional lender.

Securitization and asset-backed securities

When financial institutions provide debt such as bank loans and mortgages, the assets the institutions obtain are not tradable. In the past two to three decades, institutions have created a way to make these assets tradable through the rather cumbersomely named method of 'securitization'. What the financial institutions do is place a number of non-tradable assets of the same type into a separate legal entity, normally a trust, and then sell securities which give the holders the right to income received by the trust. The institution which originally created the debt still maintains a relationship with the borrower; interest and principal repayments will still be collected by the original lender, for example, normally for a fee charged to the trust. What the securitization achieves, however, is the removal of any risk in relation to the original loans from the original lender. The lender has effectively sold off the debt it created and does not have to show it on its balance sheet or provide capital against it.

The securities sold by a trust into which assets such as secured bank loans or mortgages have been placed are called 'asset-backed securities'. The income they offer is backed by the security taken by the original lender, which would be the value of a house in the case of a normal domestic mortgage. In some cases an original institutional lender may arrange a guarantee to back such securities in addition to the security initially provided by the borrower.

Leasing and hire purchase

Leasing and hire purchase (h.p.) are types of medium-term debt capital which can be raised in order to finance purchases of equipment. Again it is companies rather than governments who use this type of finance, and smaller companies for whom it is particularly relevant.

Under a lease or h.p. arrangement, a finance house, which is normally a specialist subsidiary of a commercial bank, will finance up to 90 per cent of the cost of equipment in exchange for the borrower, who is the user of the equipment, paying an agreed set of rentals over a specified period; the rentals are set to repay the money the finance house has laid out and also to provide a return on that money over the agreement period. The rentals are thus rather like an even set of loan repayments, as illustrated in the upper part of Table 5.1. In law the finance house actually owns the equipment, and this is the security for the finance it provides, but commercially the user of the equipment takes all responsibility for it; for example, repairing and insuring it as necessary. At the end of the rental period, the user of the equipment will own it (under an h.p. agreement), or get all the benefits virtually free from it (under a lease). Lease and h.p. finance can be arranged for a variety of terms, typically ranging from two to seven years, and on the basis of fixed or variable rates of interest. There is some flexibility in repayment schedules too, with some agreements providing for only partial capital repayment over the period of the finance, with an additional single payment, a 'balloon payment', at the end.

Leasing and h.p. are particularly useful forms of debt funding to small companies, because they come from sources which are often different from the companies' principal lenders. The percentage of cost that can be raised, at up to 90 per cent of capital cost, is also often higher than can be obtained from general lenders, who tend to work on the rule that borrowing should not be more than 50 per cent of capital expended.

Medium-term notes

Medium-term notes are a form of tradable or 'negotiable' debt. A medium-term note constitutes a written promise, a 'promissory note', from a company to repay a specified sum of money on a given future date, and in the meantime to pay interest to the holder of the note also at a specified rate and time. The interest may be either fixed or variable and the term of the note might be from one up to fifteen years. A company which creates a medium-term note will sell it in a market for such company debt. The sum the company receives for the note provides it with finance in much the same way as would a loan from a bank. The original buyer of the note may then choose to keep the security until it matures and is repaid by the issuing company, or may opt to sell it on to other investors. If the note is sold on, the price it commands may differ from its original or maturity value in the same way as a bond, and this is discussed further below.

A company wishing to issue medium-term notes will normally have to satisfy conditions laid down by financial authorities as to company size and financial standing. The notes will be issued as part of a programme whereby the issuing company commits to create a maximum volume of notes over a number of years. Over the period of the programme, the company may issue notes and repay them as required but will keep the maximum volume of notes in issue within the maximum announced at the start of the programme.

Most securities of a promissory note type are short term, and Chapter 6 provides a more detailed discussion of them.

Bonds

Bonds are tradable medium- to long-term borrowing securities issued by companies and governments. Traditionally they have offered a fixed rate of interest and a fixed sum of money on maturity, and have been issued with an original maturity of anything from one to over twenty years. Bonds differ from medium-term notes in being issued in volume on a particular date rather than over time as part of a predetermined programme.

Bonds issued by companies come under the general description of 'corporate bonds'. Another term often used to describe corporate bonds is 'debentures'. Strictly, debentures are bonds which are secured on the assets of the issuing company, the precise terms of the security being set out in a trust deed. 'Debenture' is thus a term covering a type of secured bond rather than describing all types of bonds issued by companies. Bonds issued by the UK government are called 'gilt edged securities' or 'gilts', the rather peculiar name coming from the gold edging to the documents which evidenced the existence of these bonds. Other countries use different titles for government bonds, such as Treasury bonds in the USA, Obligations assimilable de trèsor in France and Bundesanleihen in Germany.

The lending which a bond constitutes is evidenced by a document which shows all the details of the amount lent, interest payable and maturity date.

Activity 2

Figure 5.1 A specimen UK Government bond certificate. *Source:* UK Debt Management Office.

Figure 5.1 shows an example of a bond document. Try to identify from it:

1. *Who the borrower is.*
2. *How much is borrowed and in what currency.*
3. *How much interest will be paid and when.*
4. *When the bond matures and the lender will be repaid.*

1. *The 'bond issuer'.* The bond in Figure 5.1 has been issued by the UK government through, at that time, the Bank of England.

   An investor would need to know the issuer's identity in order to judge the creditworthiness of the body to which he or she was lending and thus to assess the risk of the bond. The information might also be needed if the investor had to apply for interest payments or repayment of capital at the end of the life of the bond.

2. *The 'nominal value' of the bond.* The bond we are considering here has a

'nominal' or 'par' value stated on the bond document of £1,000. This may not be the amount the bond can currently be sold for, as market conditions at the time of sale may dictate a different bond value. The nominal value is, however, the value on which interest will always be calculated. In the UK, gilts are issued with a nominal, or par, value of £1,000 per bond. In the USA, Treasury bonds are issued with a nominal value of $1,000.

In the case of most bonds, the nominal value is the sum which will be repaid by the bond issuer when the bond reaches maturity, and comes to be 'redeemed'. In some instances, however, bonds have a 'redemption value' which is different from their nominal value; it is quite common, for example, to have bonds whose redemption value is the nominal value indexed for inflation. A separate redemption value or redemption formula would need to be stated on a bond document where it differed from the nominal value.

3. *The 'coupon' or interest.* The coupon is the rate of interest paid on the bond, and is a percentage applied to the bond's nominal value. An investor will also need to know when interest is to be paid; in some cases interest is annual, but in others semi-annual. The term 'coupon' derives from the practice in the case of registered bonds of investors detaching a coupon from their bond and sending it to the issuing body each time interest falls due and can be claimed.

In Figure 5.1, the coupon rate is 6.5 per cent and interest is to be paid semi-annually on 7 June and 7 December. Thus the holder of the bond will receive £32.5 ([0.065 × 1000]/2) on 7 June and 7 December each year gross of tax.

4. *The maturity or redemption of the bond.* The bond certificate in Figure 5.1 states that the bond will be redeemed on 7 December 2003. A precise date of redemption is specified on a bond certificate, although bonds are referred to in the financial press quoting just their year of redemption e.g. 'Treas 6½ per cent 2003' for the bond in Figure 5.1. Investors need to know the maturity of a bond first in order to plan their cash flow, should they intend to hold the bond through to redemption, and also to enable them to value the bond at other times. Bond valuation is discussed further below.

The bond discussed above, which exhibits traditional bond characteristics, is termed a 'straight' or 'plain vanilla' bond. One feature of the bond market, particularly in the past 20 years, has been innovation in creating new types of bonds, the intention always being to allow a bond to be sold offering a lower overall return because its innovatory design fulfils some requirement for particular tax or risk features. Other types of domestic bonds[1] that are reasonably prevalent in the bond market are as follows:

1. *Floating rate notes/variable rate bonds and index linked bonds.* As noted at the start of our discussion of bonds, this type of debt has traditionally been issued with a fixed rate of interest. In the 1970s and 1980s, inflation rose to high levels historically and was variable. In these circumstances bonds started to be issued either with variable rates of interest (termed 'floating rate notes' if issued by companies, and 'variable rate bonds' if issued by governments) or with their interest and principal payments indexed for inflation ('index linked bonds').

2. *Deep discount or zero coupon bonds.* These are bonds which offer either a coupon which is low compared to current or expected future interest rates ('deep

discount bonds') or no coupon at all ('zero coupon bonds'). In order to attract investors to buy such bonds when the income they produce is low or non-existent, the bonds need to be sold at a value below their redemption value, i.e. 'at a discount'. The investor's return then comes partially or wholly in the form of the profit made on the difference between the bond purchase price and its redemption value.

3. *Perpetual or irredeemable bonds.* There are a few bonds in existence, mostly issued by governments in time of war, which have no redemption date. An investor buying such a bond will receive the interest on the bond 'in perpetuity', i.e. forever.

4. *Convertible bonds.* These types of bonds carry the right for the holder of the bond to convert his or her bond investment into shares (or, more unusually, into other bonds) of the issuer at a specified future date and at a specified conversion rate. The investor has no obligation to convert, and so has the security of a straight bond investment but with the opportunity to benefit from any rise in share price if that should come about over the life of the bond.

5. *Bonds with warrants.* These are similar in concept to convertible bonds, except that the bond investor has a right (through the 'warrant' attaching to the bond) to buy company shares at a specified price and future date rather than to exchange his or her bond for shares.

6. *Junk bonds.* The somewhat unattractively named 'junk bonds' were a feature of the bond market of the 1980s, notably in the USA. Junk bonds are bonds issued by less creditworthy companies and governments (those with a credit rating less than BBB). These bonds command a higher rate of return than other bonds because of their relatively high risk.

Activity 3

Suggest, with reasons, types of bonds that might be particularly suitable for a company wishing to raise finance in the following circumstances:

1. *The company is undertaking a project which is not expected to generate any cash flow for ten years, but is likely to be profitable and cash flow producing thereafter.*
2. *The company, which has relatively high borrowings compared to equity at present, is undertaking an investment into a new area of business which could transform the company into an extremely profitable venture if it proves success-ful; the downside is that the project is very risky and has a relatively high chance of failure.*

The following types of bond finance might be suitable:

1. Ten-year (or longer) zero coupon bonds might be attractive in these circum-stances, in that the company will not have to pay out interest while the project is not in a cash flow generating period. The full cost of the bond finance is only borne by the company on redemption of the bonds. Investors will only be attracted to buy these bonds, of course, if the company is viewed as a pretty safe investment or if the overall return is high, as they are having to wait a long period before they receive any return.

2. In this position, the company might consider convertible bonds or bonds with warrants. By offering bonds with the possibility of conversion into shares, the company should obtain borrowing at a lower yield than it would pay on straight debt. Investors have the enticement that, should the risky project prove successful, they will have the right to buy into the company's equity at what is likely to be a low price. However, if the project does not turn out as hoped, they have the security of being bondholders rather than shareholders, with the attached advantages of having interest paid before dividends, etc. The company might be particularly keen to see conversion of bonds into equity in future because it already has a high debt/equity ratio. Overall, issuing convertible bonds could be very attractive because it offers low-cost debt finance at present, with the possible reduction of a high debt ratio on conversion into equity later.

Bond values, inflation and interest rates

In the next three sections of this chaper, we will concentrate particularly on the relationship between bond prices, inflation and interest rates. This is not because bonds are a more important source of finance than other types of medium- and long-term debt; on the contrary, we have noted above that for many smaller companies at present the markets are not relevant to funding at all. The bond markets do have a greater effect on all our lives, however, than most of us may realize. This is because the rates of return on bonds are used by the financial authorities as a clue to future inflation. The movements of bonds can, on this basis, be the underlying reason for changes made to general interest rates, and that in turn affects companies and individuals alike through borrowing and saving rates and the state of the economy in general.

Data on medium- and long-term debt in the press

Many of the different types of debt described above are not specifically reported on in the financial press. This is because debt variants such as bank loans, leasing and h.p. are organized directly between borrowers and financial institutions and there is then no secondary trading of them thereafter. The data that are found in the press thus relate to tradable debt, and we are going to look specifically at the information published on bonds.

Figure 5.2 reproduces information that can be found in the UK press on government bonds. For the purpose of presenting data the gilts are divided into 'shorts', 'mediums' and 'longs', depending on whether they have residual maturity (i.e. maturity remaining from today's date) of, respectively, less than five years, five to fifteen years or over fifteen years. The titles of different gilts are shown in the far left column; each title includes the coupon and year of maturity of the gilt. The next two columns, moving from left to right, show two different measures of the return on the bonds, or 'yield'. The measures are called the 'interest' or 'running' yield, and the 'redemption' yield, and are discussed further below. The next four columns in the table show the price of the bond in the market the previous day, the price change during the previous day's trading and the highest and lowest price of the bond in the past 52 weeks' trading.

Two different measures of bond yield are included in the data on bonds provided to investors, because each conveys a different aspect of the return provided by a bond. The interest, or running, yield on a bond shows the coupon as a percentage of the market

Figure 5.2 Information on UK government bonds produced in the financial press. *Source: Financial Times*, 22 September 1999.

UK GILTS PRICES

	Notes	Yield Int	Yield Red	Price £	+ or −	52 week High	52 week Low
Shorts" (Lives up to Five Years)							
Treas 2½pc 1999	✠	1.25	-	199.55	+.01	199.60	194.40
Conv 10¼pc 1999		10.16	5.01	100.84	−.02	104.55	100.81
Treas 8½pc 2000	✠	8.41	5.35	101.06	−.04	103.54	101.06
Conv 9pc 2000		8.86	5.32	101.60	−.04	104.38	101.60
Treas 13pc 2000		12.28	5.51	105.83	−.02	112.21	105.83
Treas 8pc 2000		7.80	5.75	102.58	−.03	105.84	102.55
Treas Fltg Rate 2001		-	0.30	100.28	+.02	100.82	100.26
Treas 10pc 2001		9.48	5.95	105.46	−.03	110.37	105.43
Conv 9½pc 2001	✠	8.96	5.94	105.99	−.03	110.89	105.95
Conv 9¾pc 2001	✠	9.14	5.94	106.69	−.03	111.80	106.65
Treas 7pc 2001		6.87	6.05	101.86	−.05	106.51	101.68
Conv 10pc 2002	✠	9.19	6.21	108.82	−.08	116.41	108.63
Treas 7pc 2002		6.85	6.09	102.24	−.06	108.13	102.06
Conv 9½pc 2002	✠	8.79	6.21	108.13	−.08	115.64	107.93
Treas 9¾pc 2002		8.92	6.20	109.36	−.08	117.29	109.16
Exch 9pc 2002	✠	8.34	6.20	107.90	−.08	115.62	107.68
Conv 9¾pc 2003	✠	8.76	6.20	111.36	−.08	120.19	111.14
Treas 8pc 2003		7.54	6.14	106.08	−.11	114.74	105.85
Treas 10pc 2003		8.84	6.20	113.17	−.11	123.52	112.96
Treas 13¾pc 2000–3	✠	12.89	5.51	106.65	−.02	113.68	106.65
Treas 6½pc 2003		6.40	6.08	101.54	−.10	110.21	101.28
Treas 11½pc 2001–4		10.68	6.02	107.71	−.05	113.90	107.71
Treas 10pc 2004	✠	8.68	6.20	115.17	−.11	126.55	114.95
Five to Fifteen Years							
Treas 5pc 2004		5.21	6.00	95.95	−.12	98.80	95.72
Funding 3½pc 1999–4		3.79	5.32	92.36	−.09	98.98	91.01
Conv 9½pc 2004		8.26	6.03	115.00	−.14	126.43	114.78
Treas 6¾pc 2004		6.55	6.04	103.12	−.14	113.28	102.87
Conv 9½pc 2005		8.21	6.12	115.73	−.15	128.16	115.41
Exch 10½pc 2005	✠	8.63	6.12	121.72xd	−.15	135.46	121.39

	Notes	Yield Int	Yield Red	Price £	+ or −	52 week High	52 week Low
Treas 12½pc 2003–5		10.18	6.19	122.82	−.11	135.55	122.63
Treas 8½pc 2005		7.56	6.06	112.45	−.17	125.31	112.09
Conv 9¾pc 2006	✠	8.02	6.00	121.54	−.26	136.21	121.07
Treas 7¾pc 2006		7.07	6.03	109.64	−.21	122.40	109.17
Treas 8pc 2002–6		7.64	6.28	104.68xd	−.03	111.73	104.43
Treas 7½pc 2006		6.90	6.00	108.69	−.23	121.62	108.21
Treas 11¾pc 2003–7	✠	10.09	6.20	116.47	−.08	126.29	116.28
Treas 8½pc 2007		7.36	5.99	115.44	−.26	129.86	114.93
Treas 7¼pc 2007		6.69	5.93	108.44	−.26	122.55	107.91
Treas 13½pc 2004–8	✠	10.45	6.03	129.13xd	−.14	142.61	128.96
Treas 9pc 2008		7.41	5.90	121.48	−.35	138.52	120.98
Treas 8pc 2009		6.87	5.81	116.46xd	−1.03	132.91	116.46
Treas 5¾pc 2009		5.68	5.59	101.22	−.29	114.67	100.93
Treas 6¼pc 2010		5.91	5.55	105.75	−.39	118.76	105.48
Conv 9pc Ln 2011		6.96	5.58	129.27	−.50	145.31	129.05
Treas 9pc 2012		6.85	5.55	131.42	−.52	147.74	131.13
Treas 5½pc 2008–12		5.62	5.73	97.88	−.22	112.26	97.46
Treas 8pc 2013		6.39	5.41	125.21xd	−.55	139.64	124.73
Treas 7¾pc 2012–15		6.53	5.62	118.74	−.54	133.56	118.34
Over Fifteen Years							
Treas 8pc 2015		6.16	5.23	129.96	−.67	144.12	129.33
Treas 8¾pc 2017		6.18	5.17	141.58	−.76	156.08	140.80
Exch 12pc 2013–17	✠	7.37	5.55	162.81	−.50	183.80	162.44
Treas 8pc 2021		5.75	5.03	139.04	−.84	153.21	136.75
Treas 6pc 2028		5.07	4.82	118.42	−.83	131.17	115.03
Undated							
Consols 4pc		5.29	-	75.64	−.39	87.19	71.92
War Loan 3½pc		5.12	-	68.34	−.59	79.83	66.20
Conv 3½pc '61 Aft.		4.36	-	80.34xd	−.59	95.68	79.63
Treas 3pc '66 Aft.		5.66	-	52.98xd	−.59	61.93	52.16
Consols 2½pc		5.21	-	47.98xd	−.59	56.93	47.16
Treas. 2½pc		5.24	-	47.73xd	−.69	55.17	46.37

	Notes	Yield (1)	Yield (2)	Price £	+ or −	52 week High	52 week Low
Index-Linked	(b)						
2½pc '01	(78.3)	3.22	3.81	202.54xd	+.01	206.40	200.80
2½pc '03	(78.8)	2.90	3.23	201.44	+.01	207.83	200.02
4⅜pc '04	(135.6)	2.69	2.95	127.97	−.34	134.77	127.97
2pc '06	(69.5)	2.08	2.25	230.41	+.05	239.80	217.45
2½pc '09	(78.8)	2.22	2.35	209.19	+.06	221.45	197.20
2½pc '11	(74.6)	2.33	2.44	219.50	+.08	235.62	206.88
2½pc '13	(89.2)	2.33	2.42	184.05	+.10	199.07	172.59
2½pc '16	(81.6)	2.26	2.35	203.39	+.07	221.10	189.04
2½pc '20	(83.0)	2.20	2.27	203.56	+.07	221.68	185.31
2½pc '24	(97.7)	2.12	2.18	176.73	+.06	193.74	157.92
4⅛pc '30	(135.1)	2.06	2.12	174.82	+.05	193.23	155.62

Prospective real redemption rate on projected inflation of (1) 5% and (2) 3%. (b) Figures in parentheses show RPI base for indexing (ie 8 months prior to issue) and have been adjusted to reflect rebasing of RPI to 100 in February 1987. Conversion factor 3.945. RPI for January 1999: 163.4 and for August 1999: 165.5.

Other Fixed Interest

	Notes	Yield Int	Yield Red	Price £	+ or −	52 week High	52 week Low
Asian Dev 10¼pc 2009		8.20	6.66	124$\frac{31}{32}$xd	......	140$\frac{27}{32}$	124$\frac{31}{32}$
B'ham 11½pc 2012		7.99	6.50	144	......	158¾	144
Leeds 13½pc 2006		9.68	-	139½xd	......	152	138
Liverpool 3½pc Irred.		5.47	-	64xd	......	70½	55
LCC 3pc '20 Aft.		5.77	-	52	......	59	50
Manchester 11½pc 2007		8.85	6.70	130	......	151¾	130
Met. Wtr. 3pc 'B'		3.53	7.40	85	......	95	85
N'wide Anglia 3⅞pc IL 2021		-	3.67	174$\frac{31}{32}$	......	192$\frac{13}{32}$	174$\frac{31}{32}$
4¼pc IL 2024		-	3.58	169	......	182	169

● 'Tap' stock. All UK Gilts are tax-free to non-residents on application. E Auction basis. xd Ex dividend. Closing mid-prices are shown in pounds per £100 nominal of stock. Prospective real Index-Linked redemption yields are calculated by HSBC Greenwell from Gemma closing prices. ✠ Indicative price.

price of the bond. To take the example of the Treasury 8 per cent 2000, which is the fourth bond down in the table in Figure 5.2, the interest yield is calculated as follows:

$$\text{Interest yield} = \frac{8}{102.58} = 0.078 \text{ or } 7.8 \text{ per cent}$$

The interest yield is useful to a bond investor in giving the percentage annual income a bond purchase will generate. This is particularly important if an investor is borrowing to purchase a gilt, because it indicates the cash shortfall or surplus the investment strategy will imply.

The second measure of yield given in the table is the redemption yield. This yield takes into account not only the income percentage an investor will earn but also the capital gain or loss that will arise on redemption of the bond. A capital gain or loss will arise whenever a bond is sold at a price different from its redemption value. The redemption yield shows the overall return on a bond and allows an investor to compare the return the bond will offer with other investments such as shares or other forms of debt. We are not going to go into the calculation of redemption yield in detail here, as that requires techniques that are not covered in this text. We can, however, get an idea of the principle by considering again the example of the Treasury 8 per cent 2000 stock, the running yield for which we calculated as 7.8 per cent above. You can see that the redemption yield is lower than the running yield at only 5.75 per cent. Why is the redemption yield, i.e. the overall return that an investor will earn on the bond, less than the running yield? The lower redemption yield takes into account the capital loss that an investor will make on purchasing this bond (the current price of £102.58 less the redemption value of £100) in addition to the annual income generated of 7.8 per cent.

Activity 4

Referring back to Chapter 4 if necessary, compare the information provided in the financial press on bonds with that provided on equity. Consider the overall purpose of the different measures and assess the similarity or otherwise of the information provided for investors in the two different types of financial asset.

If you refer back to Chapter 4, you will recall that the two main measures given for equity investors in the press are the dividend yield and the P/E ratio. The recipricol of the P/E ratio is called the earnings yield (earnings yield = earnings per share/price per share), and this shows the overall return earned on an equity investment taking into account retained earnings and dividends.

The interest yield on bonds provides similar information to the dividend yield on shares. Both give information on the income, or cash flow, from their respective investments as opposed to the overall return.

The earnings yield on equity is comparable to the redemption yield on bonds, in that both give a broad measure of return rather than concentrating just on cash income. The redemption yield is perhaps the more comprehensive of the two measures in that it reflects future capital gains/losses; the earnings yield just represents current earnings on a share, future capital gains or losses on shares being impossible to estimate with any precision.

If you look at the data on gilts in Figure 5.2, you may notice that there is no particular pattern to the figures for interest yield shown in the table. Some bonds offer high interest yields and some low, and different investors can make their choice between them depending on whether or not they need a high current income or would rather, perhaps, have a lower income now compensated for by a capital gain later. The redemption yield column gives a different picture. You can see some sort of pattern to rates, with the shortest maturity bonds (lives of less than two years) offering yields of less than 6 per cent, gilts with a remaining maturity of two to seven years offering yields of 6–6.3 per cent and the longer-term gilts with lives of seven years upwards offering returns of around 5.5 per cent.[2] This pattern of redemption yields is the main determinant of bond prices and provides information in a wider context of what expectations investors have for interest rates and inflation in future.

Bond pricing

Referring again to the data in the table in Figure 5.2, we can note that the price, or market value, of a bond often differs from its nominal and/or redemption value. The bonds quoted in the table are all expressed on the basis of a nominal value of £100, but the prices of the bonds vary; among the mediums, the range of bond prices in the third column of figures is from around £93 to £131. What can we say about the gilts in the table to distinguish between those with a price less than and those with a price greater than par? The bonds with a low price all offer low coupons, while those with a high price offer high coupons. Roughly, it seems that any bond offering a coupon less than around 5.75 per cent is valued at less than £100 and vice versa for those offering above this rate.[3]

What is the basis for this pricing? Suppose that the government wants to issue some gilts and that at the time of issue general interest rates stand at 7 per cent and are expected to remain at a similar level over the next few years. If the government were prepared to offer a coupon of 7 per cent on its gilts, it should be able to sell the gilts at a full par value of £100 each. Investors will be prepared to pay this price because an alternative investment, which might be putting money in a bank for a number of years, would also pay them 7 per cent. Suppose, though, that once the gilts have been issued at £100, interest rates then unexpectedly rise to 8.5 per cent. Could an investor who bought a gilt for £100 sell it for the same amount? The answer is no, because the alternative investment for potential buyers of gilts is now to put their money in, say, a bank and earn 8.5 per cent. To attract buyers, the price of the 7 per cent gilts must fall so that the overall return they offer (i.e. their redemption yield) is competitive with the 8.5 per cent interest rates now generally available. When the price falls, the redemption yield on the gilt increases in two ways: first, the £7 interest paid annually now relates to a smaller investment by the buyer of the gilt and so represents a higher interest percentage; second, the gilt buyer will make a capital gain taking into account the lower price he or she now pays for the bond compared to the full nominal value still receivable on redemption from the government. Overall, the higher interest percentage and the capital gain should together offer a gilt purchaser 8.5 per cent per annum to make the investment attractive as compared to alternative financial assets.

Activity 5

Suppose current interest rates are 7 per cent and the government issues a gilt with a 7 per cent coupon redeemable in ten years' time. The gilt is sold for its par value, but then interest rates unexpectedly fall to 6 per cent. In what direction will the value of the gilt move? Can you specify a range of values within which the new gilt value is likely to be?

The value of the gilt should rise, other things being equal. This is because the gilt now offers a coupon which is higher than the rate of return offered by competitive investments. Can we say something about how far the price should rise? If the bond price rose to £116.67, then the annual interest of £7 paid on the bond would give a 6 per cent return (7/116.67 = 0.06). This must be too large a rise in price, however, because although the new purchaser of the bond gets £7 of interest, he or she will make a capital loss when the bond matures in ten years' time; the loss is the redemption value (£100) less the price he or she pays for the bond now (£116.67), or £16.67. The bond must therefore rise to somewhere between £100 and £116.67. A price of £106.25 is intuitively attractive, in that the interest yield is then 6.59 per cent (7/106.25) and the capital loss as a percentage of purchase price and averaged over the five-year life of the bond is –0.059 per cent ([106.25 – 100]/106.25 and averaged over ten years), giving a total return per year of 6 per cent. This is in fact an underestimation of value because it does not take into account that the investor will not suffer the capital loss for a full ten years. To make an accurate bond valuation, discounting techniques, taking into account time value of money, are required and such a calculation would show the bond to be worth £107.32. The calculation we have made above gives a reasonable approximation of value.

What we can note from the question above and the preceding discussion is that an unanticipated change in interest rates will bring about a change in required yield on bonds, other things being equal, and that this in turn will lead to an adjustment in bond prices. The movement in bond prices should be in the opposite direction to the change in interest rates; in other words, bond prices can be said to move 'inversely' in relation to interest rates. The price of longer-term bonds is generally more sensitive to interest rate changes than that of shorter-term bonds. The reason for this is that the changed interest rates will impact for more periods in the case of the longer-term bond and will thus have a greater effect on the current value of its cash flow.[4]

The discussion so far has related to how the price of gilts will need to alter in response to changes in interest rates, which will in turn alter the redemption yield required by investors. We noted above, however, that not all bonds seemed to be priced on the same redemption yield at any time; in Figure 5.2, there was a pattern to redemption yields, with yields on longer-term bonds being lower in the table than yields on shorter-term bonds. This must be because bond investors at the time required a lower overall return on longer-term bond investments, and the price of longer-term bonds would have had to adjust so that the coupon and expected capital gain/loss on redemption provided this. The difference in required return for different periods could arise for a number of reasons, and these are discussed in more detail in the following section.

The influence of inflation and interest rate expectations on bond prices

The pattern or relationship that can be noted between redemption yields on bonds and their residual maturity is often represented in graphical form and called the 'yield curve'; Figure 5.3 shows the form a typical yield curve would take. Yield curves are used to give borrowers and investors a picture of how rates of return on longer-term debt compare to those on shorter-term debt and to give financial authorities a market view of how interest rates are expected to move in future. The latter information is of particular interest, in that it can indicate the market's expectation of future inflation.

The pattern of redemption yields on bonds of different maturities, and thus the associated yield curves, may vary over time. Yield curves may slope smoothly upwards, as in

Figure 5.3 An upward sloping yield curve

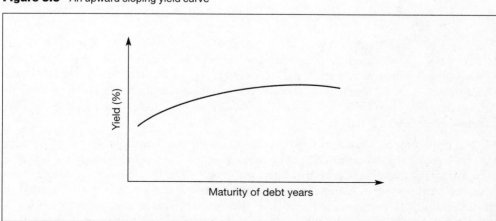

Figure 5.3, or downwards (Figure 5.4), or exhibit peaks and troughs (Figure 5.5). There are three recognized explanations for why the yield curve should take on any particular shape at any time: the expectations hypothesis, the liquidity preference theory and the segmentation hypothesis.

Figure 5.4 A downward sloping yield curve

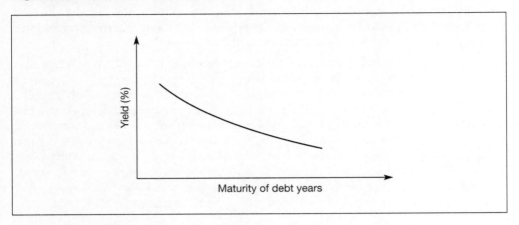

Figure 5.5 A yield curve exhibiting peaks and troughs

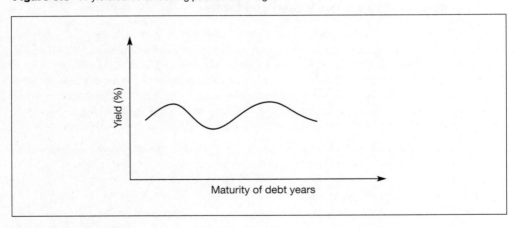

The expectations hypothesis, which was developed particularly by Fisher (1930) and Hicks (1939), attributes the relationship between yields on debt of different maturities to investors' expectations of how short-term interest rates are likely to change in future. If, for instance, there were a general market expectation that interest rates would rise in future, then the yield on longer-term debt would need to be higher than the yield on shorter-term debt to satisfy investors.

We can illustrate the impact of expectations on bond yields through an example. Say, for instance, that one-year interest rates were currently 7 per cent but were expected to increase to 9 per cent next year; the 9 per cent is called the 'forward rate of interest' for year two. An investor wishing to invest money for two years would have a choice of putting money into a two-year bond from the outset, or investing in a one-year bond now and then reinvesting the proceeds on redemption into a further one year bond, which would then mature at the end of year two. For the two-year bond to be competitive when interest rates are expected to rise, the yield on it must be higher than the current yield on one-year bonds, and the yield curve will be upward sloping. The precise yield required on the two-year bond, allowing only for the difference in interest rate expectations, can be calculated as follows:

Expected end value of
£100 investment in two one-year bonds $= (100 \times 1.07) \times 1.09 = 116.63$

$\qquad\qquad\qquad$ value of $\qquad$ reinvested
$\qquad\qquad\qquad$ investment $\quad$ in second
$\qquad\qquad\qquad$ from first $\qquad$ one-year
$\qquad\qquad\qquad$ one-year $\qquad$ bond
$\qquad\qquad\qquad$ bond

To be competitive, the two-year bond must earn an investor the same overall cash sum. Thus

$$100 \times (1 + i)^2 = 116.63$$

where i is the redemption yield on the two-year bond.

$$(1 + i)^2 = 1.1663, \text{which implies that } (1 + i) = 1.08$$

The redemption yield on two-year bonds is thus 8 per cent, while on one-year bonds it is 7 per cent, and we have an upward sloping yield curve as in Figure 5.3.

If the only factor influencing yield in relation to maturity is expectations of interest rates, we could see either an upward sloping, a flat or a downward sloping yield curve, depending on whether, respectively, people expected interest rates in future to rise, stay the same or fall. Historically, an upward sloping yield curve has generally been experienced, and such a curve (Figure 5.3) is referred to as a 'normal' yield curve. A downward sloping yield curve (Figure 5.4) is termed an 'inverted' yield curve.

The predominance of upward sloping yield curves may be explained by the liquidity preference theory. According to this theory, investors require a premium to invest their money longer term as opposed to shorter term, and this could pertain even in the absence of any expectation that interest rates would rise in the future. If you refer back to Chapter 2, you will recall that we identified differences between the requirements of borrowers and lenders. In particular, we noted that lenders typically want to tie up their money for short periods of time to preserve flexibility, while borrowers often want funds for longer periods to match the period of an investment. If you invest in longer-term bonds you can still realize your investment at any time by selling the bond prior to maturity, but as we have noted above, the value of longer-term bonds will fluctuate more than that of shorter-term bonds with changes in interest rates, and thus you will have more risk if you need to sell a long-term bond than if you need to sell a short-term one. The liquidity preference hypothesis recognizes the increased liquidity risk of longer-term debt investments and the potential mismatch of supply and demand for debt of different terms, suggesting that the result will be that debt of longer maturities will be expected to offer higher rates of interest than shorter-term debt. The liquidity preference hypothesis can thus explain an upward sloping yield curve in the absence of any expectation of interest rate increases in future. The hypothesis cannot explain downward sloping yield curves or yield curves with peaks and troughs, unless applied in conjunction with one of the other theories.

The segmentation hypothesis suggests that the shape of the yield curve is determined by supply and demand for funds in different maturity sectors of the market. The idea is that different institutions are active in particular maturity sectors only. Pension funds, for example, tend to concentrate on longer-term investments because their payment commitments (i.e. pension payments) are long term too. Commercial banks, on the other hand, have traditionally been more active in shorter-term than in longer-term lending. The yield curve can take on any possible shape depending on market conditions in each maturity sector. If the yield curve is upward sloping, this would suggest that there is a more plentiful supply of funds relative to demand in the short-term debt market than there is in the longer-term debt market. The segmentation hypothesis could explain yield curves sloping either upwards or downwards but is particularly relevant if there are peaks or troughs in the yield curve, as illustrated in Figure 5.5.

A concept associated with the yield curve is 'the term structure of interest rates'. This is a graph of one-year forward rates of interest calculated from the yield curve. We used a forward rate of interest above in our discussion of the expectations hypothesis. The forward rate was the one-year rate of interest for year two and in our example we used it to calculate what yield a longer-term bond would need to offer in order to compete with two sequential short-term bonds when interest rates were rising. Normally the calculation is the other way round. We observe the different redemption yields on short- and longer-term bonds and can use these to work out the short-term interest rates in future periods that the markets must be expecting. Returning to the numerical example we used in the expectations hypothesis section above, if we observed that two-year bonds were offering an 8 per cent yield and one-year bonds a 7 per cent yield, this would imply a forward rate for year two of 9 per cent:

$$\text{Return on two one-year bonds} = \text{Return on one two-year bond}$$

$$(1 + 0.07) \times (1 + \text{forward rate year 2}) = (1 + 0.08)^2$$

$$\text{Forward rate year 2} = 0.09$$

The term structure of interest rates provides a picture of market expectations of short-term interest rates in future and is used extensively by governments and central banks in setting interest rate policy. In Chapter 3 we discussed the purpose of monetary policy and noted that one of the main objectives was to control inflation. If the financial authorities felt that inflation was running out of control, interest rates would be raised to reduce consumer and business demand and thereby to reduce the upward pressure on prices. The real thing the financial authorities are interested in controlling here is *future* inflation, but how can they assess future inflationary pressure?

This is where the term structure of interest rates comes in. If investors expect inflation to be increasing in the future they will also expect that future interest rates will be higher than current levels; interest rates will need to be higher in future to give investors a positive real return over and above the inflation rate and/or because authorities will have raised rates in an attempt to control inflation. An upward sloping yield curve/term structure that is believed to be based on expectations of future higher interest rates thus gives a good idea of expectations of inflation and gives the financial authorities in turn a good idea of what action needs to be taken now to keep the economy on the course the government intends.

Recent British experience of the yield curve is interesting in this respect. When the UK came out of the ERM in 1992, interest rates fell quite rapidly from previously high levels (up to 15 per cent), and inflation also fell to levels of around 3–4 per cent, which was low by historical standards. The yield curve remained, however, sharply upward sloping for a number of years. The explanation seemed to be that investors believed that inflation would take off again now that the UK was outside the rigours of the ERM and that future interest rates would thus have to rise above current levels. The government and Bank of England maintained interest rates at a level which was high relative to the then current inflation in order to build credibility and persuade investors that inflation would not be allowed to take off as it had in the past. Gradually the yield curve flattened and the authorities then felt able to relax short-term interest rate policy as a result. The yield curve in the UK at the start of autumn 1999 was, in contrast, relatively flat up to seven years and then downward sloping; we saw this in the data on bonds in Figure 5.2. The current shape of the yield curve seems to be explained in part by market segmentation. Gilts are in relatively short supply because the UK government is running a budget surplus. At the same time, by tradition and as a result of some regulation, UK financial institutions, particularly pension funds, choose to hold a significant part of their investments in the form of longer dated gilts. The end result is too much demand for longer-term gilts pursuing a limited supply, and the yield on longer-term securities has been bid down as a result. At the end of August 1999, the yield on short-term gilts was around 6 per cent, but on longest-term gilts was around 1.2 per cent lower at 4.8 per cent.

Bonds are not only useful to financial authorities in providing a market view of future inflation. They are also now the principal financial asset through which monetary policy, by way of interest rate management, is carried out. Financial authorities influence short-term interest rates through government bond 'repurchase agreements', or 'repos'. Repos are arrangements entered into by bondholders whereby bonds are sold to another party but subject to an agreement for the original bondholder to buy them back at a later date. A repo provides a bondholder with short-term finance, with security being in the form of the bond underlying the agreement. Repos are thus based very much around bonds but their primary purpose is to provide short-term funding. Repos are discussed fully in Chapter 6, together with other forms of short-term debt.

International bonds

Many of the bonds issued by companies are international in nature. There are two types of international bonds, 'foreign' bonds and 'Eurobonds'. Foreign bonds are bonds issued in a country in domestic currency but where the issuer is a non-resident. Sterling bonds issued by foreigners in the UK are called 'bulldog bonds', while the equivalent foreign bonds issued in the USA are called 'yankee bonds'. The greatest volume of corporate bond issues, however, is in the form of Eurobonds. A Eurobond is a bond issued in a currency other than the domestic currency of the country where the issue takes place. It is important to note that it is the country of issue and the currency in which the bond is denominated that are the important factors in determining whether a bond is domestic or Euro; the residence of the issuer or the buyer of the bond is not relevant. The same concept applies to other forms of 'Eurosecurity', such as short-term 'Eurocurrency' loans and 'Euroequity'. In all cases the 'Euro' prefix indicates that an asset is created in a country but denominated in a foreign currency. The implication of a security being a Eurosecurity is that, because of its denomination in foreign currency, it will not be subject to control or influence by domestic monetary authorities.

Activity 6

Consider which of the following are forms of 'Euro debt':

1. *A short-term US$ loan made by a bank in the USA to a French company.*
2. *A short-term US$ loan made by a bank in London to an American company.*
3. *A bond denominated in pesetas issued on behalf of an English company by a bank located in the Bahamas.*
4. *A bond denominated in pesetas issued on behalf of a Spanish company by a bank located in London.*
5. *A bond denominated in French francs issued on behalf of a German company by a bank located in France.*

The factor which distinguishes a domestic debt from a Euro debt is the matching, or otherwise, of the currency of the debt with the place of issue of the debt.

1. This is a domestic loan despite the borrower being a foreigner. It is domestic because the currency of the loan (US$) is the currency of the country in which the issuing bank is situated (the USA).
2. This is a Eurodollar loan, because the issuing bank is in London while the loan is made in US dollars.
3. This is a truly international bond! It is a Euro peseta bond, the 'Euro' deriving from the fact that the issuing bank is located in a country (the Bahamas) other than that to which the currency of the bond attaches (Spain).
4. This is also a Euro peseta bond, even though the borrower is Spanish. Again the issuing bank is located in a country other than that from which the currency originates.
5. This is not a Eurobond because the issuing bank is French and the currency of the bond is the French franc. This bond is a foreign bond because the borrower is not French but German.

From an investor's point of view, the main differences between domestic bonds and Eurobonds are that the former are 'registered', i.e. their ownership is recorded by the issuer, and interest on them has to be paid with tax deducted. Eurobonds are thus preferable assets to hold if an investor wants his or her bond ownership to be anonymous and wants to receive interest gross. There could be wholly valid reasons for this, but some less valid ones too, such as tax evasion. Eurobonds also tend to be unsecured, while most domestic bonds have security attached.

Bond markets

In the UK, government and registered corporate bonds are traded on the London Stock Exchange. They are also traded on the relevant stock exchanges in France and Germany, but not in the USA, where the stock exchanges are for shares only.

Domestic corporate bonds are issued in similar ways to shares. Bonds might be sold through an offer for sale or could be placed directly with a number of investors. Thereafter bonds may be exchanged by investors through a relevant securities exchange, with intermediaries who deal in a company's shares also generally being prepared to trade in its bonds.

Government bonds are dealt with in markets in ways rather different from those for corporate debt. In the UK, specialist intermediaries called Gilt Edged Market Makers (GEMMS) are established to deal in gilts. GEMMS have special privileges, such as being able to deal directly with and borrow from the Bank of England. Set against this, they have to satisfy particular requirements as to the way they are established and the products in which they trade. GEMMS must, for instance, have their own capital to back their gilts trading, must always make a market in gilts and may not trade at all in shares.

Traditionally the Bank of England has been responsible for managing the national debt, and for, as is particularly relevant here, arranging the issue and redemption of gilts. In 1997 this arrangement changed on the Bank of England assuming full responsibility for conducting monetary policy. A department of the Treasury, the Debt Management Office, now organizes the issue of gilts, though the methods of issue used are the same as those traditionally employed by the Bank of England.

There are three gilt issue methods: sale by tender, sale by auction and the 'tap' method of sale. Under a sale by tender, the Treasury will announce that a certain volume of gilts will be sold on a given day with a minimum price specified. Bids are then invited for the securities. As with sales of shares by tender, once the bids have been received all gilts are allocated at a common price. If the issue is oversubscribed, the common price will be the price of the bid which clears the issue, ranking bids from the highest downwards. In the case of the issue being undersubscribed, the common price will be the minimum price specified in the tender; all bids will be accepted and any unsold gilts will be retained by the Treasury to be issued as 'tap stock'. If sale of gilts is by auction, bids are invited for gilts but with no minimum price being set; gilts are then sold to whoever bids the highest price at the auction. Sale of gilts as tap stock involves the Treasury releasing gilts that it holds on its own books in regular sales to GEMMS.

Activity 7

The Treasury announces the sale of £1 billion of gilts by tender with a minimum price of £118 per gilt. The following bids are received:

Amount (£ million)	Price per gilt
200	120
500	119.50
300	119
200	118.5

What is the common price at which gilts will be allocated to bidders?

In order to sell £1 billion of gilts and thus clear the issue, the Treasury needs to accept the bids at £120, £119.5 and £119. The common price set will be £119 and this will be paid by all who are allocated the gilts even if they bid a higher price in the tender. In this question, all bidders at £119 or above will be allocated the full amount of stock they applied for; those who bid £118.5 will be allocated nothing.

Eurobonds are traded outside recognized stock exchanges. They are normally issued by means of a 'bought deal'; this is where financial institutions, often acting in syndicates, bid against each other to acquire the whole of a bond issue and then place the bonds with other investors either immediately or over time. The same institutions then normally provide some form of secondary market in the bonds.

How important are bonds as a form of finance? For most governments, bonds are the principal means of financing public sector deficits. Governments issue a mix of short-term borrowing instruments, in the UK called Treasury bills, and gilts to finance expenditure. As virtually all governments around the world run deficits, they are universally important users of domestic bond markets. The volume of government bonds issued in the UK over recent years is shown in Table 5.2.

Table 5.2 Long-term bonds issued by the UK government (£ million)

Year	Issue
1991	11,547
1992	30,513
1993	53,147
1994	24,060
1995	22,579
1996	31,384
1997	16,711

Source: Financial Statistics, March 1999.

In 1993 the requirement to sell government bonds was particularly heavy. The volume of bonds sold has fallen in subsequent years in line with the government's reduced borrowing (see Table 3.1 for data on UK government net cash requirement).

The importance of bond finance for companies has varied over time. In the 1950s and 1960s in the UK, companies raised more bond finance than government and bonds were more important than equity to companies as a source of funds. However, in the 1970s, the UK bond market all but died away as the government started borrowing more, 'crowding out companies' with the high interest rates it offered and its attractive status as a 'safe' borrower, and as inflation soared into double figures, bringing high interest rates in its wake. The market has recovered to some extent as inflation has fallen and the government has had times of lower borrowing, as highlighted in Table 5.2. Table 5.3 shows issues of fixed interest debt by UK listed companies on the London Stock Exchange in 1997.

Although domestic corporate debt markets have revived to some extent in recent years, as discussed above, by far the greatest volume of corporate debt is issued in the form of Eurobonds. For example, in the same year that UK listed companies raised £1,835

Table 5.3 Issues of fixed interest securities by UK listed companies in 1997 (excluding preference shares)

	No. of issues	Money raised (£ million)
Convertibles	17	678.2
Debentures and loans	28	1,156.6
Total	45	1,834.8

Source: London Stock Exchange Fact File, 1998.

Table 5.4 International bond issues ($ billion)

Year	Issue
1994	482
1995	502.6
1996	782.9
1997	883

Source: Bank of England Quarterly Reviews, 1996–9.

Table 5.5 The currency composition of international bond issues in 1997

Currency of issue	Per cent of all issues
US dollar	45.2
Sterling	11.4
Deutschmark	8.3
Yen	10.2
French franc	4.5
Italian lira	4.8
Swiss franc	2.9
Ecu	2.2
Other	10.2

Source: Bank of England Quarterly Bulletin, 1999.

million of debt in the form of domestic securities, as shown in Table 5.3, they raised £43,644 million of debt in the form of Eurobonds. Table 5.4 shows issues of Eurobonds in the years 1994 to 1997; it is notable how fast the Eurobond markets grew in just these four years (72.2 per cent over the period).

The currency in which Eurobonds were issued in 1997 is shown in Table 5.5. Note from Table 5.5 the predominance of Eurodollar bonds, followed in importance in 1997 by Eurosterling and Euroyen bonds. EuroDM bonds took a smaller percentage of the total issues than has been the case in many recent years when the Deutschmark has been the second most important Euro currency.

Why have Eurobond markets grown to dominate corporate bond markets?

Eurobond markets originated in the 1950s and 1960s at the height of the Cold War. Eastern Bloc countries wanted to hold dollar assets but did not wish the assets to be located in the USA for fear of them being seized in case of all out-war. The markets were then boosted by the USA running high budget deficits that needed to be funded by sales of dollar securities, and by US lending regulations which made it attractive for American banks to set up outside the USA to conduct some business. A reason for the markets' subsequent substantial growth was oil price increases in the 1970s. Oil prices rose roughly threefold in the early 1970s and this led to oil rich nations building up huge money surpluses and oil consuming nations experiencing corresponding deficits. The Euro markets helped to recycle funds from the surplus countries to those with deficits, thereby avoiding a world financial crisis. London has always been the main centre for Eurobond issues and secondary trading, and this dominant position is retained today.

The corporate bond market is currently a source of finance in Europe only to large companies. This is because the market, as discussed above, is predominantly international and because smaller enterprises do not have the standing to be able to attract funds in these circumstances. In the USA, the domestic market is much larger and smaller companies are able to tap into it. As the European Union integrates further, a market may develop in this region to which smaller companies may be party in future.

Summary

Medium- and long-term debt has been defined in this text as debt with an original maturity in excess of one year. The different types of debt which fall into this category are bank loans and mortgages, leasing and hire purchase, medium-term notes and bonds.

Investors and borrowers wishing to choose between different types of debt need to consider the relative costs of the different debt forms, their risks, restrictions and repayment provisions. Borrowers may also need to take into account the source from which debt comes.

Bank loans and mortgages are provided by financial institutions rather than markets and can be used by borrowers to fund most types of expenditure. Finance in the form of leasing and hire purchase is medium in term and is suitable for funding the acquisition of equipment; the debt is repaid, together with a return for the debt provider, through regular rental payments. Medium-term notes and bonds are types of debt provided through markets rather than financial institutions. Medium-term notes are corporate promissory notes, or promises by a company to pay a sum of money in future, with an original maturity in excess of one year. Traditional bonds are debt securities offering a fixed rate of interest and with the principal being repaid wholly on maturity. In addition there are now many different types of bonds, including variable rate, convertible and deep discount bonds.

Data on government bonds is provided in the market pages of the financial press. Two types of bond yield are calculated: the running yield shows annual bond income as a percentage of current bond price, while the redemption yield calculates an overall return to an investor taking into account any capital gain or loss the investor will incur as well as annual income. The value of a bond will vary over time such that its redemption yield remains competitive with other financial securities available to investors. Other things being equal, bond prices will move inversely with interest rates.

A graph showing the redemption yield on bonds of different maturities is known as the yield curve. The yield curve is useful to investors in showing the relative return on debt of different terms and is also used by financial authorities to indicate expectations of future inflation. There are three principal theories which may explain the shape of the yield curve at any time: the expectations hypothesis, the liquidity preference theory and the segmentation hypothesis. An upward sloping yield curve which is considered to arise because of an expectation of future increases in interest rates, in turn caused by higher future inflation, may persuade financial authorities to increase current interest rates in order to stem inflationary pressures.

International bonds come in the form of foreign bonds, which are bonds issued by a non-resident but in domestic currency, or Eurobonds, which are bonds issued in a country in a non-domestic currency. Eurobonds are not subject to as much control from financial authorities as domestic or foreign bonds.

Domestic and foreign bonds are issued and traded through recognized securities exchanges, in the UK through the Stock Exchange. Eurobonds are traded outside any formal exchange. Issue and trading methods are generally similar to those used for shares, though government bonds tend to be subject to different arrangements. In the UK, gilts are issued by the Treasury by tender or auction, or using the tap method of issue.

Bonds are the principal source of finance to governments and are an important source of debt for large companies, particularly in the form of Eurobonds. Bonds are not currently used in Europe by smaller companies, though the creation of a larger Euro finance area may stimulate the creation of a smaller company corporate debt market.

Notes

1. Foreign and international bonds are discussed in a separate section below.
2. Ignore the yield quoted for the 'Treas Fltg Rate 2001', since this is not a fixed interest security.
3. The value of the gilts is also influenced by the precise timing of their coupon payments. A gilt which is sold 'cum dividend', i.e. where a forthcoming interest payment will be made to the new gilt owner, will be worth more than the same gilt once the interest payment has been made or where payment remains the entitlement of the previous owner.
4. The sensitivity of a bond's price to interest rates is captured in the measure 'duration'. This topic is examined in more detail in texts such as Howells and Bain (1998)

References

Fisher, I. (1930) *The Theory of Interest*. London: Macmillan.

Hicks, J. R. (1939) *Value and Capital*. Oxford: Clarendon Press.

Howells, P. and Bain, K. (1998) *The Economics of Money, Banking and Finance*. London: Addison Wesley Longman.

Questions

Note: suggested solutions are provided for questions marked *

*1. Suggest the choices a rational borrower would make between the following sets of debt alternatives:

    a)   Three alternative two-year bank loans, one with interest of 8% charged annually at the end of each year, one with interest charged at 2% at the end of each quarter, and one with interest charged at 0.67% at the end of each month.

    b)   An unsecured bank loan of £10,000, which could be used to finance the purchase of a piece of equipment, or h.p. finance of £10,000 which could also be used to purchase the equipment. Both the loan and the h.p. have an APR of 7% and have identical repayment profiles.

    c)   Debenture finance, where the whole of the debenture issue becomes repayable in 10 years' time, and a secured bank loan, where the loan is repayable in full at the end of 10 years but where there are provisions for early repayment at the borrower's request without penalty. Both the loan and the debenture have an equivalent annual cost of 6%.

*2. Consider the following information for two UK government bonds:

	Coupon	Market value	Redemption yield
Bond A	6%	£110	7%
Bond B	4%	£95	7.5%

Calculate the interest yield on each of the bonds and explain the relevance of this yield measure as opposed to the redemption yield also supplied in the question.

3. The Board of a small company is considering how to finance the purchase of some equipment and the extension of some buildings which the company occupies. These forms of finance are being considered – medium-term bank loans, lease, and hire purchase finance. Write a report to the Board explaining the main characteristics of each debt finance product.

*4. Put yourself in the position of a company treasurer who is responsible for arranging an issue of straight bonds of the company. Explain how you would go about deciding the bond price.

5. The following information on gilt bond yields is found in a current issue of the *Financial Times*:

	Redemption yield
Shorts (1–5 years)	6%
Mediums (5–15 years)	7%
Longs (over 15 years)	9%

Sketch a yield curve to represent the data and give possible explanations for why the yield curve should be shaped as it is.

6

Short-term debt capital

LIKE LONGER-TERM DEBT CAPITAL, short-term debt tends to command much less prominent coverage in the media than equity. This is because the markets, particularly for short-term tradable debt, appear at first sight not to have much relevance for individual savers and borrowers, because only larger companies and public bodies use them directly. This is not to say that short-term borrowing and lending is less important than other types of funding. Virtually all participants in financial markets will need to use this finance at some time and to some extent, but many transactions will be arranged privately outside formal markets and as such remain largely uncommented upon.

The markets for tradable short-term debt are often referred to as 'the money markets'. This title is in some ways misleading, in that it might suggest a wider financial role than the specific function of the markets, which is the issue and subsequent trading of debt products with an original maturity of less than one year. The money markets have never had a physical 'home', but instead are characterized by huge sums of money being lent via phone agreements between participating institutions. Small companies and individuals have traditionally not played a part in these markets because the sums transacted are so large (normally in excess of £0.5 million per transaction). Borrowers and lenders of smaller sums of money have instead used financial intermediaries, such as banks and building societies, as a channel for their funds. Although the total sums borrowed and lent through intermediaries in this way will be highly significant, this less formal 'market' for short-term funds is not transparent, and there is therefore little specific reporting on it in the financial press. Although borrowers and lenders of smaller amounts of short-term funds have traditionally not participated directly in formal money markets, this situation is to some extent changing. Access to the money markets has been opened up to retail trade through 'money market funds'. These operate rather like investment trusts in the equity market in attracting small investments from numerous individuals or small companies and then investing them *en bloc* on the money markets. Money markets in future may thus have a wider role to play as a short-term home for funds than their traditional one.

There is one aspect of short-term borrowing and lending which always has commanded extensive media comment; this is the short-term rate of interest, which has an influence on so many in setting the cost of variable rate loans, short-term deposits and mortgages. The short-term rate of interest, often referred to in media comment as just 'the' rate of interest, is, as we noted in Chapter 3, one of the principal tools of economic policy used by governments and financial authorities, and changes made to it are often highly controversial. Financial authorities seek to influence short-term interest rates through intervention in markets for short-term debt. Thus, although money markets have, until recently, seemed remote from the lives of ordinary people, the markets have always had a significant but indirect influence, in being the principal vehicle through which control of short-term interest rates is exerted.

Learning objectives

In this chapter, we will look at the different types of short-term debt available, both within and outside formal money markets, and at the form of return which is offered to investors in such products. We will also cover how financial authorities intervene in short-term debt markets to influence interest rates. Notable points to come out of the chapter are:

- how to compare the quoted rates of return on different types of short term-debt product;
- what trading activities financial authorities take to raise or lower short-term interest rates;
- how markets operate for different forms of short-term debt product.

The main characteristics of short-term debt products

In Chapter 5, we discussed the principal factors to be taken into account when choosing between different forms of longer-term debt, namely the return on/cost of the debt, its risk, repayment provisions and debt source. The same factors will apply when considering different types of short-term debt product. Repayment provisions will tend, however, to be less relevant in the choice between the different types of debt we are considering here, in that, particularly in the case of the shortest-term debt arranged for just a few days or months, the debt will tend always to be repaid in a single lump sum at the end of the debt term. It will often not be feasible to have any more complicated repayment arrangements, bearing in mind the short period for which the debt is out-standing.

We noted too in Chapter 5 that the return on debt can come in many forms. The most common form is interest, and most, but not all, medium- to long-term debt products pay some level of interest, or have interest included in other periodic debt payments, such as the rent paid under hire purchase or lease agreements. Many short-term debt products, particularly tradable products, do not pay interest at all, but instead offer investors a return in the form of 'discount'. Interest is often not offered on the products because it would be a relatively small amount in relation to principal, bearing in mind the short term of the debt, yet could be administratively costly to arrange, because the debt products may change hands several times in the course of their relatively short lives. Investors will of course not be willing to put their money into debt products offering no interest unless they see a return being earned in another way. Instead of paying interest to an investor, many short-term debt products offer a return in being issued for a price which is less than their maturity value. The difference between the issue price and the maturity value is termed 'the discount' on the product, and it provides a profit to the investor in place of an interest payment.

Let us look at an example of how discounts work. As a lender of funds, I might be offered a bank deposit which would last a year and give me 10 per cent interest payable in full at the end of the year. An alternative use of my money might be the purchase of a money market product. I might be able to buy a money market security which had a one-year life and which would repay £100 when it matured for £90.91; the difference between the issue price of the security and its maturity value is the discount, and in this example is £9.09. The money market security pays me no interest as such, but in its place I make a profit in the form of the discount. In fact these two investments yield the same annual return of 10 per cent, and there may therefore be nothing to choose between them. Below we examine how discount can be compared with interest paid on other debt products.

Short- and longer-term debt

So far our discussion has started to consider how different short-term debt products might be compared in order to make a choice between them. It should be emphasized, however, that this is not the only debt choice that lenders have to make. In this text, short-term and longer-term debt products have been covered in separate chapters because some of their characteristics are most usefully studied in this way. There is, however, no firm cut-off between debt of different terms. Borrowers may want to choose debt of a certain maturity to match the term of their borrowing requirements; investors too might have a particular period of investment in mind. Both groups of participants in the debt markets are likely to have some flexibility, though. A company wishing to borrow in the medium term might, for example, be persuaded to borrow short term and then look to renew the borrowing at a later date if the cost of short-term debt were considerably lower than that of longer-term debt. An investor wanting to maintain liquidity might wish to tie money up for less than a year, but might nevertheless put money in longer-term tradable securities, knowing that the investment could be sold before the securities would fall due for repayment. We should also not forget that longer-term debt transforms itself into shorter-term debt as the date of its redemption comes closer; a bond, for example, issued with an original maturity of, say, 15 years, becomes a short-term debt product when its outstanding maturity is less than one year. There will, therefore, in practice always be considerable continuity between the markets for debt of different terms, and this needs to be borne in mind when considering financial markets as a whole.

Different types of short-term debt

In order to study the different types of short term debt, we will begin by considering domestic products, and will separate these into two broad categories:

- *Non-money market debt products.* These are forms of non-tradable debt made available by financial intermediaries and used by corporate and individual borrowers of any size; overdrafts and short-term loans fall into this category.
- *Money market debt products.* Wholesale debt products, some of which are tradable, created in recognized and relatively formal debt markets, and providing short-term funds to public bodies and larger corporations; bills, inter-bank deposits, certificates of deposit, commercial paper and security sale and repurchase agreements ('repos') fall into this category.

Non-money market debt products

Overdrafts

An overdraft is a form of debt funding whereby a user of funds is permitted to borrow up to a pre-set amount at any time during an agreed period. The arrangement is flexible for the borrower in that the amount borrowed can fluctuate according to need, with the overdraft perhaps increasing at times when the borrower has particular demands for cash, but then reducing at other times when cash comes in and can be used to repay the borrowing. The fact that funds are only borrowed as and when required, instead of a set amount of loan being drawn down and then remaining in place throughout a loan agreement period, can also make overdraft financing cost-effective. Interest, which will normally be variable rate, will only be calculated on the overdraft according to the amount borrowed on a day-to-day basis, so money is only paid for when it is actually needed and used.

Technically, overdrafts are a form of funding with the shortest possible term, in that, although facilities are generally offered for an agreed period, say six months without formal review, the borrowing is also legally repayable on the lender's demand. If a borrower's circumstances deteriorate or the lender is unhappy with the lending arrangements for other reasons, the overdraft facility can thus be withdrawn immediately. In practice, lenders try to avoid taking such action except in extreme circumstances, and many borrowers use overdrafts more like medium- to long- than short-term finance; the overdraft facility is continually renewed and the funds it provides may be used to fund the persistent cash needs of business or personal life.

Overdrafts may be secured on stated assets or be offered as unsecured lending. Repayment provisions will also vary. If the facility tends to be continually renewed, there may be no repayment provisions at all. In other cases, the borrower may agree to pay off the overdraft over a set period. There is also no firm rule as to what fees will be charged. Overdafts may be offered to individuals without any fees at all. Corporate borrowers will normally be charged a review fee where the overdraft is operated on a longer-term basis.

Overdrafts are a common form of finance in the UK and Germany. In the USA, overdrafts are not permitted by law.

Short-term loans

In addition to offering overdraft facilities, banks will also offer somewhat more formal loan arrangements in the form of different types of term loans and lines of credit. These differ from overdrafts in that the lending institution commits to make available funds over a future agreed period, and such lending cannot be withdrawn on demand by the lender. Term loans, which have been discussed in relation to longer-term borrowing in Chapter 5, may be used by individual or corporate borrowers. Lines of credit are a form of short-term debt used only by companies.

Standby credits arise when a bank commits to lend funds to a borrower up to a certain limit and at any time within a given period. It is up to the borrower whether and when these funds are used, but once the credit has been drawn down and then repaid, the funds cannot be used again in the lending period. A revolving credit is similar to a standby credit, but offers the borrower greater flexibility. Again funds are committed by a bank for a period, but the borrower now has the opportunity to draw down funds, then repay them, then draw down funds again, providing all the time that the borrowing remains within the agreed revolving credit limit. Standby and revolving credits are normally unsecured and offered with variable rates of interest. Fees will be charged for arranging the facilities and also for committing funds, whether or not these are used.

Money market debt products

Money market debt products offer alternative forms of short-term investment and borrowing to the finance provided through financial intermediaries such as overdrafts and short-term loans.

For instance, consider a company with a shortage of cash in the short term, perhaps because credit has been offered to a customer, such that payment for sales will not be received for a number of months. The company could alleviate its cash shortage by taking out an overdraft facility with its bank. An alternative for the company, however, would be to sell money market securities. The typical form that such a security would take would be an 'IOU', i.e. a piece of paper promising to pay whoever holds it a certain sum of money on a specific date in the future. The IOU in the case we are considering here might be issued by the company needing finance itself or by its customer; in both cases, to fit in with commercial cash flow, the promise to pay under the IOU would be linked with the date when payment for goods would normally be expected. Our company waiting for payment from its customer for, say, three months, could issue securities promising to pay a given sum in three months' time. The securities which carry this right to receive a sum of money in the future are valuable and can thus be sold by the company in the money markets. When the company receives funds from its customer, these can be used to redeem the securities issued three months previously. The company thus secures short-term funds in a way equivalent to borrowing on overdraft. From the point of view of the buyer of the securities, he or she is acquiring a short-term investment which will be similar to putting money on deposit with a bank. We considered a lender making a choice between a money market security and a bank deposit earlier in this chapter.

One big difference for an investor between a money market product and an ordinary bank deposit is that the former will, in many cases, be tradable. If a product is tradable the investor is not tied to keeping funds invested for a whole period in the way he or she would be with a bank deposit. The value of a money market product when sold will depend on the length of time the product has to run until its maturity and the rate of interest available on competitive products at the time of sale. If general interest rates in an economy remain unchanged through the life of a money market product, we would expect the market value of the product gradually to increase as maturity approaches, and eventually on maturity to equal maturity value. If you refer back to the example of a money market product given above, a product could be sold for £90.91 and be redeemed for £100 one year later, and this would provide an investor with a 10 per cent return. What will happen to the value of that product if it were sold in six months' time? If interest rates stayed at 10 per cent, the value of the product should rise, because a new owner of the product should need a discount representing only half a year's interest at 10 per cent in order to persuade him or her to invest their money. It would actually make sense for the product to be worth £95.24 in these circumstances, with interest being calculated on a simple basis. If interest rates on competitive products change over the life of a money market asset, this will have an additional effect on its market value. The higher competitive interest rates, the lower the market value of money market products, other things being equal. Market values fall with higher interest rates on competitive products because new buyers of money market assets need a greater discount to compensate them for interest forgone on other investments. If, for instance, interest rates were 12 per cent in six months' time when our illustrative money market product came to be sold, its value would be only £94.34. Its value has still risen compared to its issue price, because of the elapse of time, but the increase is not as great as it would have been had interest rates remained unchanged or have fallen.

Bills

Bills are a form of finance used by companies and governments and are in the form of an IOU, as described above. Traditionally, bills were used to help to finance trading abroad, and the typical bill issued by a company, a 'commercial bill', takes the form of an IOU issued by the company's foreign customer in connection with international trade. An example of a bill is shown in Figure 6.1.

Figure 6.1   An example of a bill of exchange. *Source:* National Westminster Bank plc

---

5 February 2000   £35,000.00

On 5 February 2002 for value received, pay against this bill of exchange

to the order of **ABC Limited** the sum of

Thirty Five thousand pounds sterling

Effective payment to be made in **Sterling** without deduction for and free of any taxes, impost, levies or duties present or future of any nature

Drawn on XYZ Limited	Drawn by ABC Limited
address	address

Accepted

(XYZ Limited signatures)   *(ABC Limited signatures)*

The way a bill works is that the exporter makes out a document, the 'bill', which records that the importer owes him or her a given amount payable on a given date, and the importer signs this in agreement. In Figure 6.1, the exporter is ABC Ltd and the importer XYZ Ltd. The exporter can then sell the bill in the bill market, providing him or her with immediate funds. The importer will redeem the bill a few months later, having by that time received the goods from the exporter and having thus been able to trade with them in the way desired. Like many money market debt products, bills do not pay interest to investors, but instead are sold at a discount to their maturity value, in the way discussed above.

Commercial bills normally have maturities from one to six months, though more unusually they may be issued for a full year. Banks sometimes act as guarantors of commercial bills, which means that a bank guarantees repayment to a bill purchaser in the event of the commercial bill issuer defaulting on the debt. The existence of the bank guarantee should mean that the risk for the investor in the bill is reduced and that the bill can thus be sold on a smaller discount than otherwise. The borrower under the bill arrangement benefits from selling on a lower discount in the market, and thus the guaranteeing bank can in turn charge a fee for its guarantee service. Where a bank guarantees a bill in this way it is said to 'accept' the bill and the bill is then referred to as a 'bank bill'. Commercial bills accepted by banks of the highest standing are termed 'eligible bills'. These bills are 'eligible' in the sense that the financial authorities are prepared to buy them should there be a shortage of funds in the money markets and should the investor owning the bills wish to convert the investment into cash.

Governments are also active in issuing bills, though the finance raised in this way is obviously not related to trade. Government bills are called, in the UK, 'Treasury bills', and are issued by the government to meet short-term needs for finance. Local authorities also issue bills to finance their spending on local services etc.

Commercial paper

Commercial paper operates in just the same way as a commercial bill, in that it is essentially an 'IOU' issued by a company without provision for interest and to be sold in a market at a discount. Strictly, bills are issued in connection with trade debts and by the receiver of goods in a commercial transaction (as with the example of the exporter and the importer above) but commercial paper is issued by a borrowing company itself and to finance a general shortage of cash. In the case of a bill, a trade payment should satisfy the redemption of the bill, but with corporate paper an investor has to rely on general company cash flow to provide repayment on the paper's maturity. As a result of the borrowing arising with commercial paper being unconnected with any commercial trade receipts, only larger companies with good credit standing can participate in this market. Indeed, in most countries companies wishing to issue corporate paper have to be authorized to do so. In the UK, issuing companies have to have a stock market quotation and capital per the balance sheet of at least £25 million.

Certificates of deposit

These are in essence tradable bank deposits. The 'certificate' is a document evidencing the existence of a bank deposit and it is tradable, so that, in effect, the bank deposit can be transferred between different owners before it comes to be repaid. This is one money market security which does not operate on the basis of discounts. Interest is paid in the normal way on the bank deposit but the price of the certificate of deposit will vary in the market depending on how the rate of interest on the deposit, which is fixed, compares with general interest rates. Certificates of deposit are issued by banks as a means of encouraging the making of short-term deposits.

Inter-bank and other wholesale money market loans

These are not strictly money market *securities*, in that they are not tradable.

Inter-bank loans are, as the name suggests, large, short-term loans made between banks to balance their liquidity positions. The loans are unsecured and not evidenced by any certificate which could otherwise be traded. The loans do not operate on a discount basis, with interest being charged in the normal way. The inter-bank market is the largest of the money markets by volume of loans transacted and is also important because the market rate of interest for borrowers acts in many countries as a reference rate by which many other rates of interest are decided. In the UK, the three-month borrowing rate in the inter-bank market is called the London Inter Bank Offer Rate, or LIBOR, and many commercial or individual loans will have an interest rate specified as a given percentage above LIBOR.

Non-bank participants in the money markets, such as local authorities and specialist money market institutions called discount houses (discussed further below), also make loans and take deposits. Deposits taken by discount houses are secured by holdings of securities, such as commercial or Treasury bills.

Sale and repurchase agreements ('repos')

Repos are agreements under which one party agrees to buy a financial security, such as a bill or a bond, but with the proviso that the other party will buy the security back at a pre-agreed price and on a pre-agreed date in the future. The price at which the security is sold now will be lower than the price at which it will be bought back in future; the difference provides the current acquirer of the bill or bond with a return for what is effectively a short-term loan with the financial asset bought and sold back acting as loan security.

Repos have been common in continental Europe for some time, and are the preferred product for monetary intervention by central banks. In the UK, the Bank of England traditionally used other products, notably the outright sale and purchase of bills, to exert monetary control. From the mid-1990s, gilt repos have been inceasingly used by the Bank of England to influence interest rates both to make monetary control more effective and to bring the UK more in line with the rest of Europe.

Data on money market products and evaluation of different forms of return

Figure 6.2 shows the data provided on money market instruments in the *Financial Times*. The figure shows rates of return on the different types of money market product discussed above for different terms ranging from overnight to one year.

The first thing to note is that there are two rates quoted for each product for each period. Thus if we take the three-month rates for inter-bank deposits we can see a quotation of '5⁷⁄₁₆–5⁵⁄₁₆'. The first rate is the percentage interest rate at which funds could be borrowed in the market for a period of three months. Borrowing rates are called 'offer' rates, and the 5⁷⁄₁₆ rate is in fact the influential LIBOR, discussed above. The second rate is the rate paid on funds lent in the market, and this is termed the 'bid' rate. The difference between the bid and offer rates provides a profit to dealers in the market and is termed the 'spread'.

An investor wishing to put money into some form of money market product and wishing to compare the different rates of return available on these and other assets can use the data provided in Figure 6.2 but needs to be aware of a number of issues in order to carry out an analysis.

Figure 6.2 Data on short-term debt products provided in the financial press. *Source: Financial Times,* 22 September 1999.

UK INTEREST RATES

LONDON MONEY RATES

Sep 21	Over-night	7 days notice	One month	Three months	Six months	One year
Interbank Sterling	$6\frac{1}{8} - 4\frac{1}{2}$	$5\frac{1}{8} - 4\frac{7}{8}$	$5\frac{3}{8} - 5\frac{1}{4}$	$5\frac{7}{16} - 5\frac{5}{8}$	$5\frac{13}{16} - 5\frac{11}{16}$	$6\frac{5}{8} - 6\frac{3}{8}$
Sterling CDs	-	-	$5\frac{1}{8} - 5\frac{1}{4}$	$5\frac{3}{8} - 5\frac{5}{8}$	$5\frac{11}{16} - 5\frac{11}{16}$	$6\frac{1}{8} - 6$
Treasury Bills	-	-	$5\frac{1}{2} - 5\frac{3}{8}$	$5\frac{5}{8} - 5\frac{3}{8}$	-	-
Bank Bills	-	-	$5\frac{5}{8} - 5\frac{1}{2}$	$5\frac{3}{4} - 5\frac{5}{8}$	-	-
Local authority deps.	$4\frac{7}{8} - 4\frac{3}{8}$	$5\frac{1}{8} - 4\frac{15}{16}$	$5\frac{1}{4} - 5\frac{1}{8}$	$5\frac{1}{2} - 5\frac{3}{8}$	$6 - 5\frac{7}{8}$	$6\frac{5}{16} - 6\frac{3}{16}$
Discount Market deps	$5 - 4\frac{13}{16}$	$5\frac{1}{4} - 5\frac{1}{16}$	-	-	-	-

UK clearing bank base lending rate 5¼ per cent from Sep 8, 1999

First of all, interest rates on short-term debt products are normally expressed in terms of 'simple' interest. Simple interest just means expressing the total amount of interest paid in a period and not taking into account when the interest is paid. In Chapter 5, where we considered longer-term debt, we noted that the timing of interest payments was important because this could affect the total amount of return that an investor could earn. We considered an investor having a choice of putting money on deposit with a bank and earning either 10 per cent interest paid at the end of the year or having 2.5 per cent interest paid on the deposit every quarter. The latter alternative made the most money, because, as interest was earned every quarter, it would be rolled into the deposit and would then earn further interest itself in subsequent periods. The timing of interest is thus important when investments run for long periods and the accumulation of interest is highly significant. When investments run for short periods, however, the impact of receiving interest at different times is much less dramatic and interest therefore tends to be expressed on a 'simple' basis, noting just the amount rather than the timing of payments. It might nevertheless be important to take into account the way interest was being quoted if you were comparing, say, a one-year inter-bank deposit with another bank deposit paying interest monthly.

The potential pitfalls with analysing data from Figure 6.2 do not end with appreciating the precise basis on which interest is quoted. We noted above that some money market products offer interest while others are sold at a discount; we also have repos, which have a difference between sale and repurchase price that is not, in precise terms, either interest or discount. Rates of return on money market products in the press also tend to be quoted on different bases; the rates in Figure 6.2 for Treasury and bank bills are annualized rates of discount, while the other rates shown are annualized simple interest rates. It is important to appreciate that there is a difference between the two and to be able to convert them to equivalent rates so that a valid comparison can be made between different products.

Discount rates on money market products express the total discount offered with reference to the maturity value of the security:

$$\text{discount rate} = \frac{\text{maturity value of security} - \text{issue price of security}}{\text{maturity value of security}} \tag{1}$$

Thus, if as an investor I am offered a bill with a maturity value in one year of £100 at a price of £90, the discount is £10 and the quoted discount rate is 10 per cent, calculated as follows:

$$\text{discount rate} = \frac{100 - 90}{100} = 10 \text{ per cent}$$

However, 10 per cent is not the rate of return I get on this investment and cannot be compared directly with returns offered on other products. I do not have to put up £100 now to earn a £10 profit; I only have to pay £90, i.e. the issue price of the security. The rate of return I make is 11.1 per cent, calculated as follows:

$$\text{rate of return} = \frac{\text{maturity value of security} - \text{issue price of security}}{\text{issue price of security}} \tag{2}$$

$$= \frac{100 - 90}{90} = 0.111 \text{ or } 11.1 \text{ per cent}$$

If I were comparing the proposed money market investment with, say, a bank deposit, I should compare the 11.1 per cent return calculated from equation (2) with whatever interest rate the bank offers me.

The example just considered used money market products with a maturity of one year. If products with shorter maturities are considered, annualized discount and interest rates can be calculated as follows:

$$\text{annualized discount rate} = \frac{\text{maturity value of security} - \text{issue price of security}}{\text{maturity value of security}} \times \frac{1}{\text{maturity of security as proportion of one year}} \tag{3}$$

$$\text{annualized interest rate} = \frac{\text{maturity value of security} - \text{issue price of security}}{\text{issue value of security}} \times \frac{1}{\text{maturity of security as proportion of one year}} \tag{4}$$

To take an example, suppose a six-month bank bill was being sold in the market at £96. The annualized discount rate could be calculated using equation (3):

$$\text{annualized discount rate} = \frac{100 - 96}{100} \times \frac{1}{1/2} = 8 \text{ per cent}$$

The rate of interest to which this discount is equivalent can then be calculated from equation (4):

$$\text{annualized discount rate} = \frac{100-96}{96} \times \frac{1}{1/2} = 8.33 \text{ per cent}$$

In practice the proportion that a security bears to a year would be calculated on a daily basis. The number of days for which the security would be outstanding would be divided by 365 days in the UK and by 360 days in continental Europe and the USA.

How can we connect discount rates and simple interest rates for a security? It can be seen that the two fractions for discount rate and interest rate above have the same numerator (maturity value – issue price) but different denominators (maturity value for the discount rate and issue price for the interest rate). Thus if we have a discount rate for a security, we can get the interest rate simply by multiplying the discount rate by maturity value/issue price; this has the effect of changing the denominator in the way we want.

$$\text{interest rate} = \text{discount rate} \times \frac{\text{maturity value}}{\text{issue price}} \tag{5}$$

or

$$\text{discount rate} = \text{interest rate} \times \frac{\text{issue price}}{\text{maturity value}} \tag{6}$$

Activity 1

The relevance of being able to appreciate the difference between discount and interest rates really becomes apparent when you are trying to compare the rates offered by alternative securities. Consider an investor with two alternative investments: one is a three-month Treasury bill quoted at an annual discount of 8 per cent, while the other is a one-year local authority deposit offering an interest rate of 8.5 per cent. Which yields the higher return?

To compare the two investments, we need to express the returns they offer on an equivalent basis. We could do this by finding either the discount rate or the interest rate attributable to both for the same period. Finding the interest rate is probably better, because that is then comparable with the return offered by other assets, such as a bank deposit.

We already know that the local authority deposit offers 8.5 per cent annual interest. Our task is thus to convert the Treasury bill discount into an annual interest rate. To do this, let us consider a Treasury bill unit with a maturity value of £100.

The three-month discount on the bill will be:

(8 per cent of £100) × 3/12 = £2

Thus the issue price of the bill will be £98 (£100 less the £2 discount) and the maturity value £100.

We now have the information to use equation (5) above.

$$3 \text{ month interest rate} = 3 \text{ month discount rate} \times \frac{\text{maturity value}}{\text{issue price}}$$

$$= 0.08 \times (3/12) \times (100/98) = 0.0204$$

We can now get an annual interest rate by multiplying the three month interest rate by 12/3 i.e. $0.0204 \times 12/3 = 0.0816$, or 8.16 per cent.

In this case the local authority deposit offers the greater return. It should be noted that these securities were issued for different periods (one for a year and one for three months), so expectations of interest rate changes would need to be taken into account as well as other factors noted in Activity 2.

Activity 2

In Activity 1, we found that the local authority deposit offered a higher rate of return than the Treasury bill. Although this was only a hypothetical example, you might actually see this sort of difference in rates on securities issued by these borrowers – can you explain why?

You would expect Treasury bills to offer slightly lower rates of interest than local authority deposits because central government will be regarded as a marginally more secure borrower than local authorities. Other factors might also come into play, such as the liquidity in the Treasury bill market compared to that in the local authority market; generally, the Treasury bill market might be expected to be the more active and thus the more liquid, which will be seen as an advantage to investors and thus might encourage them to accept slightly lower rates of return.

Considering other money market instruments, banks or large companies would in most cases be considered slightly more risky as borrowers than government or local authorities, so you would expect some rate premium on money market instruments issued by them. Markets with non-tradable and non-secured forms of debt – for example, inter-bank loans – would also be expected to offer lenders a slightly higher rate of interest than other products to compensate investors for the slightly higher risks they are exposed to through lack of security and liquidity.

Of course, rates do not always neatly reflect the risk position that you would expect in each market; particular supply and demand conditions in different market sectors can lead to rate anomalies at certain times.

Activity 3

Suppose that in addition to the local authority deposit and the Treasury bill, our investor also wanted to consider investing money short term by acting as the buyer in a gilt repo. Suppose an arrangement could be entered into whereby gilts with a current market value of £100 could be bought now for £97 subject to an agreement that they would be bought back in one month's time for £97.66. How does the rate of return on the repo compare with the other investments?

We know already that the local authority deposit offers a return of 8.5 per cent and the Treasury bill a return on an equivalent basis of 8.16 per cent. What annualized simple interest rate does the repo represent? The investor is required to pay £97 now in return for getting £97.66 in one month's time. The one month rate of interest is thus:

$$\frac{97.66 - 97}{97} = 0.68 \text{ per cent}$$

The annualized rate of interest = 12×0.68 per cent = 8.16 per cent. The repo rate is in this case the same as the return on Treasury bills.

The role of financial authorities in short-term debt markets

Financial authorities participate in markets for short-term debt in order to control interest rates and to ensure that the banking system has adequate liquidity. The first reason for participation relates to the carrying out of monetary policy and the second to the supervision and regulation of financial markets. A third and generally subsidiary reason for involvement might be in order to fund government borrowing through the issue of short-term government debt; governments generally, however, rely more on longer- than on shorter-term debt for funding. All the above mentioned functions of financial authorities are discussed in Chapter 3.

What form does the participation of financial authorities in the money markets take? In order both to influence interest rates and ensure the liquidity of the banking system, financial authorities in virtually all countries engage in 'open market operations'. Open market operations mean the financial authorities buying and selling securities, such as bills and repos, 'on the open market', i.e. just as any other market participant.

Suppose, for instance, that the financial authorities wanted to bring about an increase in short-term interest rates. The first thing the financial authorities will need to do is create a requirement for financial institutions to seek funds from them. If financial institutions need funds, then the financial authorities will be in a position to supply those funds at the rate they wish to see prevailing in the markets. The way a need for funds can arise in the money markets is shown on the left-hand side of Figure 6.3. A shortage of funds in the money market arises on some days relatively automatically. Large payments from the private sector to the government may be due (for instance, for tax), and this could make institutions short of funds. Alternatively, previous short-term financing arrangements, such as repos, may be coming to an end and institutions will be seeking to renew them. The authorities can also engineer a shortage of funds in the money markets by selling securities (generally Treasury bills) that institutions participating in the market have an obligation to buy. Market participants would have to use cash in order to acquire the securities, and this would make them short of liquid funds. The authorities can then offer funds back to the market to alleviate the funds shortage, but at the rate of interest they now wish to see in the market. One way that funds could be provided to the market would be by the financial authorities offering to buy bills held by other institutions; when the bills are acquired by the authorities, cash transfers back from the authorities to the other participants in the market and the shortage of liquidity is resolved. In this case the discount offered on the bills would be set to reflect the new interest rate the authorities wished to bring about; calculations equating the disount rate to the required interest rate similar to those we carried out in activities above would be used. Similarly, the authorities might use repos to bring about a rate change. The

Figure 6.3　The conduct of open market operations by the financial authorities

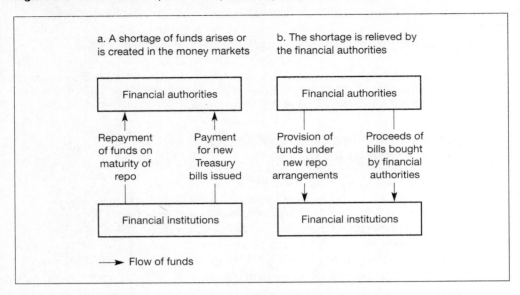

authorities would offer to enter into repos as a buyer in the arrangement, but with repurchase prices being set to reflect the new level of interest rates now considered suitable. The right-hand side of Figure 6.3 shows a funds shortage being relieved by the financial authorities in the ways outlined above.

Open market operations can also be used to relieve a shortage of funds in the money markets at times when the financial authorities are not seeking to change interest rates. The authorities can provide funds in the ways outlined above but at discounts or repo prices reflecting current rather than changed market interest rates.

Financial authorities can influence interest rates or provide liquidity to the money markets other than through open market operations. Most authorities have the power to act as 'lender of last resort'. This role would see the authorities lending directly to market participants rather than trading in securities to bring about the same result. In recent years, open market operations have been used to a much greater extent than direct lending. The intention is for the market to be seen to be operating freely as far as possible.

Characteristics of money markets

Traditionally money markets have been divided into the 'primary' or 'discount' market and 'secondary' or 'parallel' markets. The primary market is the market for short-term debt in which the central bank or other financial authority participates as an issuer of securities and as a provider of market liquidity. Secondary markets are markets set up to operate alongside the primary market but often involving more specialized participants.

In the UK, the primary market has traditionally been the market where Treasury and commercial bills have been traded. Specialized institutions unique to the country and known as 'discount houses' have acted as intermediaries in the market. The role of the discount houses, which were relatively few in number and located near to the Bank of

England, was to act as a buffer between the wider banking sector and the central bank. If, for instance, the Bank wanted to bring about a change in interest rates, it would do this by trading bills only with the discount houses. The discount houses would pass on any rate changes through the returns they in turn offered on deposits made with them. This specialized role of the discount houses and the discount market has been gradually eroded since 1996 as the Bank of England has been increasingly prepared to trade directly with a much wider range of financial institutions and in a wider range of securities.

Parallel markets in the UK include the inter-bank market and the commercial paper market. In both cases the markets offer particular classes of borrowers and lenders the opportunity to manage their liquidity without having to route money through the primary market. Figure 6.4 illustrates how bank liquidity positions can be adjusted through either the primary or the parallel money markets. A commercial bank with surplus funds (Bank A) could place those funds on deposit with a discount house via the primary market. The discount house might then lend the funds to another bank with a shortage of funds (Bank B). An alternative, however, is for the bank with surplus funds to lend funds directly to the bank with a funds shortage via the inter-bank market.

Figure 6.4 Adjustment of banks liquidity through either primary or parallel money markets

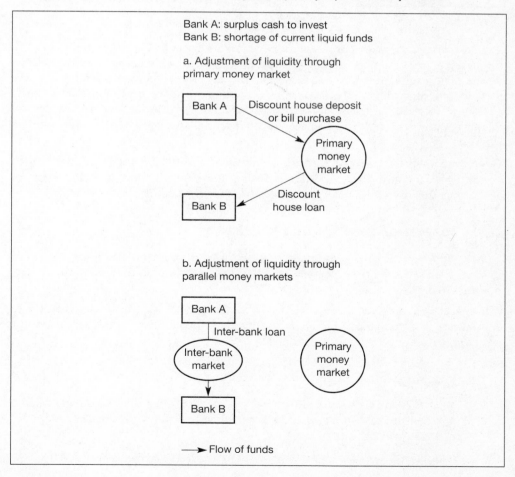

How or why did the parallel markets originate? In some cases the markets came about to try to get round monetary regulations. For example, the inter-company market in the UK, which deals in deposits between different companies, grew up at the end of the 1960s at a time when bank lending to companies was restricted by the Bank of England in an attempt to control money supply. The market circumvented the controls by enabling companies in need of funds to borrow from companies with surplus funds without getting involved with the banks and their accompanying restrictions. The local authority bill market similarly evolved in response to government restrictions on local authority funds (Goacher, 1990).

Table 6.1　The amounts outstanding at the end of November 1997 in various UK money markets (£ billion)

Market	Amount
Inter-bank	135
CD	100
Gilt repo	72
Treasury bills	3
Eligible bills	21
Commercial paper	8

Source: Bank of England Quarterly Bulletin, February 1999.

Table 6.1 shows the size of different money markets in the UK at the end of 1997. The three largest markets by far are the inter-bank market, the CD market and the gilt repo market. The last has grown from a negligible size in 1995 to represent 21 per cent of the total shown in the table; its growth reflects the increasing focus of financial authority activity in this area of the money markets. In early 1999, more than 50 per cent of financial authority intervention in the money markets was conducted through the repo market.

Government bills are issued through auctions in a similar manner to government bonds. In most countries the bills are initially sold to a restricted range of institutions (in the UK the discount houses and banks) but may then be sold on more widely.

International money markets

Another name for these markets is the Eurocurrency markets. These are global markets for unsecured bank deposits which offer interest rather than discount and are not tradable.

Euromarkets in general were considered in Chapter 5 specifically in relation to Eurobonds, and the same principles as to what determines a Euro and what a domestic asset apply to short-term debt instruments.

Activity 4

Refer back to the section on Eurobonds in Chapter 5. Using the same basis for definition, how do you think a Eurocurrency deposit will differ from a domestic bank deposit. Give examples of each.

A Eurocurrency deposit is a deposit made with a bank located outside the country to which the currency of the deposit relates. A dollar deposit with a bank located in London is a Eurodollar deposit; the bank where the deposit is made is not located in the country to which the currency of the loan relates. Similarly, a deposit of Deutschmarks made in a French bank located in the USA is a EuroDM deposit.

A domestic deposit is made in the currency of the country in which a bank is located. A sterling deposit with a UK bank located in London is a domestic deposit. So is the same deposit made with a French bank located in London.

The importance of a deposit being Euro or domestic lies in its supervision or otherwise by domestic financial authorities. For example, the Bank of England effectively controls sterling interest rates applicable to loans in the UK but does not influence or supervise foreign currency, or Euro, loans.

The reasons for the establishment and subsequent growth of Euromarkets are discussed in Chapter 5.

Summary

The same factors need to be considered for short-term debt as for longer-term alternatives, namely cost/return, risk and repayment provisions. Most borrowers and lenders have some flexibility in their choice of debt term and therefore there is no firm cut-off between typical short-term debt products and their longer-term counterparts.

Many short-term debt products do not pay interest for reasons of administrative convenience. A return is provided to investors in short-term debt products by way of a discount, which is the difference between the price a security is issued or bought at and its value on redemption. In many cases, short-term debt products are tradable, and their market value will vary according to the time before maturity and the interest rate offered on competitive products. Other things being equal, the higher are short-term interest rates, the lower will be the market value of money market products.

Overdrafts and various types of short-term loan are examples of non-money market short-term debt products. As money market products are wholesale, these are the only forms of short-term debt finance suitable for individuals and small or medium-sized companies. Larger companies use these forms of finance but can also tap the money markets.

Bills, commercial paper, certificates of deposit and repos are examples of tradable money market products. Bills and commercial paper are in essence corporate IOUs. Return on them comes in the form of discount rather than interest. Certificates of deposit are tradable bank deposits and pay fixed rate interest in the normal way. Repos are arrangements under which one party sells a security, such as a bond, to another party, but with the first party agreeing to buy the bond back at a future date at a price agreed now; the arrangement is like a loan to the first party secured by the bond. Bills and commercial paper are issued by companies to finance overseas trade and general short-term business needs. Bills are also used by governments to meet short-term shortages of funds. Repos are used by banks to produce short-term funds and are also used by financial authorities to control interest rates.

Inter-bank loans are non-tradable money market products. They are short-term, unsecured loans between banks, and are the most important money market product in terms of market turnover. The inter-bank money market is also important in providing a reference interest rate, LIBOR in the UK, which is used to set the rate of interest paid in many other loan arrangements.

In order to compare the attractiveness of different short-term debt products, it is important to express the return they offer on an equivalent basis. Discount or repo profit is most usefully converted to an equivalent annual interest rate in order to do this.

The financial authorities participate in money markets in part as fund raisers but also in order to influence short-term interest rates. Changes in interest rates are brought about through either repos or purchases and sales of bills, which are together known as open market operations. Financial authorities may also undertake open market operations in order to provide liquidity to financial institutions in instances of shortage.

Money markets can be categorized into primary and secondary, or parallel, sectors. The primary market is the sector of the market in which the financial authorities participate and in the UK focuses on trading of the best quality bills and repos. The secondary markets, which include the inter-bank markets, offer opportunities for financial institutions and commercial companies to manage their liquidity without routeing funds through the primary markets.

A Eurocurrency deposit is a deposit made in a bank which is located in a country other than the country to which the currency of the deposit relates. The significance of a deposit being Euro in nature is that it will not be subject to the monetary supervision of the country in which it is located.

Reference

Goacher, D. (1990) *The Monetary and Financial System* (2nd edn). London: The Chartered Institute of Bankers.

Questions

Note: suggested solutions are provided for questions marked *

1. Explain how the issue by a company of commercial paper or bills can replace the need for overdraft finance.

2. Discuss the benefits and drawbacks for an individual or company of funding by overdraft rather than a term loan.

*3. The following rates are quoted on a particular day in respect of the interbank market:

	Overnight	One month	Three months
Interbank Sterling	5¾–5	5⅞–5⅝	5½–5⅜

a) What percentage rate of interest would be paid by a bank wishing to borrow funds in the market for three months?

b) What percentage return would a bank get by lending money in the market overnight?

c) What is the percentage spread for intermediaries in the market on one-month money?

*4. A fund manager wishes to place £10m in the money markets for one month. The following rates for one month money are quoted:

	One month
Sterling CDs	6½–6⅛
Bank bills	6¼–6

Which of the products offers the higher rate of return to the fund manager?

5. Explain the main differences between the primary and secondary money markets in the UK.

7

The derivatives markets

NO FINANCIAL MARKETS HAVE PROVOKED more debate and controversy over the past ten years than the derivatives markets. These are markets of extremes in so many respects – they are the newest and fastest growing financial markets, and in many cases the most physical and 'colourful' of all the markets operating. The derivative products trading in the markets also exhibit extreme characteristics: they offer the greatest potential return of all financial assets to investors, but bring with them the greatest potential risk. Herein too lies the controversy surrounding the derivatives markets; trading within them has brought about some of the most spectacular losses and corporate collapses of the past decade, most notably the demise of Barings Bank in London in 1995 and the crises among 'hedge funds' following various stock market falls in autumn 1998. Whether the reason for these corporate debacles can be laid at the door of derivative products and the markets in which they are traded, or instead with companies and investors misunderstanding and misusing those products, has been at the core of market controversy. This is a subject to which we will return later in the chapter.

Derivatives are financial assets in their own right but are based on (derived from) other underlying financial assets, such as shares or bonds. For the most part, derivatives take the form of contracts to buy or sell underlying assets in the future; in some cases, though, derivative products achieve an alteration to or an exchange of the cash flow from an underlying asset rather than an actual change in asset ownership.

Derivative products include forward contracts, futures, options and swaps. In this chapter we will look at the nature of different derivative products, at the way the products are traded and at the structure of derivatives markets.

Learning objectives

The purpose of this chapter is to make clear the nature of derivative products and in particular:

- the overall function of derivatives;
- the risk/return characteristics of different derivative products;
- how derivatives are traded;
- why derivatives have lead to so many corporate scandals.

The function of derivatives markets

Before we get into examining derivative products and markets in more detail, one general point is worth emphasizing. The derivatives markets are fundamentally different in their function, from the point of view of fund raisers, from all the markets we have studied up to now. In the case of shares, bonds and money market instruments, all allow companies or governments to raise money through their issue. Derivatives, when they are issued, do not raise funds for such parties, although they can sometimes be used as part of funding packages to make it easier for fund raisers to sell other types of securities. What, then, is the point of these derivatives markets? One of the main functions of the derivatives markets is to allow market participants to *manage risk*. Through the buying and selling of derivatives, risk can be transferred from one party to another in the market or perhaps eliminated altogether. From an investor's point of view, the function of derivatives markets is more similar to that of other financial markets; the markets provide alternative assets into which investors can put their money in competition with shares, bonds, etc., as well as providing risk management opportunities as outlined above.

These are points which will be explained further in the rest of the chapter, but it is worth keeping in mind the somewhat peculiar nature of derivatives markets in the closer study of them in this chapter.

History

Derivatives markets have been around in some form or another for centuries. The earliest trades centred mostly on commodities; in the seventeenth century there were derivatives markets allowing future purchases and sales of rice in Japan and of tulip bulbs in Amsterdam. Markets in financial derivatives (contracts to buy or sell assets such as shares or bonds in future) have only developed in the twentieth century and most notably over the past thirty years; this makes the markets youngsters compared to share or bond markets, which have generally been operating in Western developed economies for several centuries.

Financial derivatives markets were originally developed in the USA. The world's two largest derivatives markets were developed in Chicago in the 1970s, the Chicago Board of Trade (CBOT) and the Chicago Mercantile Exchange (CME) , and the Chicago markets have remained dominant in foreign exchange derivatives to this day. The spur for these markets' growth was uncertainty in foreign exchange markets following the abolition of fixed exchange rates in 1972. Derivatives markets in other parts of the world have developed over the 1980s and 1990s and deal particularly in derivatives based on interest rates and share prices. The UK market, the London International Financial Futures and Options Exchange (LIFFE), was originally established in 1982 as a futures exchange, but was merged ten years later with the UK options exchange. The French market, the Marché à Terme International de France (MATIF), was opened in 1986, while the German exchange, the Deutsche Terminborse (DTB) started in 1990; this market has since merged with the Swiss derivatives market to become Eurex. Derivatives markets also operate in other European countries and Asia, and increasingly in less financially developed countries; in 1998, there were over 60 derivatives exchanges established worldwide. Perhaps because of their relative youth or perhaps because the products they offer suit the particular requirements of their time, derivatives markets have shown spectacular growth; LIFFE, for instance, has seen business increase from under two million contracts a day to over 15 million in less than ten years (*The Economist*, 5 July 1997).

Forward contracts

To get an idea of the basic characteristics of derivatives, we can start by considering forward contracts. A forward contract is an agreement entered into by two parties for one party to buy and the other party to sell a particular asset at some time in the future; the precise date at which the sale will take place and the price operating under the sale are agreed now. Say, for instance, that I own some UK government gilts. I could enter into a forward contract to sell those gilts in three months' time for a set price per gilt. The gilts I own are financial assets, but so too is the forward contract based on them. Depending on how prices of gilts move in the future, my forward contract might prove to be advantageous to me, i.e. an asset, or disadvantageous, i.e. a liability. The contract might thus have a positive value (if it is an asset to me) or a negative value (if it proves to be a liability). The forward contract is an example of a derivative product, in that it is a financial product derived from another underlying financial asset (my gilts), and in that its value depends on movements in the price of the underlying gilts.

Activity 1

Let us put some numbers on the example of a forward contract outlined above. Suppose my gilts are currently valued in the gilt market at £100 each and that I own 100 gilts. If the forward contract I enter into binds me to sell all 100 gilts in three months' time for £110 each, what is the forward contract worth when it comes to be carried through if gilts in three months' time are each worth, alternatively:

1. *£120*

2. *£90?*

(Note that what is being asked here is what the forward contract *is worth, not what my gilts in conjunction with the forward contract are worth.)*

1. In three months' time, under my forward contract, I will have to sell gilts which have ended up being worth £120 for the contract price of £110; I therefore lose £10 on every gilt in comparison with what I would have made without the forward contract. In this case, the forward contract has ended up being a liability. If I could trade the contract in a forward contracts market, I would be prepared to pay to get out of it. Rationally, I should be prepared to pay up to £1,000 (100 × £10) to get out of the contract, and we can therefore say that −£1,000 is the worth of my forward contract in three months' time.

2. If gilt prices end up in three months' time being £90, my forward contract turns out to be an asset. As a result of having the contract, I can sell gilts worth £90 in the secondary gilt market for £110. The forward contract makes me an extra £20 on each gilt, and as it relates to 100 gilts, the contract's total value is £2,000 (100 × £20). If there were a market in forward contracts, it could reasonably be expected that someone else would be prepared to pay me this price for the contract because, even if they did not own gilts themselves, they could buy up

gilts in the gilt market for £90 and then sell them under the forward contract for £110; someone could therefore pay me £2,000 for my contract and still break even.

In the note to Activity 1, it was stressed that you should consider the value of the forward contract and not of the contract and the gilts combined. As a result of entering the forward contract, I will, with certainty, receive £11,000 for my gilts (100 × the forward contract price of £110). Without the contract I would have recieved, under (1), £12,000 (100 × £120), or, under (2), £9,000 (100 × £90). Held in conjunction with gilts, the forward contract *eliminates risk*, in that I know for certain what I will receive for my combined investment of gilts plus forward contract, whatever happens to the price of gilts in future. If I held a forward contract on its own, however, I would be in a *risky* position, in that, taking the example above, the contract could end up being worth −£1,000 or +£2,000. Later in the chapter we will see that, held in isolation, derivative products are among the most risky financial investments available.

This example thus shows how forward contracts:

1. Can have a value, and can therefore be considered as financial assets independently of the underlying securities (gilts, in the case we looked at) to which they relate.
2. Can be used, in conjunction with holdings of other assets, to manage risk.
3. Can be held in isolation, as a financial investment with a high risk.

Points (2) and (3) above emphasize the connection between all derivatives and risk. Derivatives are in fact only worth creating if the price of the underlying asset to which they relate is risky. Think again about the example of a forward contract on gilts that we considered above. If the price of gilts in three months' time were known with certainty, forward contracts would have no purpose; someone wanting to sell gilts would know exactly what he or she would get for the gilts in the future spot market anyway and would not be prepared to enter a forward contract for any lesser price, while someone wanting to buy gilts would also be sure of the future spot price and would not be prepared to pay any more under a forward contract. The end result would be that everyone would wait to transact until the time they actually wanted to exchange assets and forward contracts would not exist. Derivative products thus rely crucially on the existence of risk.

One final point before we leave this activity relates to the marketability of forward contracts. It was mentioned in Activity 1 that if there were a market for forward contracts, then, depending on price movements of underlying assets, particular forward contracts could have a positive or negative market value. Forward contracts are not, in fact, market traded assets, but bespoke or 'over the counter' contracts agreed between a particular buyer and seller. Usually, forward contracts are arranged to suit the individual commercial requirements of one or other party to the agreement, and delivery of the underlying assets takes place at the end of the contract period. An example might be where a trading company had arranged to sell goods abroad, with foreign currency being received in a number of months' time. The company might enter into a forward contract with its bank to sell the foreign currency for domestic currency, so as to fix, in domestic currency terms, the price it will get for its goods. When the company receives the foreign currency from its customer, this currency will be actually exchanged for domestic curreny by the company's bank. In these circumstances, the company is using the forward contract to remove the commercial risk it would otherwise be exposed to from its trading actions; in other words, the forward contract is being used to hedge the company's commercial risk.

Futures

Futures contracts are very similar in nature to forward contracts, their main difference being that they are standardized contracts that can be traded in a futures market. Contracts are standardized in terms of the quality and quantity of underlying financial assets, and the future dates to which the contracts relate. To take an example, you could, on an individual basis, enter into a forward contract based on any gilt and any contract time period; you might not be able to sell on that contract easily, however, if there were no recognized market dealing in that particular gilt or maturity date. The contracts traded on LIFFE are constructed around particular gilts and particular maturities.[1] The concentration on fewer types of contract saves market participants time and cost in researching different products and creates relatively large product markets. The latter point helps to ensure liquidity for investors wishing to trade in contracts before they mature. The downside of futures contracts as compared to forward contracts is that they are less likely to give a perfect hedge for commercial risks. An example of a forward currency contract was given above, when a trading company arranged to sell foreign currency to its bank precisely to match the receipt of currency it expected from its customer. If, alternatively, the company used the futures market to hedge its risk, it might have a slight mismatch in the quantity and maturity of contracts because of the standardized nature of the futures market. The imperfection of the hedge would need to be weighed against the likely additional cost of the customized forward contract.

Another difference between forward contracts and futures is that futures are rarely settled by delivery of the underlying asset. If a trader has entered into a contract to buy (have delivered) a particular quantity of an asset in the future, then, when the contract comes to be settled, the trader's position can be 'closed out' by him or her entering into an offsetting contract to sell (deliver) the same quantity of asset at the same time in the future; the underlying asset is never actually exchanged under this arrangement. The existence of a clearing house in the market assists the settlement of contracts without delivery, as discussed later in this chapter.

A futures contract under which a market participant will buy an asset in future is called a 'long' contract. Similarly, a futures contract which binds a party to sell in future is called a 'short' futures contract.

Valuing forward contracts and futures

Like forward contracts, futures contracts, taken in isolation, can have a positive or negative value at any time. The positive value attributable to one party to a futures contract is the negative value attributable to the other party. To illustrate this, let us go back to Activity 1. We noted that, if the forward contract price was £110 and the gilt price ended up at £120, the contract for the seller was worth –£1,000. The contract for the buyer would be worth precisely the reverse, i.e. +£1,000, because the buyer would now be in a position to acquire gilts for £110 which he or she could then sell in the market for £120, giving a total profit of $100 \times £10$ or £1,000.

Activity 2

Construct a graph showing the value, on maturity, of a forward contract or future to buy a single gilt for £110 against the value of the underlying gilt. On the x axis of your graph, you should show the price of a gilt, and on the y axis the value, from the point of view of the future gilt buyer, of the forward contract based on that gilt.

Now construct a similar graph showing the position of the seller under the forward contract.

Comment on your results.

Note that the two graphs in Figure 7.1 are mirror images. This illustrates the fact that the gilt buyer's profit under the forward contract, or future, is the gilt seller's loss, and vice versa. Note too the possible extent of profits and losses for gilt sellers and buyers. The potential profits for gilt buyers and losses for gilt sellers are unlimited, as the price to which the underlying gilt can rise is unlimited. Technically the losses for gilt buyers and profits for gilt sellers are limited by the fact that the gilt cannot have a value less than zero; still, there is a lot of money to be made or lost before that distant floor is reached.

Figure 7.1 The value of a future/forward contract for a buyer and a seller under the contract

a. The value of a future/forward contract for the buyer under the contract, where the gilt is to be exchanged for £110.

b. The value of a future/forward contract for the seller under the contract, where the gilt is to be exchanged for £110.

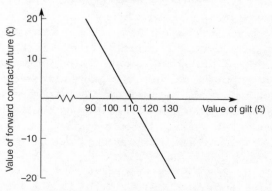

Futures contracts, if held in isolation from commercial assets, the risk of which they hedge, are highly risky. This can be seen from the diagrams you have just produced. Take the example of someone entering into a contract to buy a gilt at £110 and assume that just before the futures contract comes to expire the gilt price stands at £120. This would mean, and you can see this on your graph, that the value of the buyer's futures contract would be £10. Now suppose that the gilt price rises to £130; this represents just over an 8 per cent increase in gilt value. What happens to the value of the buyer's future? It increases by £10 to £20 – not, perhaps, at first sight a dramatic increase in absolute value, but in percentage terms quite impressive! The value of the future has increased *100 per cent* on the back of an 8 per cent change in gilt value. These are the sort of possibilities that entice investors into futures. Of course, futures are not all about big gains: if gilt prices decrease £10 (an 8 per cent fall in investment value for gilt investors) the investment value of futures buyers is wiped out altogether.

The characteristic of many derivative products of producing large percentage gains or losses as a result of much smaller percentage price movements of the underlying assets is referred to as the 'gearing' or 'leverage' of the derivative assets. If, for instance, an investor believed that a particular share was likely to rise in value over the near future, he or she could back that belief either by buying the share itself or by buying a derivative, such as a long futures contract. There is a significant difference in the capital required for each of these strategies. In the case of buying the share itself, the full share value will have to be invested now. If the futures strategy is followed, a much smaller investment will be required because the future has a much smaller individual value than the share.[2] This means that an investor with limited capital may be able effectively to place more 'bets' on the share price going up by using futures than by buying the underlying assets themselves, and hence the description of derivatives as 'highly geared' investments.

The above discussion and activities are concerned with the value of futures and forward contracts on maturity. As we have already noted, futures contracts are often traded before maturity. How is a market value arrived at for contracts in these circumstances? A detailed discussion of the valuation of futures before maturity is beyond the scope of this book. We can make a general observation that the value of a futures contract at any time is very closely influenced by the spot price of the underlying asset to which it relates. To take an example, an investor expecting the value of an underlying asset to rise can either invest in the underlying asset itself or take a long futures contract, binding them to buy the same underlying asset in future. If an investor decides to follow the futures contract alternative, some costs of investing directly in the underlying asset will be saved, but at the same time some benefits from owning the underlying asset directly will also be forgone. An example of a cost saved would be the cost of borrowing capital to buy the asset outright; an example of benefits forgone would be any return that the underlying asset might yield during the period of ownership, such as a dividend or interest payment. Since both the purchase of a long futures contract and the direct investment in the underlying asset have the same eventual outcome of providing a holding of the underlying asset, the value of the futures contract is limited by the costs and benefits of the alternative strategy of investing directly in the underlying asset. Prices in spot and futures markets are thus irrevocably linked together.

Types and uses of futures contracts

Futures contracts are traded which relate to interest rates, share prices, share indices and currencies.

The structure of futures relating to share prices and currencies are straightforward. In both cases there are underlying assets – shares and currencies – which are traded in spot markets, and the futures are drawn up simply to be contracts to buy or sell given quantities of the underlying assets at set future dates. What about interest rates and share indices though? The risk of interest rate movements or of general share price movements is just the sort of thing many companies and individuals would want to hedge against, but in both cases there is no directly related underlying asset; you cannot, after all, carry out a spot trade to buy or sell interest rates. Futures contracts therefore either have to be drawn up around another underlying asset which reflects movements in the economic variable people wish to hedge against, or have to be designed separately from any spot traded financial securities. Short-term interest rate futures and share index futures are examples of the latter. Short-term interest rate futures are designed as contracts to buy or sell short-term bank deposits at given interest rates, with the deposits starting at some agreed point in the future; they are always settled in cash rather than an actual bank deposit being 'delivered'. To take an example, one short-term interest rate futures contract might be for the delivery of a 7 per cent one million Eurodollar deposit which would last three months and be created in one month's time. An investor at risk of interest rates going down, perhaps because the return on some of his or her investments would then go down, could enter into such a futures contract as the party to acquire the Eurodollar deposit in future; this is going long in the futures contract. If interest rates do go down, the investor's return on investments will go down as feared, but he or she will make money on the futures contract to offset this. The futures contract will be valuable because it gives the investor entitlement to a deposit at 7 per cent even though general interest rates have ended up lower than this. The one million Eurodollar deposit will not be created, but the investor will instead be paid the cash value of the futures contract on maturity. Similarly to interest rate futures contracts, share index futures are constructed to be contracts to buy or sell the market index, with settlement again being in cash.

Activity 3

Longer-term interest rate futures are structured around the agreed sale or purchase of gilt edged securities. For instance, say the treasurer of a company with a long-term loan, the interest on which varies with general interest rates in the country, is concerned that general interest rates might rise and that his company might therefore end up paying more interest and have lower profits as a result. He can hedge this risk by entering into a contract to sell gilts in future – can you explain how?

To see how this hedge works, you need to recall that the value of gilts moves inversely with interest rates (see Chapter 5 if you need to refresh your memory on this). Thus if interest rates go up, the price of gilts will go down.

If there is no general market expectation that interest rates will rise, the company should be able to enter freely into a futures contract to sell gilts at their current value in several months' time. If, though, interest rates do go up, at the time the futures contract expires gilts will have fallen in price and the company will be able to buy up gilts cheaply and sell them at a profit under the futures contract. The profit made offsets the company's loss as a result of having to pay higher interest on its loan – a typical hedge.

Most of the examples we have used so far have involved market participants using futures markets to hedge commercial risks. The markets also provide ideal opportunities for two other types of trading activity – speculation and arbitrage.

Speculation was discussed in Chapter 2. Briefly, it is where a risky investment is entered into with the hope of profit, the investment normally being made without relation to any underlying industrial or commercial activity. Derivative products are particularly attractive financial assets to speculators because they allow them to bet on the markets without using up much capital (the gearing aspect of derivatives mentioned above). Speculators can therefore make spectacular gains from a small capital base if they turn out to have got their bets right – or spectacular losses if their bets turn out to be wrong.

Arbitrage is where market professionals trade on small discrepancies in market pricing. The aim is always to buy assets in the market which is underpricing and to sell the assets in the market which is overpricing, thereby realizing a profit. The activity of arbitrageurs should force prices back to equilibrium by boosting demand in lower priced markets and boosting supply in higher priced markets. The existence of futures markets provides arbitrageurs with opportunities to exploit any pricing differences between forward markets and futures markets – for example, in foreign exchange or interest rates – in that these are two markets in essentially the same product. Arbitrage opportunities also arise if there is any variance in pricing between futures markets and spot markets; the relationship between futures prices and spot prices is explained in the section on valuing futures before maturity above.

Activity 4

Suppose a futures contract exists for the exchange of 500 gilts (£50,000 nominal value) at a price per gilt of £105. Just before maturity, the spot price of gilts of the relevant maturity is £100. The value of the futures contract in the futures market to the short seller is £2,475. What arbitrage strategy can be carried out to profit from any market discrepancies?

For the markets to be in equilibrium, the value of the futures contract ought to be £2,500 (the £105 gilt selling price less the £100 spot value of gilts × 500). To profit from the market discrepancies, an arbitrageur should buy the short gilt contract for £2,475 and buy 500 gilts in the spot market for £100 each. He or she could then sell the gilts on maturity of the futures contract for £105 each, making a risk-free profit of £25. This example does not allow for transactions costs, which might in reality wipe out any potential profit.

Options

The third type of derivative we can consider is options. In commercial terms, futures have greater significance than options. Most derivatives exchanges start by trading futures and then introduce options only at a later date. The volume of futures trading tends to remain much greater than that of options; taking figures for LIFFE in 1991, options trading was less than a quarter of futures trading in terms of contract numbers (Cobham, 1992). In finance in general, however, options are proving to be probably the more interesting product. The study and increased understanding of options has been one of the most important developments in financial theory in the past twenty years, and is considered to be one of the most likely bases for future progress (Brealey and Myers, 1996). Options are thus important not just for providing a method for managing or speculating on risk but also for giving us an insight into how many wider financial and commercial decisions are made.

An option is a financial asset which gives the holder the right to buy or sell an underlying asset on a future date at a price (the exercise price) agreed now; a contract which gives the holder the right to buy an asset in future is called a call option, while a contract giving the right to sell an asset is called a put option.

In the definition above, it is stated that an option is a right to buy or sell an asset on a particular date. To be more precise, contracts which give an option which can be exercised only on a particular date are called European options; options also exist which give the right to buy or sell at any time up to a particular date, and these are called American options. The use of 'American' and 'European' is somewhat misleading, as both kinds of options are sold in both continents, either 'over the counter' or through futures and options exchanges. Most options sold on futures and options exchanges are American options.

From the point of view of an investor considering buying an option or entering into a future, the two products have a fundamental difference. From the diagrams you produced above, you saw that a future or forward contract can end up being a liability or an asset for either party to the contract; the amount that can be made or lost is virtually limitless, and the investment in isolation is thus very risky. From the point of view of a holder of an option, however, the option can *never* be a liability as it confers *the right* but *not the obligation* to acquire an asset; the worst that can happen is that the holder's investment proves worthless.

Activity 5

Let us put some figures on options, as we did on forward contracts, to bring home the nature of the option product. Consider that you hold an option to acquire a single share in A plc for £10. How much will that option be worth on expiry (i.e. when the contract is mature) if A plc shares end up selling in the secondary share market at that time for:

1. *£8.*

2. *£9.*

3. *£10.*

4. *£12.*

5. *£15?*

1. If A plc shares end up being worth £8, it will not be sensible for you to exercise your option. Under the option, you would have to pay £10 to acquire an A plc share. Why pay this much when you can pick the shares up in the secondary share market for only £8? What you should do is simply let your option lapse.

The option therefore ends up being worthless. It does not end up having a negative value, as a future would have done, because no one can force you to go through with the option trade.

2.   Again the option is worthless, because shares are still cheaper in the secondary market than they are under the option contract.

3.   Still the option is worthless. You make no profit from buying shares under the option for the exercise price of £10 as compared to buying them in the open market for £10. In this instance it makes no difference whether you exercise the option or let it lapse.

4.   Now the option is worth something. It is worth £2 on expiry, because the option gives the holder the right to buy a share for £10 which can then be sold again immediately in the secondary share market for £12.

5.   If the share price ends up at £15, the option is worth £5, which is the then share value of £15 less the exercise price under the option of £10.

Where an option would have a positive value if it were exercised now, it is said to be 'in-the-money'. This situation arises where the exercise price of the option is below the spot price of the underlying asset in the case of a call option (as illustrated in parts (4) and (5) of Activity 5). Where an investor holds a put option, the option would be in-the-money if the option exercise price were above the spot price of the underlying asset. An option is said to be 'at-the-money' if the option holder would break even if the option were exercised now, and 'out-of-the-money' if a loss would be made on current exercise.

Activity 6

Plot your results from Activity 5 on a graph which will show the value of a call option just before expiry against the value of an underlying share. On the x axis show the value of the A plc share and on the y axis the value of the call option.

Now perform the same operation for a put option. Assume that you have an option to sell an A plc share for £10 and show how the value of this option varies with share price.

If you consider the graphs in Figure 7.2, investing in options looks too good to be true. The investment can never be worth less than zero but there is still the chance to make a profit if share prices are high (in the case of a call option) or low (in the case of a put option). If you then think of the position of the seller of options, who is often termed the 'option writer', his or her position on expiry is just the mirror image of the option holder, as shown in Figure 7.3.

Unlike option holders who have the right but not the obligation to carry through a purchase or sale under the option contract, the option writer is contractually required to uphold his or her side of the bargain should the option holder choose to exercise. From the diagrams in Figure 7.3, you can see that option writers lose money on calls if share prices end up above the exercise price and lose money on put options if the share price ends up below the exercise price – and they never seem to make any money at all. Of course, this position does not make financial sense, and the missing bit in the option jigsaw is the option premium; this is the price an option writer charges to create an option. Taking the option premium into account, the option writer makes a profit equal to the premium if he or she creates an option which is then not exercised by the option holder. The position for the option writer is represented in Figure 7.4.

Figure 7.2 Values of options, just before expiry, to sell/acquire A plc share for an exercise price of £10

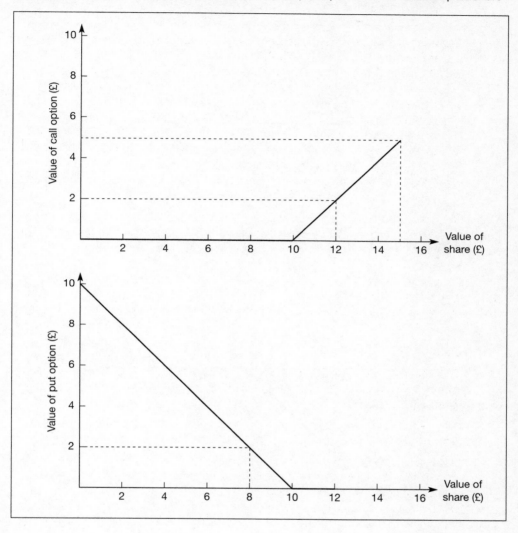

Activity 7

Suppose that the options referred to in Activities 5 and 6 commanded premia of £0.5 and £0.4 for a call and put respectively. Now produce graphs showing the overall profit of a call and put buyer depending on the underlying value of A plc shares.

The overall profit or loss of option buyers is shown in Figure 7.5.

Something that comes out of the diagrams showing the profits of option buyers and sellers (Figures 7.4 and 7.5) is that risk in the case of options is not symmetrical. What is meant by that is that option buyers are in a position of limited risk; the most they can lose is the premium thay have paid for their options, while their potential gain is effectively limitless. Option writers, on the other hand, have a maximum profit of the premium, but a limitless potential loss.[3] This is not to say that investing in options is not

Figure 7.3   The profit/loss of the writer of options on A plc shares with an exercise price of £10 on expiry of the options

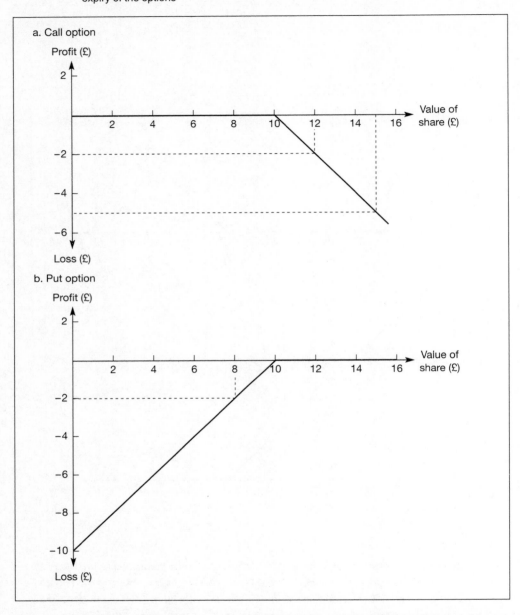

risky; as with futures, investors are still more likely to see big percentage gains and losses on investment than they are with, say, bonds or shares, but the position of option writers carries even greater risk.

Uses and types of option

So far options have been considered as isolated investments in their own right. As with futures, they can be used in conjunction with other assets to hedge risk. In intro-

Figure 7.4 The profit/loss of the writer of options on expiry, taking into account the receipt of premium payments

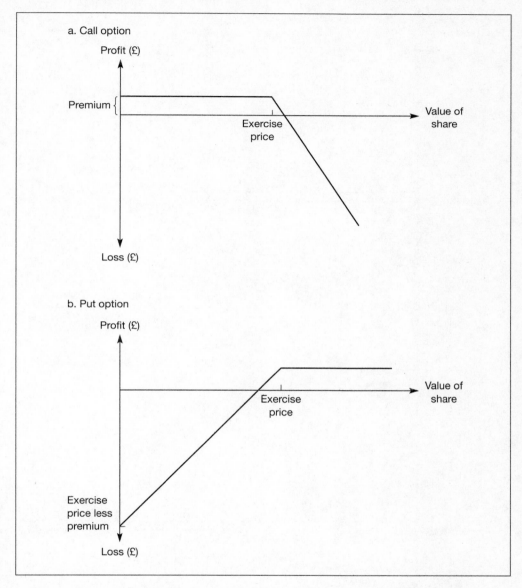

ducing forward contracts and futures, we considered how a company expecting to receive foreign currency in relation to a sale of goods abroad could sell the currency forward effectively to fix in domestic currency terms the profit it would make on its commercial trade. An alternative risk management strategy for the company would be to take out currency options to protect the company from exchange rate losses, while still leaving it in a position to benefit from exchange rate gains. Specifically, the company could acquire an option to sell foreign currency in future (a put option); this would protect the company in case of a depreciation of the foreign currency and thus would give a floor to the amount the company would receive in terms of its own

Figure 7.5 The profit/loss of the buyer of call and put options on A plc shares held to expiry and with an exercise price of £10

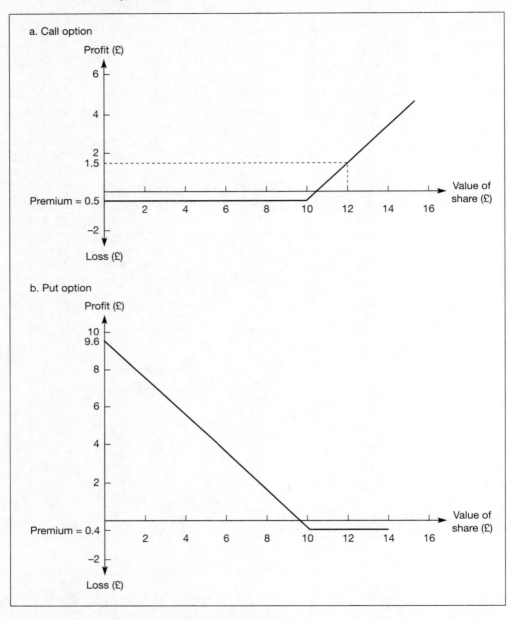

currency for the goods sold. If, however, the foreign currency were to appreciate against the domestic currency, the company would let its put option lapse and sell the foreign currency it received on the open market to make an exchange profit. Of course, getting rid of downside risk while maintaining upside does not come free. While the company may have been able to enter into a future or forward contract at little or no cost, it will have to pay a premium to acquire a put option.

Options are thus an alternative risk management tool to futures or forward contracts. They will be particularly attractive to hedgers who feel uncertain as to which way markets might move and want to protect against the adverse impact of risk, while maintaining the chance to profit from advantageous market changes. Options are sold on exchanges relating to shares, share indices, currencies and interest rate futures contracts.

One useful aspect of options is that they can often be combined together to create a package which allows market participants to hedge against or speculate on risks that are not exhibited directly in any spot traded underlying financial asset. An example of such an option package is a 'straddle'. A straddle is created where an option writer simultaneously sells a put and call option on an underlying asset; both options have the same expiry date and exercise price. An example of a straddle would be where an option writer sold a call and put option on a share with an exercise price equal to the current share price of £1.10, the expiry date for both options being three months' time. The option writer is speculating that the share price will not prove to be volatile over the options' life. If the share price remains at £1.10 over the next three months neither option will be exercised and the option writer will make a profit equal to the two option premia charged. If the share price moves a little the profit will be reduced by any loss made on the exercise of either option by its holder. This situation is illustrated in Figure 7.6, which is made up by combining earlier diagrams of puts and calls.

Figure 7.6 The profit/loss on a straddle for the writer of options, where the exercise price of call options written is £1.10

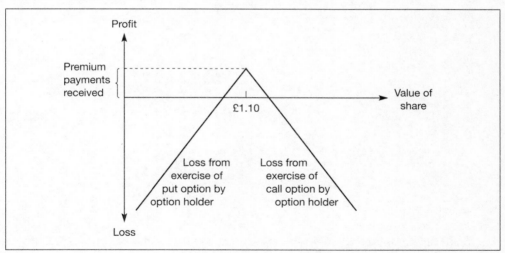

As well as trading as financial assets to be used for hedging, speculation and arbitrage, options can be included in finance raising packages to make the sale of other securities more attractive. Convertible bonds, which were explained in Chapter 5, are an example of this. Convertible bonds are corporate long-term borrowing instruments carrying the right for the holder to convert his or her investment into shares at a price fixed at the outset. The bonds can be considered as ordinary, or 'straight', bonds plus a call option on shares.

As options are always an asset and never a liability to the holder, the inclusion of conversion rights in the bond package should make the investment more attractive than straight bonds. Convertible bonds should thus sell on a lower coupon rate than comparable straight bonds. The saving in coupon payments makes convertible bonds potentially attractive forms of fund raising to companies wishing to preserve current cash flow.

Data on options in the financial press and option valuation

Figure 7.7 shows an extract from the *Financial Times* of 22 September 1999 showing options on individual shares traded on LIFFE.

Figure 7.7 Data on share options provided in the financial press. *Source: Financial Times*, 22 September 1999.

LIFFE EQUITY OPTIONS

		Calls			Puts		
Option		Oct	Jan	-	Oct	Jan	-
ASDA	200	21	23½	-	-	-	-
(*220)	220	1	4	-	-	-	-
Option		Oct	Jan	Apr	Oct	Jan	Apr
Abbey Natl	950	62	108	131	25	60½	89½
(*983)	1000	35½	83½	107	48½	85	115
Allied Domecq	550	50	70½	86½	5	19½	28½
(*592)	600	18½	42	58½	24½	41	51
Ald Dom ex	330	27	42½	53	6	17½	24½
(*349½)	360	10½	27	38½	20	32	39½
Allied Zurich	700	38½	70	91½	18	45	57
(*716)	750	14	45½	65½	45½	69	80½
AstraZeneca	2500	118½	213½	282	49½	122½	166
(*2551)	2600	58½	163½	230½	98½	172	214
BAA	600	41	58	73½	6½	22½	30½
(*632)	650	13	32	48	29	46½	54½
BAT	500	23	48½	61	17½	37	52
(*504)	550	6	28	40½	50½	66½	82½
Barclays	1600	74	154	201½	59½	120	171
(*1608½)	1700	31½	108	152	117	174½	222
Bass	750	33	57½	75	17½	48	62
(*762½)	800	11½	35	53½	46½	78	91
Boots	700	29	49	75½	18½	40½	54
(*705)	750	9½	26	53½	49½	68	82½
Br Airways	360	19½	33	46	10	25½	33½
(*368)	390	6½	20½	33	27½	43	50
BP Amoco	1050	63	109	138½	23½	60	82
(*1085½)	1100	35	83	115½	45	84	106½
British Steel	140	15½	18½	23½	1½	6½	9
(*153½)	160	4	9½	14	10	16½	19½
Cable & Wire	650	41	70½	91	18½	38½	55½
(*671½)	700	18	45½	65½	42	63½	79
CGU	900	49½	88½	108½	28½	56½	82
(*918)	950	26½	64	89	55½	82	107
Glaxo	1600	73½	154	196	47	104	149
(*1619½)	1700	29½	104½	143½	104	153½	196½
HSBC 75p	700	32½	65	88½	24½	49½	71½
(*705)	733	17½	49	-	43	66½	-
Halifax	649	47	75	-	9½	29½	-
(*684)	699	19	48½	-	31½	53	-
ICI	600	51½	80½	95	11	33½	51½
(*636½)	650	23	54	69	32	56	76
Land Secur	800	38	59½	81½	12	33½	47
(*820½)	850	11½	35½	57	38	60	72½
Marks & S	300	33	44	55	3	13½	21½
(*328½)	330	13½	27½	39½	13½	27	35½

		Calls			Puts		
Option		Oct	Jan	Apr	Oct	Jan	Apr
Natl Grid	420	20½	32½	46½	7½	20	26
(*430½)	460	4½	15	29	32	43	48½
Natl Power	460	25½	45	57½	21	43	53
(*462)	500	11	29½	42	47	68	76½
NatWest	1050	50½	102	138	42½	82	106
(*1054)	1100	29½	78	114½	71½	108	132½
Reed Intl	360	36	54	65	6	18½	29½
(*388½)	390	17½	38½	50	17½	32½	44½
Reuters	850	58½	100	129½	15½	47	74
(*889½)	900	30	74	105½	36½	70½	99
Royal Bk Scot	1150	53½	113½	150½	45½	92	115
(*1153½)	1200	32	89½	126½	74½	118	141
Royal/Sun Al	419	45	66	-	4½	21	-
(*458)	459	18½	44	-	18	37½	-
Safeway	240	11½	20	26½	7½	17	22
(*243)	260	4	11½	18½	20	29	33
Sainsbury	390	17½	33	45	12½	29	36½
(*392½)	420	6	20½	32	30½	46	52½
Securicor	550	46	100½	118½	½	24½	36
(*593)	600	8½	78	94½	13½	47	59½
Shell Trans	460	19	38½	51½	15½	30	43½
(*467)	500	5½	21	35	42	52½	65
SmKl Bchm	750	40	75½	100	28½	57½	74
(*758)	800	17½	51½	74	57½	83½	98½
Std Chartd	750	57	102	135	28½	63½	88
(*777½)	800	31½	79	118½	52½	90	112½
Thames Wtr	900	30½	65	81	24	49½	65½
(*900½)	950	11½	43½	59	56	78	94
Vodafone	1300	89	130	173½	41	90	118
(*1322½)	1350	44	106	149½	66½	115½	143½
Woolwich	317	13½	-	-	9½	-	-
(*319½)	346	3½	-	-	28½	-	-
Option		Nov	Feb	May	Nov	Feb	May
Allce & Leics	750	58	76½	92½	21½	39½	56½
(*772½)	800	25½	51	67½	47	64	81½
Anglo Amer	3000	218½	325½	398	111½	191	258
(*3076)	3100	161	276½	347	161½	241	306½
Blue Circle	360	25½	43	47½	17½	27½	40½
(*365)	390	13	29	34½	35	44½	58
Brit Aero	390	40½	55½	64	12	22	30
(*418½)	420	22	38½	48	23½	35	43½
Brit Telecom	900	80	112	140½	36	65	83
(*937)	950	53	87	118½	59	89½	108½

		Calls			Puts		
Option		Nov	Feb	May	Nov	Feb	May
Cadbury Sch	425	26	41	-	18	28	-
(*429½)	450	15	29	-	32	41½	-
Carlton Comm	420	29½	48½	60½	17½	30½	38½
(*429)	460	13	31	42½	40½	53	60½
Diageo	600	47½	68	80	18	31	43½
(*635½)	650	19½	48	55½	41	54	68½
Gallaher	420	35	47½	53	15	22	32
(*437½)	460	15½	28½	34	36	43	54
GEC	550	61½	81½	95	16	30	40
(*591)	600	32	54	70½	36	53	64½
Hanson	460	39	58½	63½	17	29½	35
(*479)	500	20	39	44½	37½	50½	55
Hilton	200	19½	27½	31½	6½	12	17
(*211½)	220	9	17½	22	16	22	27½
Impl Tobacco	700	68½	88½	108	16	38½	53½
(*747)	750	39	54	82	36½	63	78½
Invensys	300	21½	33	42½	15½	26	32½
(*303½)	330	9	20½	30	33½	43	49½
Kingfisher	600	52½	73½	86½	20½	34½	47½
(*630½)	650	26	49	61½	45	60	72½
Lasmo	140	11	19½	21½	8	15	17½
(*142)	160	4	12	14	21	27	30
Legal & Gen	180	15	22	27	2½	7½	10½
(*191)	200	4½	11½	17	12	17	21½
P & O	900	65½	102	123½	40½	66½	87
(*922½)	950	42	78	99	66	89½	113
Prudential	850	81	114	136½	25	50	69½
(*899)	900	52	87	111	46	72	93
Rentokil Init	220	20½	39½	34½	6	11	16
(*233½)	240	8½	28½	24½	15½	21	26
RTZ	1000	87½	128½	151	40	70	97
(*1040½)	1050	61½	104½	126½	63½	94	122½
Rolls-Royce	200	23½	31	35	4	9	12½
(*218)	220	11½	26	24½	12	18	22
Tesco	180	12½	18	26	8	11½	19½
(*184½)	200	4½	8½	17½	20½	22	31
Utd Biscuits	180	18½	22½	25½	5	7	12½
(*192)	200	8	12	16	14½	16½	23½

		Calls			Puts		
Option		Dec	Mar	Jun	Dec	Mar	Jun
BG	360	28½	38½	45	17½	23½	30
(*371½)	390	15½	25½	31½	34½	39½	46
Bk Scotland	650	88½	97½	117	36	56½	74½
(*680)	700	45	74	94	61½	82½	100½
BSkyB	550	44½	61	75	20½	33	42
(*567)	600	21½	37½	51	48	59½	67½
Brit Biotech	30	9	10½	14½	4	5½	8½
(*34½)	35	6½	8½	13	6½	8½	12
Centrica	161	11	-	-	9	-	-
(*161)	181	4	-	-	22	-	-
Dixons	1000	108	147	181½	78	108	131½
(*1019)	1050	81½	124	159	102½	134	158
EMI	460	37½	53½	65½	26½	39	48
(*466)	500	20½	36	48	49½	61½	70
Freeserve	130	20½	28½	35	13	19½	24½
(*136)	140	16	24½	31	18½	25	30
Granada	525	48	-	-	26	-	-
(*538½)	550	34	52	58½	38½	56½	56½
GUS	500	58	68½	88	19	33½	43½
(*532)	550	31½	44	64½	42	59	72½
LloydsTSB	700	83½	104	123	26	47	64½
(*749)	750	55½	78	98½	47½	71½	89
Lonrho	500	84	73½	83	10	20½	27½
(*548)	550	33½	44½	56	29	42	50
Norwich U.	480	27	36½	54½	26½	34½	50
(*460)	500	12½	24	39½	52½	59	75
Orange	1100	100½	138½	180½	42½	67½	87
(*1145½)	1150	74	114	145½	65½	92½	112
Railtrack	1150	88	122½	159	59½	82	129½
(*1164)	1200	61½	98	135	85	107	155½
Scot Power	550	62	74	87½	11½	20	31½
(*598½)	600	30½	46	60½	31½	41½	54
Tarmac	110	8½	11½	-	3½	6	-
(*116½)	120	4	7	-	9	11	-
Telewest	220	22	31½	39½	17	24	29½
(*222½)	240	13½	23	30½	28½	35½	40½
Tomkins	260	26	34	41	12½	20½	25½
(*270½)	280	16	24	31½	22½	30½	36
Unilever	546	60	-	-	14	-	-
(*588½)	596	31½	-	-	35	-	-
Whitbread	750	48½	76½	88	35	53½	67
(*756)	800	28	54	64	63½	80½	95½

* Underlying security price. Premiums shown are based on settlement prices.
September 21 Total contracts, Equity & Index options: 50,423 Calls: 21,959 Puts: 28,464

The option prices shown in the *Financial Times* table are, in columns three to five, in relation to call options and, in columns six to eight, in relation to put options. Taking the second share shown in the table, Abbey National (a UK bank), Abbey's most recent share price (983p) is shown in parentheses under the company's name. Prices of calls and puts on the share are then shown for an exercise price of 950p (the same row as the company's name) and 1000p (the row one below). The first call price quoted is for an option with an expiry date of October 1999, the next of January 2000 and the last of April 2000; prices are quoted for put options for the same expiry dates.

We can note a number of points from the table with respect to the value of options prior to maturity:

1. Call options are worth more the lower the exercise price of the option. The October Abbey call option with an exercise price of 950p is worth 62p, while the

October call with an exercise price of 1000p is worth only 35.5p. This makes sense because a call gives the right to buy the share, and buying will be preferable at a lower price per share.

2. Put options are worth more the higher the exercise price of the option. The October Abbey put with an exercise price of 950p is worth 25p, while the October put with an exercise price of 1000p is worth 48.5p. The argument is the reverse of that with calls; if you are selling an asset in future, gaining a higher price is preferential to a lower one.

3. Options are worth more than their value if exercised immediately. Take, for example, the October 950p call option on Abbey. If this option were exercised now, it would yield a gain of 33p (the current value of the share in the secondary share market, 983p, less the exercise price of 950p); this value is termed the 'intrinsic value' of the option. The option is, however, worth, at 62p, considerably more than its intrinsic value. The reason why is that there is a chance that Abbey shares will rise higher than their current price, making the option more valuable still. The additional value of an option over and above its intrinsic value is called the 'time value' of the option.

4. Options have a value, provided that they still have some time to run, even if they would be worthless if exercised now. This is related to (3) above; the value of the option is wholly time value and reflects the chance that share prices will change over the remaining life of the option and thus make it valuable. For an example of this, consider the Abbey puts with an exercise price of 950p. All these puts have a value in the options markets (from 25p to 89.5p as shown in the table), but they would be worth nothing if exercised now (they are out-of-the-money), because the price the options allow an investor to sell at (950p) is less than the spot market price of shares (983p). The value of the put options reflects the fact that there is a chance that Abbey National shares will fall in price to below 950p over the remaining life of the options, thereby making them profitable to exercise.

5. The value of both put and call options is greater the greater the length of time they have left to run. This can be seen from the table by comparing the values of puts and calls with the same exercise price and on the same share but with different expiry dates. Taking Abbey calls with an exercise price of 950p, note that calls with an expiry date of April 2000 are worth more than twice as much as calls with an expiry date of October 1999 (131p versus 62p). Options are worth more the longer they have to run because then there is a greater chance that share prices will move to make the options valuable. Expressed more formally, the time value on long dated options is worth more than that on short dated options, even though both types of options may have the same intrinsic value.

The above points arising out of the *Financial Times* data indicate the sort of variables that determine the value of options before maturity, in particular the influence of the time left to run on the option and the relative values of exercise price and current share price. Option valuation models have been developed based on these and other variables and are used actively by traders in the options markets. The detailed discussion of these models is, however, beyond the scope of this book.

Swaps

It was noted at the beginning of this chapter that most derivatives involve the exchange of underlying assets in the future but that some products achieve instead an exchange of or alteration to asset cash flow without an actual change in ownership. Swaps are an example of the latter form of derivative and can be defined as the exchange of cash flows on defined underlying assets or liabilities. The purpose of a swap is to change the exposure of the parties to the swap to variables such as interest rates or currency fluctuations. Swaps can thus be seen as risk management tools in the same way as futures and options.

Swaps are conducted through an intermediary, such as a bank, rather than being traded on derivatives markets; in this aspect they are more similar to forward contracts than to futures and options. Swaps based on financial assets are the newest form of derivative in use, only being developed from the beginning of the 1980s. Contracts have, however, been increasingly standardized to reduce costs and provide greater pricing transparency.

The most common forms of swaps are interest rate swaps and currency swaps. In an interest rate swap, the parties to the contract agree to exchange their interest payment obligations. The following is an example of an interest rate swap which achieves the exchange of fixed rate for floating rate interest obligations.

Company A takes out a £10 million bank loan, the terms of which are that interest will be 2 per cent above LIBOR, with the principal repaid in ten years' time.

Company B issues ten-year bonds with a nominal and redemption value of £10 million, the terms of which are that the coupon is fixed at 12 per cent.

The companies swap their interest obligation, probably through a bank as swap broker, such that Company A pays the 12 per cent fixed coupon on Company B's bonds, while Company B pays the floating rate interest on Company A's bank loan. Company A remains legally responsible for making interest and principal repayments on the £10 million bank loan, while Company B remains responsible for payments on the bonds; the default risk to lenders is thus unaffected by the swap arrangements.

A fee will be paid by both parties to the bank; additional payments may also be agreed at the outset from one company to the other if the interest payments on one loan would be valued in the market as less than those on the other loan.

It is reasonable to ask why a swap market needs to exist at all, and specifically why, in the example above, Company A does not issue its own bonds and Company B borrow from a bank, as that combination seems to be what the companies both ultimately want. Market imperfections are what drive the swap market and explain examples like that of A and B above. Company A may not be well known in the corporate bond market but want to benefit from relatively low rates for fixed interest funding in that market. Company B might have an established presence in the market, resulting in its bonds commanding better rates than those of Company A. Company B can profit from its reputation in the bond market by arranging bond finance and then swapping its obligations in the swap market, as outlined above. The bank involved as swap broker also benefits from the arrangement. It earns a fee but does not have to use any of its own capital in the swap arrangements.

Currency swaps involve the exchange of payments in one currency for payments in another currency. Currency swaps may be used by a company wishing to adjust its currency exposure, in terms of either the currency receipts it expects to generate or the currency payments it needs to make.

Most of the world's swap business is centred on London and New York. Interest rate swaps are the largest part of the market, with currency swaps having only about a fifth of interest rate volume (Cobham, 1992). More complex swaps, which include, for example, an option for one or other party to the swap to cancel the arrangement, are also becoming more common.

The markets in which derivatives are traded

The largest derivatives markets are unlike most other current financial markets in operating principally from physical locations. These derivatives markets are what is termed 'open outcry markets', where traders shout or signal buy and sell orders to each other across 'pits' on the trading floor. The markets present a spectacular sight, with the different coloured jackets of the traders signifying the different institutions they represent and positively frenzied activity at times of market volatility. The two largest derivative markets, based in Chicago, LIFFE and many Asian derivatives markets operate from a physical trading floor, but some of the later markets to be developed, notably the DTB and MATIF, use screen-based trading. The cost advantages of screen-based trading appear gradually to be winning out in the competitive battle between the markets, and floor-based markets are increasingly introducing screen-based systems alongside their more traditional trading methods. LIFFE did have plans to move its base from near Cannon Street station to more extensive premises near London Bridge; the idea of the move was to provide a larger trading floor. These plans had to be abandoned when the market found itself increasingly losing out to the lower cost German/Swiss Eurex market. There are now plans for LIFFE to become a company and to operate a fully screen-based system. The move to become a company is intended to make it easier for capital to be raised to invest in new systems and for change to be introduced without less disruption from individual market members.

Another trend in derivatives markets is for link-ups between exchanges from different countries. In June and August 1999 respectively, link-ups were announced between the Chicago Board of Trade and Eurex, and between the Chicago Mercantile Exchange and LIFFE. As global capital markets become ever more competitive, alliances to expand the scope of trade and reduce costs seem to be the action most exchanges are looking to take.

Trading payments

In the absence of formalized futures and options markets, one risk that participants in the market would face in addition to the risk of changes in value of derivative products would be the risk of default of the opposite party to any contract. To remove this risk and thus encourage derivatives trading, futures and options markets operate a 'clearing house' system. Under this system, a market clearing house is interposed between the parties to any market contract, such that each party is legally bound to the clearing house rather than to the original opposite party to the contract. To take an example, a company wishing to hedge a future receipt of foreign currency might enter into a short futures contract, with an individual market trader (called a 'local') being the counterparty to the transaction. Once the contract had been made, the market clearing house would be interposed between the two parties, such that the company and the local would have their respective short and long currency futures contracts with the clearing house rather than with each other. The default risk attaching to the original parties to the contract has thus been replaced by that of the clearing house. The clearing house in most markets is either an institution owned by the derivatives market itself or a subsidiary of large financial institutions, and its creditworthiness will be beyond doubt. Thus participants in futures and options markets will be able to trade without the fear of default risk.

The stability of the clearing house is also protected by rules to establish the creditworthiness of market participants and by a system of stage payments on any market contracts entered into. To protect against default from traders with the clearing house, rules are laid down requiring any participants in the market to have minimum levels of capital to back their trading activities. A system of 'margin payments' also operates, which means that traders have to pay for any losses they incur at the beginning and during a contract period rather than waiting until maturity; this reduces the chance of traders building up large loss positions that they are then unable to meet at the end of a contract. On entering into a futures contract, both parties have to pay an 'intial margin', which will be determined by taking into account the maximum expected daily loss that might be expected on the contract; this anticipated loss will in turn depend on how volatile the underlying asset is expected to be over the course of the futures contract. Typically the initial margin will be between 1 and 5 per cent of the value of the underlying assets to which the futures contract relates. Over the course of the contract and as the price of the underlying asset moves, the parties then have to deposit more margin, if their trading position shows a loss, or can withdraw margin, if their position shows a gain. This process is called 'marking to market', and any additional margin deposited is known as 'variation margin'. Writers of options also have to make margin payments to reflect their risk of making large losses on their contracts. Many markets do not require margin from options buyers, as the most the option holder can lose, as we have seen above, is the option premium. LIFFE does require option buyers to make margin payments, however, but the option premium on this market is not payable until the end of the contract period.

Regulation

Derivatives exchanges have rules, in the same way as exchanges for other financial assets, to regulate who may trade in the market and the way trading is to be carried out. In the UK, for example, LIFFE is a Recognised Investment Exchange under the 1986 Financial Services Act. The rules of the exchange have to ensure that trading is carried out in an orderly way and that participants in the market are afforded some investor protection. Members of the exchange are also authorized and monitored for their capital adequacy by the Financial Services Authority.

Controversy surrounding derivatives

Derivatives have been the products at the centre of some major financial collapses or losses in the 1990s. In the UK in 1995, Barings Bank, one of the oldest and most respected financial institutions in the country, was brought to the brink of collapse by losses of £860 million incurred in the futures and options markets of Japan and Singapore. One year later, NatWest had to announce losses of £90 million sustained as a result of mispricing of options by one of its traders. Banks have not been the only institutions to suffer, though; a German industrial company, Metalgesellschaft, lost US$1 billion through oil futures in 1993 and an American group, Procter and Gamble, US$102 million on interest rate swaps in 1994.

Perhaps, though, potentially the most serious losses from derivatives trading were those that arose in autumn 1998 at the time of the global financial crisis that followed the collapse of Asian security markets. Hedge funds, which are unregulated investment funds aimed at the very rich and based mostly in the USA, revealed huge losses as a result of the fall in the prices of various financial assets, particularly bonds of countries with lower credit ratings. One bail-out had to be organized by the Federal Reserve in the USA; a consortium of banks put up over £2 billion to save Long Term Capital Management from collapse in October 1998. The rush by hedge funds to sell off assets to maintain liquidity was blamed for a dramatic fall in the dollar in the same month and for threatening the stability of the whole US stock market.

How did some hedge funds lose so much money so quickly? Hedge funds are somewhat misleadingly named, in that hedging, as we have seen above, is normally associated with lowering or eliminating risk. These funds, however, have tended to invest to earn high returns, but with a high risk as a consequence. Different funds pursued different investment strategies, so it is difficult to generalize about the funds as a group. The essence of most strategies, however, was to try to spot, using financial models, assets that were underpriced relative to similar assets and then to make investments, often through derivatives, to try to capitalize on those value discrepancies. For instance, a fund might consider one country's bonds to be underpriced compared to another country's bonds. The fund would take a long future position in the bonds which were considered undervalued and simultaneously a short position in the overvalued bonds. There is an element of hedging here, in that the fund has offsetting positions in bonds as a whole, and should therefore be insulated from risks of, say, a general switch of investment away from bonds and into shares, but there is an exposure to, or a speculation on, the relative value of bonds moving in the way the fund managers predict. As a result of the geared nature of derivative products, funds could see big profits but also big losses as a result of much more modest movements in underlying asset values. In addition, many funds geared up the investment further by borrowing many times their own capital to invest in derivative and other financial products.

Up to mid-1998, most hedge funds earned handsome returns, often over 40 per cent a year for their investors. A high fee was also normally charged by the managers of the fund for this performance (around 20 per cent of the return earned).

Many of the positions the funds took in 1998 relied on the risk premium of securities of less financially developed countries decreasing compared to securities of economies like the USA and Europe. Generally this tended to happen over the 1990s, with investors apparently becoming more sanguine about risk and thus requiring less of a return compensation for taking it on. However, with the financial crisis in Japan and the rest of Asia in 1997–8 and the problems then experienced by Russia and Brazil, investors became more wary of risk and the premium required from risky assets became greater. The speculation undertaken by hedge funds thus suddenly became hugely loss-making, the losses being magnified by the geared nature of the derivatives some funds had invested in and the amount of borrowing they had taken on. The problems of hedge funds at one stage looked to threaten the stability of the whole financial system as the fear was that a sale of assets by these organizations could lead to a panic flight from financial securities. The Federal Reserve's swift action in arranging a rescue package for LTCM seemed in the end to stave off the worst consequences of some hedge funds' problems, and world markets went on to recover much of the value lost in 1998.

Do the losses incurred through derivatives outlined above mean that these are dangerous products that we would all be better off without? Derivatives can undoubtedly perform a very useful economic function. As we have seen, they can enable people to manage risk relatively cheaply and easily. They can be used to create a wider choice of funding instruments – for example, as part of convertible bonds or bond/warrant packages – than would otherwise be available. Derivatives have also been argued to assist in pricing in spot markets, because expectations of future prices revealed by derivatives markets can then be factored into spot prices. There can be a downside to this 'price discovery' role of derivatives markets, however. If confidence in spot markets falls, then participants can act on this with relatively little capital investment by going short in futures markets. Falling prices in futures and options markets then rapidly force down prices in spot markets, perhaps making the spot markets more volatile than they would be in the absence of derivatives products. Heavy trading in derivatives markets has been cited as one factor in the 1987 stock market crash.

Most of the problems with derivatives arise when they are used not for hedging or arbitrage but for speculation. Losses can be made when people speculate on any asset but bigger losses can be made more quickly when people speculate on derivatives because of the geared nature of these assets. The biggest financial catastrophes have arisen when the risks being undertaken have not been fully recognized. Barings and the current problems with hedge funds are prime examples of this. In the Barings case, spectacularly high profits from derivatives trading in the Far East were not questioned by the bank's management until too late. Once the bank had collapsed, it was found that trading which had been thought to focus around low-risk arbitrage was in fact pure, and not very successful, speculation. Similarly, for most of their existence, hedge funds have provided well above average returns to their investors. Insufficient questions were asked, even by the funds' financially sophisticated participants, as to why. Hedge funds employed mathematicians and, in LTCM's case, two Nobel Prize winners responsible for developing the foremost model for valuing options to devise their investment strategies. The traditional trade-off between investment risk and return looked, perhaps, to have been overcome by the employment of financial wizards who could read the markets better than anyone else. The eminence of the management teams may have masked some of the risks that were being run. As markets have undergone major shocks and some of the assumptions on which models have been based have apparently changed, above average profits have been turned into above average losses and the traditional link between return and risk seems to have been present all the time.

Derivatives have thus often been the products on which spectacular losses have been made, but not, it would be argued here, the cause, in themselves, of those losses. What would be likely to prevent future losses from occurring? Some have argued for a restriction on the use of derivatives. What might be more effective would be risk management systems in financial and commercial organizations which fully recognized exposures to different markets and economic variables and a financial regulation system which adequately took such risk factors into account. The risk presented by derivatives would be just a part of this system.

Summary

Derivatives are financial products which are created from other underlying risky financial assets. They revolve around the future exchange of underlying assets or achieve an alteration to the future cash flow from underlying assets. Derivatives include forward contracts, futures, options and swaps.

Derivatives are different from other financial products studied so far in that they are not used primarily to raise money for companies and governments, but to manage risk. Held in conjunction with commercial contracts or other financial assets, derivatives can reduce or eliminate risk. As individual financial assets, however, derivatives are high-risk/high-return investments. They also require relatively little capital for investment and thus present ideal opportunities for speculators.

Forward contracts and futures both represent binding contracts to trade financial assets in future. As stand-alone investments, these products can have either a positive or negative value to a party to the contract, depending on the way prices of the underlying assets move over the life of the future. Options are contracts giving the holder the right but not the obligation to buy or sell financial assets in future. Taken in isolation, options have limited risk for holders but risk similar to that of futures for option writers. Swaps are arrangements to exchange interest rate or currency liabilities between parties to the contract. Unlike options and futures, swaps are arranged through an intermediary rather than being market traded.

Derivatives exchanges are unlike most other financial markets in being in many cases physical markets, though this may change in the future as automated trading becomes more prevalent. Most markets operate a clearing house system which removes default risk for market participants. Margin payments have to be made to the clearing house during the derivatives contract period.

Derivatives have been in existence in some form for centuries but have grown in financial importance in the last 30 years of the twentieth century. Although the markets offer useful risk management opportunities, the products they trade have also been involved in notable corporate collapses. What appear to be needed are regulatory systems which can take into account the full risk associated with derivatives trading and other assets.

Notes

1. LIFFE contracts in fact use notional gilts, i.e. gilts that do not actually exist in the spot gilt market, as the underlying asset for gilt futures. A range of gilts similar to the notional underlying gilt can be used to settle the futures contract on maturity. This device is used to prevent the futures market on an actual gilt getting too large in relation to the volume of the gilt in issue. Most futures are organized to have four maturity dates spaced evenly over the year, usually March, June, September and December.

2. See also the margin arrangements for investing in futures later in the chapter.

3. This is assuming that the options are written in isolation and not as part of a broader hedging strategy.

References

Cobham, D. (1992) *Markets and Dealers: The Economics of the London Financial Markets.* London: Longman.

Brealey, R. A. and Myers, S. C. (1996) *Principles of Corporate Finance*, 5th edn. London: McGraw-Hill.

Questions

Note: suggested solutions are provided for questions marked *

1. Explain the main characteristics of forward contracts, futures, options and swaps. In what ways are futures different in principle from:

   a) forward contracts; and
   b) options?

*2. Gregory enters into a forward contract with Sophie under which Gregory will buy Sophie's 5,000 shares in Halifax plc for £7 each in three months' time. What will the contract be worth to each party to it on maturity if Halifax shares are worth at that time:

   a) £7.30
   b) £6.80
   c) £7?

   Graph your results.

*3. The following data are provided in December in the financial press in respect of options on Zplc shares:

		Calls				Puts	
	Jan	Apr	Jul		Jan	Apr	Jul
Zplc 500	60	75	90		10	25	33
(550) 600	14	33	42		64	80	93

   a) What price would an investor have to pay to acquire an option to buy a Zplc share for 500p, exercisable up until the following April?
   b) Which of the options shown in the table are in-the-money?
   c) What is the intrinsic value of a put option with an exercise price of 600p and an expiry date of July? What is its time value?
   d) Why are July call options worth more than January call options in the table?

*4. Samantha buys 1,000 April calls on Zplc shares with an exercise price of 500p. Using the information in Question 3, what is Samantha's overall profit/loss on the transaction if she holds the options to maturity and if at that time Zplc shares are each worth:

   a) 480p
   b) 550p
   c) 600p
   d) 650p?

Graph your results either for the whole transaction or considering a single Zplc share.

5. Comment on the risk and return characteristics of derivative products making particular reference to recent cases of corporate derivative losses.

8

The market for foreign exchange

THE FOREIGN EXCHANGE MARKETS (often referred to as the 'forex' markets) are non-physical markets which operate 24 hours a day and have a turnover which is huge in comparison with that of other financial products and even in comparison with the total volume of world trade. The markets are sometimes shown on television news at times of notable currency fluctuations, with dealers in vast rooms of computers frantically shouting seemingly unintelligible instructions down phones and to each other. For most people this will seem an odd world, far removed from their daily lives and from reality in general. Yet, similarly to bond and money markets which can appear equally distant from everyday life, forex markets have an impact on all of us, and not just in terms of the amount we can buy when we travel abroad on business or holiday.

What are forex markets all about? For a start, their function is unlike that of most of the other financial markets we have looked at, in that they are not concerned with the channelling of funds around an economy, and in particular not with the raising of funds to meet financial deficits. The markets' function is to allow the trading, or 'exchange', of the money used in one country or geographical area for the money used in another country or area. The forex markets are thus wholly secondary markets, in that the products traded within them, namely the different domestic currencies, are not produced by the forex markets themselves but are instead issued by governments or central banks.

In what ways do forex markets have an influence on all of us? We will see below that changes in the value of foreign currencies affect not only the wealth and purchasing power of individuals travelling or living outside their home country, but also the very ability of companies to compete around the world. Politically, the value of a currency can be important too, and nowhere is this more true at present than in Europe, where the future currency of the area is probably the most important, and controversial, political issue of the time.

In this chapter we will consider the meaning and determination of different exchange rates and the nature of the forex markets. A number of exchange rate regimes which have operated around the world at different times are then considered.

Learning objectives

The purpose of this chapter is to explain the nature of foreign exchange and the markets in which it is traded. The political arrangements which impinge on foreign exchange markets are also covered. Specific points to note are:

- the meaning of spot and forward exchange rates and data on them reported in the financial press;
- the influence of inflation and interest rates in determining exchange rates;
- the interrelationship between exchange rates and the prices of other financial assets;
- the effect of changes in exchange rates on individuals, companies and governments;
- how forex markets are structured and the different uses made of them;
- the purpose and efficacy of different exchange rate regimes.

Exchange rates

As explained in the introduction to this chapter, the function of the forex markets is to enable the currencies of different countries or areas of the world to be traded against each other. When units of one currency are exchanged for units of another currency, the relative values of the two products in the exchange have to be determined, and this is where exchange rates come in.

An exchange rate is the price of a unit of money used in one country or area expressed in the money of another country or area.

Thus, we can express the value of £1, being a unit of the money used in the United Kingdom, in terms of the money of, say, the United States (US dollars, US$) or the European currency area (euros). Using data from 30 August 1999, £1 could be exchanged for US$1.588, or, alternatively, for 1.519 euros. These exchange rates are written as follows:

US$1.588/£

1.519 euros/£

An exchange rate places a value on a unit of currency in just the same way that a price might be expressed for any other good or service. Imagine, for instance, that you are a resident of the USA. A hamburger might cost 50 cents, a Coke 25 cents and one unit of UK money, i.e. £1, $1.588. These are three alternative products all of whose values are being expressed in the domestic currency, US$. US dollars are in this case acting as a unit of account in allowing the values of the different items to be stated and compared. The complication that arises with exchange rates as compared to the pricing of other products comes from the fact that the item being valued – in our example £1 – is a form of money itself and can thus also act as a unit of account in just the same way as US dollars. This means that as well as quoting the value of £1 in terms of US dollars, as above, we might just as validly quote the value of US$1 in terms of pounds. This leads to the same exchange rate being quoted in two different ways. For instance, the exchange rate quoted above of US$1.588/£ can alternatively be expressed as £0.63/US$, which is calculated as follows:

US$1.588 = £1

US$1 = £1/1.588 = £0.63

It is traditional to place the single unit of currency being valued at the end of the exchange rate expression, so the £/US$ exchange rate calculated above is expressed as £0.63/US$.

From the point of view of the residents of a particular country, expressing the price of one unit of foreign currency in terms of the home currency is called a 'direct quotation' of the exchange rate; this form of the exchange rate uses the home currency as a traditional unit of account. Expressing the value of one unit of the home currency in terms of foreign currency is called an 'indirect quotation', and treats the foreign currency as a unit of account. From the point of view of US residents, the direct quotation of the US$/£ exchange rate is US$1.588/£, and the indirect quotation is £0.63/US$. In most countries the direct form of quotation is used, but in the UK the indirect form is adopted.

Activity 1

The exchange rates quoted in the UK on 30 August for the French franc and the Japanese yen against the pound were FF9.963/£ and ¥177.357/£. What are the associated direct quotations for each currency against the pound?

To find the direct quotations for the two currencies against the pound, we calculate the reciprocal of the indirect quotations.

FF9.963 = £1
FF1 = £1/9.963 = £0.1004

¥177.357 = £1
¥1 = £1/177.357 = £0.0056

Activity 2

This is a supplementary activity arising out of Activity 1. What exchange rate for the Japanese yen against the French franc is implied by the exchange rates given in Activity 1? Quote the rate in both the direct and the indirect form from the point of view of a French resident.

In Activity 1, we have set down two expressions giving the value of £1 in terms of French francs and Japanese yen. These expressions are:

FF9.963 = £1
¥177.357 = £1

As both FF9.963 and ¥177.357 are equal in value to £1, then the following equality should also hold:

FF9.963 = ¥177.357

The indirect ¥/FF quotation gives the value of FF1 in terms of yen. This is calculated as follows:

FF1 = ¥177.357/9.963 = ¥17.802

The direct quotation gives the value of ¥1 in terms of FFs. This is calculated either by taking the reciprocal of the indirect quotation or by working directly from the FF/¥ identity we derived from Activity 1. Taking the latter approach:

¥1 = FF9.963/177.357 = FF0.0562

The yen/franc rates calculated in Activity 2 are termed 'cross exchange rates', in that they are exchange rates calculated from two other rates quoted in the forex markets. Some of the less prominent currencies around the world, sometimes known as the 'exotic currencies', may not have exchange rates quoted in the markets against many other currencies, but cross exchange rates can be calculated provided that exchange rates are quoted in the markets against the more dominant currencies, such as the US dollar.

The importance of exchange rates

Changes in interest rates or exchange rates in a country are probably the two items of financial news which command most prominence in media reporting. The relevance of interest rates has been discussed in Chapters 5 and 6, but what are the impacts of a change in exchange rates?

Individuals

If an exchange rate changes, the value of the money of one country is altered in terms of the value of the money of another country, and this affects the amount of goods and services that the residents of those countries can buy from each other. For instance, say the US$/£ exchange rate starts off as US$1.58/£, but that it then alters to US$1.65/£. After the change in exchange rates, someone holding pounds can get more dollars in exchange than before. This means that, providing that the prices of goods and services in the USA remain stable in dollar terms, US goods and services will become cheaper to holders of sterling. The opposite is true for holders of US dollars wishing to buy goods and services in the UK. US dollars can now be exchanged for fewer pounds, and this makes UK goods and services more expensive to Americans. Changes in exchange rates can thus affect the spending power of people travelling abroad on holiday or to work and could also affect where people choose to concentrate major purchases. An example of the latter is Europeans travelling to the USA to do Christmas shopping, or British people travelling to mainland Europe in order to stock up on food and wine.

It is not only individuals who are affected by a change in exchange rates; companies, investors, financial authorities and governments can all find their fortunes boosted or dented by what happens in the forex markets.

Companies

Companies are affected by changes in exchange rates because these have an impact on their ability to compete in foreign markets, if they are exporters, or on the cost of goods and services bought in from abroad, if they are importers. Imagine, for example, a company in the UK manufacturing fridges. The components for the fridges are acquired or made in the UK and the fridges assembled using UK labour. The company sells some of its fridges in the UK and some in mainland Europe, predominantly Germany. The price the company places on its fridges is set in sterling and is calculated to give a percentage mark-up on costs. Suppose that our fridge company is trading quite satisfactorily at home and in Europe when the £/DM exchange rate alters significantly, making the pound worth more in terms of Deutschmarks. What effect does this have on our company? The sterling price of the company's fridges is now higher in terms of Deutschmarks than it was before, and this is going to discourage people in Germany from buying the company's products. Not only will our company find it harder to trade abroad, however. Any German fridges being imported into the UK will now be cheaper, because their price, as stated in Deutschmarks, will convert into fewer pounds; the home market for fridges is also, therefore, likely to be more competitive. What can the company do to maintain its trading position? The problem is that its costs – components and labour – are priced in sterling and are therefore unaffected by the change in exchange rates. In the short term all the company can do is maintain current prices and probably lose some turnover, or cut prices and lose some profit margin. In the longer term, it could look to acquire some components abroad in order to benefit from the stronger pound or even to locate production abroad to benefit from lower priced labour.

Activity 3

Cooling Company Ltd is a company producing fridges in the UK for sale at home and in Germany.

The cost of producing one fridge is £300. A mark-up of 30 per cent is then applied, giving an ex factory selling price of £390. Allowing for the average costs of distribution around the UK and to Germany, the selling price of Cooling Company's fridges is £420 in the UK and £450 in Germany.

The main product which competes with the Cooling Company fridge is a fridge produced in Germany. The selling price of the German fridge is DM1262 in the UK and DM1306 in Germany.

Consider the competitiveness of Cooling Company at exchange rates of DM2.97/£, DM3.5/£ and DM4.2/£.

At DM2.97/£ Cooling Company's price for a fridge in Germany converts to DM1336.5 (£450 × 2.97). This is 2.3 per cent above the German rival's price. The sterling price of the German company's fridge is £425 (DM1262/2.97), 1.2 per cent above Cooling Company's price. These relatively small price discrepancies may be sustainable if consumers in the two countries are prepared to pay small price increments for products they perceive to be marginally different.

At DM3.5/£, Cooling Company's price in Germany is DM1575, and the German competitor's price in the UK is £360. The German company's prices are now so much below Cooling Company's (17 per cent lower in Germany and 14 per cent in the UK) that Cooling Company would probably have to cut prices in order still to sell goods. Prices could be cut to match those of the German company while still retaining some profit margin.

At DM4.2/£, Cooling Company's original prices are 31 per cent above the German competitor's in Germany and 28 per cent above its prices in the UK. In order to match prices Cooling Company would have to cut its UK price to £300 (DM1262/4.2) and its

German price to £311 (DM1306/4.2). At these prices, however, Cooling Company loses money on every fridge it sells, as production and distribution costs are £330 for UK sales and £360 for German ones.

The situation depicted in the last part of Activity 3 may at first seem extreme, in that a company has seen itself move from a position of profit to one of loss simply as a result of changes in the exchange rate. This in fact is exactly the situation that many UK exporting companies found themselves in in 1998–9, during which period sterling was around 30 per cent higher in value against the Deutschmark, as compared to its lowest values in the earlier 1990s. Over the period, companies have had to adjust to the position by either improving their products or cutting costs. In contrast, a prior situation in which UK companies' competitive situation was drastically improved by a change in exchange rates was in 1992, when sterling was forced out of the European Exchange Rate Mechanism (ERM). The currency fell by around 20 per cent in value against the Deutschmark over the remainder of the year, and this made it far easier for UK firms to compete abroad and at home. The exchange rate was one of the most significant factors in bringing the UK out of the economic recession of the early 1990s.

Governments and monetary authorities

If companies' prospects can be significantly affected by exchange rates, so too can those of governments and financial authorities. It is beyond the scope of this book to discuss in detail the impact of exchange rates on monetary and wider economic policy, but we can at least indicate the areas in which exchange rates can be important.

In some countries, maintaining a particular exchange rate *vis-à-vis* another currency is the central tenet of monetary policy as a whole. This tends to be the case especially in smaller or less developed economies, where a stable exchange rate may be necessary to maintain vital external trade or to avoid repayment of foreign capital becoming too expensive. Maintaining a particular exchange rate may also be undertaken in order to 'borrow' the monetary policy of another country. Why this should be will become clearer when we discuss the determinants of exchange rates below, but for now we can say that pursuing a policy of a stable exchange rate with another country should ensure that in the long term the inflation rate in your country should not exceed the inflation rate of the other country. This idea was behind the focus of UK economic policy in the mid-1980s. Although currencies were not formally linked, the UK government aimed to maintain a stable exchange rate between sterling and the Deutschmark. The potential benefit of this was that the UK would then adopt Germany's monetary discipline, and as Germany had a considerably better inflation record than the UK, this could be expected to yield benefits in the longer term in the form of greater stability and higher growth. The mirroring of German monetary policy was also one of the attractions for many countries of entering the ERM, this time with a formal linking of currencies which then should also link inflation rates.

Another reason why exchange rates might be particularly targeted by some governments or financial authorities is to try to achieve a balance in the goods and services that a country sells overseas as compared to those it buys. If a country sells goods and services overseas broadly equal in value to those it buys in from abroad, this can be referred to as a position of 'balance of payments equilibrium'. A government might want to achieve balance of payments equilibrium in order to maintain the production of goods and services in the home country and to prevent the country building up too high a level of foreign borrowing. A high level of foreign borrowing could make the country unstable, should foreigners lose confidence in the country and not want to renew debt, and could also represent an unacceptable burden of repayment on future generations.

How could a change of exchange rates affect the balance of payments of a country? This has in fact already been illustrated from a microeconomic viewpoint by Activity 3. We saw that when the value of the home currency increased in value *vis-à-vis* other currencies, which is termed the home currency 'appreciating', the prospects for the home countries' exports became poorer and those for imports from other countries improved. The converse is also true. If the value of the home currency fell in terms of other currencies, which is termed the home currency 'depreciating', exports would be encouraged and imports discouraged. Thus a country with a balance of payments deficit – that is, a position where imports exceed exports and foreign borrowing is being incurred to finance the difference – could be assisted by its currency depreciating. Governments in some cases try to bring about a currency depreciation specifically in order to boost demand for home-produced goods and services or to correct a balance of payments deficit. A currency depreciation which is deliberately brought about by government is termed a currency 'devaluation'.

So far we have considered why governments or financial authorities might choose to target a country's exchange rate specifically to achieve monetary or economic goals. In many developed countries at present, however, exchange rates are not a specific target. Instead, interest rates are selected as the prime tool of policy and, as we shall see below, this rules out targeting exchange rates too. In these circumstances the authorities will still need to watch what happens to exchange rates, however. If exchange rate changes are such that the position of companies competing abroad or the balance of payments of the country as a whole become unacceptable, monetary policy may have to be altered to deal with the exchange rate problem. The position of UK exporting companies in 1998–9, during which time sterling was at a historically high level against the Deutschmark, has been mentioned above. The strength of sterling was largely an unintended by-product of the Bank of England's policy of maintaining relatively high interest rates in order to control inflation. The plight of exporters did lead to vociferous calls for a change in interest rate policy at various stages. In the event, the Bank of England refused to alter its course specifically to reduce the value of sterling, but interest rates came down anyway as inflationary fears receded.

One further way in which changes in exchange rates can affect the conduct of monetary policy is by potentially influencing the amount of foreign investment money flowing into or out of a country. The importance of possible future movements in exchange rates to investors is explained further in the sections below. The basic idea is that if investors expect a currency to appreciate in future they will be encouraged to invest their money in that currency, other things being equal. Capital flowing into or out of a country can affect longer-term interest rates, which can then make it more difficult for financial authorities to bring about the interest rate structure they believe is necessary.

The final point on the importance of exchange rates to governments and perhaps to people as a whole is that currencies are often a matter of national pride. The value of a country's currency *vis-à-vis* others can be taken as one benchmark of a country's success or failure. Many a minister or even entire government has been forced out of office on the back of a tumbling value of the country's currency; witness the resignation of Norman Lamont in the UK following the exit of sterling from the ERM in 1992. On the other hand, the intense pride of the Germans in their strong and stable currency has been notable in the progress of Europe towards monetary union.

Data on exchange rates in the financial press

Figure 8.1 is an extract from the *Financial Times* showing the data produced on exchange rates in the UK.

The exchange rate data fall into three main parts. The first set of data, headed 'pound spot', shows the rates of exchange for different currencies against the pound. As is customary in the UK, the quotations given are in the indirect form, i.e. the rates show how much foreign currency can be exchanged for £1. The second set of data, headed 'dollar spot', shows the rates of exchange of currencies around the world against the most dominant world currency, the US dollar, again in the indirect form.[1] The final section of the data shows cross exchange rates, calculated from the dollar spot table, for different currencies.

Figure 8.1   Data on exchange rates provided in the financial press. *Source: Financial Times.*

POUND SPOT FORWARD AGAINST THE POUND

Aug 27		Closing mid-point	Change on day	Bid/offer spread	Day's Mid high	Day's Mid low	One month Rate	One month %PA	Three months Rate	Three months %PA	One year Rate	One year %PA	Bank of Eng. Index
Europe													
Austria*	(Sch)	20.8988	−0.0360	892 - 083	20.9187	20.8638	20.8579	2.3	20.7722	2.4	20.3838	2.5	101.8
Belgium*	(BFr)	61.2671	−0.1055	390 - 952	61.3260	61.1650	61.1473	2.3	60.8963	2.4	59.7572	2.5	101.1
Denmark	(DKr)	11.2892	−0.0178	840 - 944	11.3033	11.2708	11.2698	2.1	11.2312	2.1	11.0631	2.0	103.9
Finland*	(FM)	9.0302	−0.0156	261 - 343	9.0390	9.0150	9.0125	2.4	8.9756	2.4	8.8077	2.5	79.6
France*	(FFr)	9.9625	−0.0172	579 - 671	9.9720	9.9458	9.943	2.3	9.9022	2.4	9.717	2.5	104.2
Germany*	(DM)	2.9705	−0.0051	691 - 718	2.9743	2.9644	2.9647	2.3	2.9525	2.4	2.8973	2.5	101.6
Greece	(Dr)	495.902	−0.9110	507 - 296	496.462	494.674	497.708	−4.4	501.138	−4.2	509.406	−2.7	61.0
Ireland*	(I£)	1.1962	−0.0020	956 - 967	1.1973	1.1941	1.1938	2.4	1.1889	2.4	1.1667	2.5	91.2
Italy*	(L)	2940.75	−5.0700	940 - 210	2943.57	2935.82	2934.99	2.3	2922.95	2.4	2868.28	2.5	74.3
Luxembourg*	(LFr)	61.2671	−0.1055	390 - 952	61.3260	61.1650	61.1473	2.3	60.8963	2.4	59.7572	2.5	101.1
Netherlands*	(Fl)	3.3470	−0.0057	454 - 485	3.3501	3.3414	3.3405	2.3	3.3268	2.4	3.2645	2.5	100.2
Norway	(NKr)	12.6111	−0.0615	024 - 198	12.6761	12.5778	12.6243	−1.3	12.6381	−0.9	12.6381	−0.2	93.8
Portugal*	(Es)	304.487	−0.5240	347 - 626	304.771	303.972	303.892	2.3	302.644	2.4	296.983	2.5	90.9
Spain*	(Pta)	252.702	−0.4360	587 - 818	252.940	252.290	252.208	2.3	251.172	2.4	246.474	2.5	75.7
Sweden	(SKr)	13.2296	−0.0149	174 - 417	13.2528	13.1909	13.2077	2.0	13.1646	2.0	13.0032	1.7	82.9
Switzerland	(SFr)	2.4322	−0.0045	305 - 338	2.4345	2.4287	2.4241	4.0	2.4078	4.0	2.3372	3.9	105.4
UK	(£)	-	-	-	-	-	-	-	-	-	-	-	103.1
Euro	(€)	1.5188	−0.0026	181 - 195	1.5207	1.5160	1.5158	2.3	1.5096	2.4	1.4813	2.5	85.57
SDR†	–	1.167923	-	-	-	-	-	-	-	-	-	-	-
Americas													
Argentina	(Peso)	1.5872	+0.0010	867 - 877	1.5905	1.5843	-	-	-	-	-	-	-
Brazil	(R$)	3.0653	+0.0337	619 - 686	3.0690	3.0364	-	-	-	-	-	-	-
Canada	(C$)	2.3721	−0.0120	705 - 736	2.3845	2.3614	2.3717	0.2	2.3706	0.2	2.3628	0.4	78.7
Mexico	(New Peso)	14.8952	+0.0866	825 - 078	14.9113	14.8310	15.1185	−18.0	15.5848	−18.5	17.9379	−20.4	-
USA	($)	1.5878	+0.0014	873 - 883	1.5907	1.5845	1.5883	−0.4	1.5894	−0.4	1.5909	−0.2	107.3
Pacific/Middle East/Africa													
Australia	(A$)	2.5102	−0.0041	084 - 119	2.5218	2.4996	2.5099	0.1	2.5087	0.2	2.5013	0.4	80.7
Hong Kong	(HK$)	12.3284	+0.0112	243 - 324	12.3485	12.3032	12.3436	−1.5	12.3709	−1.4	12.5291	−1.6	-
India	(Rs)	69.0693	+0.0393	317 - 069	69.1800	68.9290	69.3539	−4.9	69.961	−5.2	72.8029	−5.4	-
Indonesia	(Rupiah)	12067.29	+98.27	380 - 079	12227.60	11971.30	12126.82	−5.9	12317.09	−8.3	13251.41	−9.8	-
Israel	(Shk)	6.7438	−0.0033	352 - 523	6.7550	6.7057	-	-	-	-	-	-	-
Japan	(Y)	177.357	+0.2250	254 - 461	177.840	176.530	176.632	4.9	175.132	5.0	167.792	5.4	141.3
Malaysia‡	(M$)	6.0337	+0.0056	984 - 026	6.0439	6.0219	-	-	-	-	-	-	-
New Zealand	(NZ$)	3.0924	+0.0106	893 - 955	3.1160	3.0825	3.0918	0.3	3.0911	0.2	3.094	−0.1	88.1
Philippines	(Peso)	63.1151	+0.0576	364 - 938	63.3523	62.9200	63.3128	−3.8	63.7659	−4.1	66.8011	−5.8	-
Saudi Arabia	(SR)	5.9551	+0.0058	524 - 577	5.9654	5.9425	5.9574	−0.5	5.9634	−0.6	5.9795	−0.4	-
Singapore	(S$)	2.6802	−0.0036	786 - 818	2.6930	2.6746	2.6741	2.7	2.6634	2.5	2.6177	2.3	-
South Africa	(R)	9.6697	+0.0009	627 - 767	9.6838	9.6612	9.7297	−7.4	9.8414	−7.1	10.2468	−6.0	-
South Korea	(Won)	1877.57	−10.9800	619 - 896	1897.27	1875.26	-	-	-	-	-	-	-
Taiwan	(T$)	50.5794	+0.0224	587 - 001	50.6813	50.4742	50.58	0.0	50.6829	−0.8	51.1125	−1.1	-
Thailand	(Bt)	60.8049	−0.0872	460 - 637	60.9920	60.7180	60.8009	0.1	60.8862	−0.5	61.7073	−1.5	-

† Rates for Aug 26. Bid/offer spreads in the Pound Spot table show only the last three decimal places. Sterling index calculated by the Bank of England. Base average 1990 = 100. Index rebased 1/2/95. * EMU member. The exchange rates printed in this table are also available on the internet at http://www.FT.com.

Figure 8.1 (continued)

DOLLAR SPOT FORWARD AGAINST THE DOLLAR

Aug 27		Closing mid-point	Change on day	Bid/offer spread	Day's mid high	Day's mid low	One month Rate	%PA	Three months Rate	%PA	One year Rate	%PA	J.P Morgan index
Europe													
Austria*	(Sch)	13.1621	−0.0347	602 - 640	13.1892	13.1238	13.1321	2.7	13.0701	2.8	12.8135	2.6	101.2
Belgium*	(BFr)	38.5862	−0.1017	806 - 917	38.6660	38.4740	38.4982	2.7	38.3164	2.8	37.5643	2.6	101.1
Denmark	(DKr)	7.1100	−0.0177	089 - 110	7.1270	7.0900	7.0955	2.5	7.0668	2.4	6.9545	2.2	102.9
Finland*	(FM)	5.6873	−0.0150	864 - 881	5.6990	5.6707	5.6743	2.7	5.6475	2.8	5.5367	2.6	78.7
France*	(FFr)	6.2744	−0.0166	735 - 753	6.2873	6.2561	6.2601	2.7	6.2305	2.8	6.1082	2.6	103.4
Germany*	(DM)	1.8708	−0.0050	705 - 711	1.8747	1.8654	1.8665	2.8	1.8577	2.8	1.8213	2.6	101.1
Greece	(Dr)	312.320	−0.8600	170 - 470	313.110	310.920	313.355	−4.0	315.32	−3.8	320.22	−2.5	60.6
Ireland*	(I£)	1.3275	+0.0035	273 - 276	1.3313	1.3247	1.3305	−2.8	1.3368	−2.8	1.3636	−2.7	-
Italy*	(L)	1852.09	−4.8900	183 - 236	1855.91	1846.70	1847.87	2.7	1839.14	2.8	1803.04	2.6	74.0
Luxembourg*	(LFr)	38.5862	−0.1017	806 - 917	38.6660	38.4740	38.4982	2.7	38.3164	2.8	37.5643	2.6	101.1
Netherlands*	(Fl)	2.1079	−0.0056	076 - 082	2.1122	2.1018	2.1031	2.7	2.0932	2.8	2.0521	2.6	100.2
Norway	(NKr)	7.9425	−0.0460	395 - 455	7.9801	7.9240	7.9482	−0.9	7.952	−0.5	7.9445	0.0	92.4
Portugal*	(Es)	191.766	−0.5060	739 - 794	192.160	191.210	191.329	2.7	190.425	2.8	186.688	2.6	91.3
Spain*	(Pta)	159.153	−0.4190	130 - 175	159.480	158.690	158.79	2.7	158.04	2.8	154.938	2.6	75.1
Sweden	(SKr)	8.3320	−0.0170	270 - 370	8.3540	8.3097	8.3155	2.4	8.2833	2.3	8.174	1.9	82.4
Switzerland	(SFr)	1.5318	−0.0042	312 - 323	1.5354	1.5271	1.5262	4.4	1.515	4.4	1.4692	4.1	105.1
UK	(£)	1.5878	+0.0014	873 - 883	1.5907	1.5845	1.5883	−0.4	1.5894	−0.4	1.5909	−0.2	102.7
Euro	(€)	1.0455	+0.0028	453 - 456	1.0485	1.0429	1.0479	−2.8	1.0529	−2.8	1.074	−2.7	-
SDR†	-	0.73464	-	-	-	-	-	-	-	-	-	-	-
Americas													
Argentina	(Peso)	0.9996	−0.0003	996 - 996	0.9997	0.9995	-	-	-	-	-	-	-
Brazil	(R$)	1.9305	+0.0195	290 - 320	1.9330	1.9140	-	-	-	-	-	-	-
Canada	(C$)	1.4939	−0.0090	934 - 944	1.5008	1.4894	1.4931	0.6	1.4915	0.6	1.4852	0.6	78.1
Mexico	(New Peso)	9.3810	+0.0460	760 - 860	9.3875	9.3755	9.5185	−17.6	9.806	−18.1	11.276	−20.2	-
USA	($)	-	-	-	-	-	-	-	-	-	-	-	108.8
Pacific/Middle East/Africa													
Australia	(A$)	1.5809	−0.0040	803 - 815	1.5876	1.5758	1.5805	0.3	1.58	0.2	1.5794	0.1	80.5
Hong Kong	(HK$)	7.7644	−0.0001	643 - 645	7.7646	7.7640	7.7714	−1.1	7.7838	−1.0	7.8759	−1.4	-
India	(Rs)	43.5000	−0.0150	900 - 100	43.5270	43.4800	43.665	−4.6	44.02	−4.8	45.765	−5.2	-
Indonesia	(Rupiah)	7600.00	+55.00	500 - 500	7700.00	7550.00	7635	−5.5	7750	−7.9	8330	−9.6	-
Israel	(Shk)	4.2473	−0.0059	432 - 513	4.2650	4.2235	-	-	-	-	-	-	-
Japan	(Y)	111.700	+0.0400	670 - 730	111.950	111.330	111.21	5.3	110.195	5.4	105.47	5.6	143.1
Malaysia‡	(M$)	3.8000	-	200 - 200	3.8000	3.8000	-	-	-	-	-	-	-
New Zealand	(NZ$)	1.9476	+0.0049	463 - 489	1.9619	1.9451	1.9458	1.1	1.9441	0.7	1.9445	0.2	-
Philippines	(Peso)	39.7500	-	500 - 500	39.8600	39.6400	39.8615	−3.4	40.122	−3.7	41.992	−5.6	-
Saudi Arabia	(SR)	3.7505	+0.0002	500 - 510	3.7515	3.7499	3.7508	−0.1	3.7522	−0.2	3.7588	−0.2	-
Singapore	(S$)	1.6880	−0.0038	875 - 885	1.6950	1.6870	1.6836	3.1	1.6758	2.9	1.6455	2.5	-
South Africa	(R)	6.0900	−0.0050	875 - 925	6.0950	6.0850	6.1258	−7.0	6.1922	−6.7	6.4413	−5.8	-
South Korea	(Won)	1182.50	−8.0000	200 - 300	1194.00	1181.05	-	-	-	-	-	-	-
Taiwan	(T$)	31.8550	−0.0150	520 - 580	31.8600	61.8400	31.845	0.4	31.89	−0.4	32.13	−0.9	-
Thailand	(Bt)	38.2950	−0.0900	700 - 200	38.3900	38.2500	38.28	0.5	38.31	−0.2	38.79	−1.3	-

† SDR rate per $ for Aug 26. ‡ Official rate set by Malaysian government. The WM/Reuters rate for the valuation of capital assets is 4.22 MYR/USD, a discount of 20% on the official rate. Bid/offer spreads in the Dollar Spot table show only the last three decimal places. UK, Ireland & Euro are quoted in US currency. J.P. Morgan nominal indices Aug 26: Base average 1990=100 Bid, offer, mid spot rates and forward rates in both this and the Dollar table are derived from THE WM/REUTERS 4pm (London time) CLOSING SPOT and FORWARD RATE services. Some values are rounded by the F.T. * EMU member. The exchange rates printed in this table are also available on the internet at http://www.FT.com

CROSS RATES AND DERIVATIVES

EXCHANGE CROSS RATES

Aug 27		BFr	DKr	FFr	DM	I£	L	Fl	NKr	Es	Pta	SKr	SFr	£	C$	$	Y	€
Belgium*	(BFr)	100	18.43	16.26	4.848	1.952	4800	5.463	20.58	497.0	412.5	21.59	3.970	1.632	3.872	2.592	289.5	2.479
Denmark	(DKr)	54.27	10	8.825	2.631	1.060	2605	2.965	11.17	269.7	223.8	11.72	2.154	0.886	2.101	1.406	157.1	1.345
France*	(FFr)	61.50	11.33	10	2.982	1.201	2952	3.360	12.66	305.6	253.7	13.28	2.441	1.004	2.381	1.594	178.0	1.525
Germany*	(DM)	20.63	3.800	3.354	1	0.403	990.0	1.127	4.246	102.5	85.07	4.454	0.819	0.337	0.799	0.535	59.71	0.511
Ireland*	(I£)	51.22	9.438	8.329	2.483	1	2459	2.798	10.54	254.6	211.3	11.06	2.033	0.836	1.983	1.328	148.3	1.270
Italy*	(L)	2.083	0.384	0.339	0.101	0.041	100	0.114	0.429	10.35	8.593	0.450	0.083	0.034	0.081	0.054	6.031	0.052
Netherlands*	(Fl)	18.31	3.373	2.977	0.888	0.357	878.6	1	3.768	90.97	75.50	3.953	0.727	0.299	0.709	0.474	52.99	0.454
Norway	(NKr)	48.58	8.952	7.900	2.355	0.948	2332	2.654	10	241.4	200.4	10.49	1.929	0.793	1.881	1.259	140.6	1.204
Portugal*	(Es)	20.12	3.708	3.272	0.976	0.393	965.8	1.099	4.142	100	82.99	4.345	0.799	0.328	0.779	0.522	58.25	0.499
Spain*	(Pta)	24.24	4.467	3.942	1.175	0.473	1164	1.324	4.991	120.5	100	5.235	0.962	0.396	0.939	0.628	70.18	0.601
Sweden	(SKr)	46.31	8.533	7.530	2.245	0.904	2223	2.530	9.533	230.2	191.8	10	1.838	0.756	1.793	1.200	134.1	1.148
Switzerland	(SFr)	25.19	4.642	4.096	1.221	0.492	1209	1.376	5.185	125.2	103.9	5.439	1	0.411	0.975	0.653	72.92	0.624
UK	(£)	61.27	11.29	9.963	2.971	1.196	2941	3.347	12.61	304.5	252.7	13.23	2.432	1	2.372	1.588	177.4	1.519
Canada	(C$)	25.83	4.759	4.200	1.252	0.504	1240	1.411	5.317	128.4	106.5	5.577	1.025	0.422	1	0.669	74.77	0.640
USA	($)	38.58	7.110	6.274	1.871	0.753	1852	2.108	7.943	191.8	159.1	8.332	1.532	0.630	1.494	1	111.7	0.956
Japan	(Y)	34.54	6.365	5.617	1.675	0.674	1658	1.887	7.111	171.7	142.5	7.459	1.371	0.564	1.337	0.895	100	0.856
Euro	(€)	40.34	7.433	6.560	1.956	0.788	1936	2.204	8.304	200.5	166.4	8.711	1.601	0.658	1.562	1.046	116.8	1

Danish Kroner, French Franc, Norwegian Kroner, and Swedish Kronor per 10; Belgian Franc, Yen, Escudo, Lira and Peseta per 100. * EMU member.

Let us consider what information the different parts of the table give us, starting with the data headed 'pound spot'. The first column of the table lists the countries for whose currencies a rate is quoted against the pound, and the next column gives a shortened version of the names of those countries' currency units. The third column of the data, headed 'closing mid-point', gives what might popularly be termed '*the* exchange rate' for the relevant currency against the pound. It is a 'spot' rate of exchange determined by trading in the forex markets at the end of the previous day. What 'spot' means is that the quotations are for an exchange of currencies which will take place immediately.[2] The single spot rate quoted is in fact an average of the bid and offer prices for the currency at the end of the previous day's trading, i.e. an average of the prices at which dealers were prepared to buy the currency (the bid) or sell it (the offer). The actual bid and offer prices are shown in the fifth column of the table. The change of the mid-point quotation as compared to the previous day is shown in the fourth column and the highest and lowest mid-point quotations in the day in the sixth and seventh columns.

Activity 4

Find from the pound spot table in Figure 8.1 the mid-point quotation for the US dollar against the pound. How has the mid-point figure been calculated from the bid–offer spread?

The US$/£ exchange rate is quoted as US$1.5878/£. The associated bid–offer spread is quoted as 873–883. As stated at the bottom of the table, the bid–offer spread shows the last three decimal places of the full bid or offer quotation. This means that dealers in the forex markets must have been prepared to buy £1 in exchange for US$1.5873 and to sell £1 for US$1.5883. We know the figures must be this way round because dealers will always buy (bid) at a lower price than they will sell (offer) in order to make a profit. The mid-point quotation is just an average of the bid and offer prices:

$$1.5878 = (1.5873 + 1.5883)/2$$

The data in columns eight to thirteen of the pound spot table relate to 'forward' exchanges of currency.

Forward contracts have been discussed in Chapter 7, together with other financial derivatives. A forward foreign exchange contract is an agreement to exchange one currency for another at a particular exchange rate, but with the exchange actually taking place at some time in the future. Forward foreign exchange contracts can be entered into in major currencies for periods of one, three or six months or a year. Longer periods may also be arranged between individual parties.

The data in Figure 8.1 show that if on 27 August 1999 (being the date to which the data reported on 30 August related) you had wanted to arrange to exchange pounds for US dollars in one month's time you could have done so at a mid-point rate of US$1.5883/£. Note that the amount of US dollars exchangeable for £1 in one month's time (1.5883) is greater than the amount exchangeable now (1.5878). The US dollar is thus more valuable in terms of pounds in the spot market than it is in the forward market; in this situation the US dollar is said to be at a forward 'discount' against the pound. If the US dollar had been worth more in terms of pounds in the forward market than in the spot market, it would be said to be at a forward 'premium'. The figures headed '% PA' next to each of the forward exchange rates show the premium or discount at which a currency stands, converted into a yearly rate.

Activity 5

Find from Figure 8.1 one European currency which was trading at a discount, one month forward against the pound, and another European currency which was trading at a premium over the same period. State the amount of discount or premium in each case, and see if you can work out how the associated annual percentage rates quoted in the table have been calculated in each case.

The only two European currencies trading at a discount against the pound, one month forward, were the Greek drachma and the Norwegian krona. If we take the drachma, we can work out the percentage discount over one month as follows:

percentage discount = $(497.708 - 495.902)/495.902 = 0.0036$

We can then convert this to an annual rate by multiplying by twelve. We do this because the percentage discount we have just calculated relates to a period of one month.

annual percentage discount = $12 \times 0.0036 = 0.0437$ or 4.4 per cent,

as shown in the pound spot table. The minus sign in the table shows that this is a percentage *discount*.

The Austrian schilling stands at a premium one month forward against the pound. The percentage premium over one month is:

$20.8988 - 20.8579/20.8988 = 0.002$

The annual percentage premium is this number multiplied by 12, which comes to 2.35 per cent. You may note that a number of European currencies have the same percentage premia against the pound as the Austrian schilling, and that this applies over all forward periods. This is because these currencies are part of the euro zone and are thus, effectively, one currency.

The final column of the pound spot table, headed 'Bank of Eng. Index', shows how the value of different currencies has changed against the pound since 1990. An index value of 100 would mean that the value of the currency had not changed at all against the pound. A value below 100 means that the relevant currency has depreciated against sterling, and vice versa for a number above 100. Thus the Greek drachma has depreciated by 39 per cent against the pound since 1990 (100 – 61), while the Deutschmark has appreciated by 1.6 per cent per cent (101.6 – 100).

The last section of the data provided on exchange rates, headed 'cross rates and derivatives', shows cross rates of exchange calculated for different currencies from their actual exchange rates against the US dollar. You can see the indirect quotation for a currency, i.e. how many units of other currencies can be exchanged for one unit of the currency in question, by looking along the row starting with the name of the country to which the currency relates.[3] Thus indirect quotations for the US dollar against other currencies are shown in the row with 'USA' in the first column; the rates quoted should be exactly the same as those shown in the column headed 'closing mid-point' in the dollar spot table. To get a direct quotation against a currency, just look down the column headed by the name of the country to which the currency relates. The cross rates quoted have been calculated from the mid-point spot quotations of different currencies against the US dollar and are shown to fewer decimal places than the quotations in the other tables.

Activity 6

From the table headed 'cross rates and derivatives' find how many Deutschmarks could be exchanged for one Dutch florin on 26 August 1999. Find the corresponding rate of how many florins could be exchanged for one Deutschmark. How can one rate be derived from the other?

How has the rate showing how many Deutschmarks can be exchanged for one florin been calculated from the US dollar spot exchange rates quoted in Figure 8.1?

To find how many Deutschmarks could be exchanged for one Dutch florin, we need to look along the row titled 'Nertherlands' until we reach the column headed 'DM'. We find that DM0.888 exchanged for Fl1. To find how many florins could be exchanged for DM1, we look along the row starting with Germany and find the column headed 'Fl'. The exchange rate shown is Fl1.127/DM. We could find the second rate from the first by calculating a reciprocal:

DM0.888 = Fl1
DM1 = Fl1/0.888 = 1.126

(There is a slight difference in the rate calculated above and the Fl/DM rate quoted in the table due to rounding.)

The cross rates have been calculated from the dollar spot table. From that table we have:

$1 = DM1.8708, and
$1 = Fl2.1079

Thus DM1.8708 = Fl2.1079
Fl1 = DM1.8708/2.1079 = 0.8875

The determination of exchange rates

We have looked at how to interpret data on spot and forward exchange rates in the financial press. What we have not discussed yet is how a particular spot rate of exchange is arrived at by the currency markets or how the markets then determine what relation the forward exchange rate should bear to the spot rate. These are the matters we are going to consider in this section. What we will find at the end of the section is that the value of a country's currency is an economic factor which links many other financial variables – the inflation rate in the country, its interest rates and the value of other financial products traded within its markets.

Exchange rates and inflation

One common-sense way for the values of two countries' currencies to be established is to look at what goods one unit of each of the currencies can be exchanged for in its own country. For example, imagine one good was dominant in trade and consumption around the world, say loaves of bread. If one loaf of bread could be bought for £0.80 in the UK and for $1 in the USA, it would make sense for £0.80 to be equal in value to US$1, and the exchange rate for the two currencies, £0.8/US$, would thus be established. If the £/US$ exchange rate were different from this value, it would be cheaper for consumers to buy bread in one country than in another, and purchases should switch from the more expensive to the cheaper country. This process of arbitrage should then exert a pressure on the exchange rate to return to its equilibrium value. Setting the value of currencies in this way so as to equalize the products which can be bought in each case is the basis of an exchange rate theorem known as 'the purchasing power parity theorem'.

So far we have considered purchasing power parity in relation to spot rates of exchange. The theorem can also tell us something, however, about how the expected future exchange rate should compare to current spot rates, and this is where the inflation rate in a country comes in. Continuing with the example of pounds and dollars above, imagine that over a period of a year the inflation rate in the UK is expected to be 10 per cent and the inflation rate in the USA 5 per cent. The price of a loaf of bread in the UK would therefore be anticipated to rise over a year to £0.88 (i.e. to £0.8 × 1.1) and in the USA to US$1.05 (i.e. to US$1 × 1.05). The exchange rate in a year's time that would preserve purchasing power parity would thus be £0.88/US$1.05, or, converting this rate to an amount of pounds per single dollar, £0.84/US$. Note that the expected future exchange rate sets the pound at a discount to the dollar, or, in other words, the pound is expected to depreciate against the dollar. It will always be the case that, if purchasing power parity is to be maintained, a country with a relatively high inflation rate will have a depreciating currency.

Purchasing power parity is an idea which has intuitive appeal. In practice it may not always apply rigorously, however. For a start, it may be possible for the price of goods, converted into a common currency, to remain different in two countries. Imagine, for example, that the price of bread in the UK and the USA was as set out originally above, i.e. £0.80 in the UK and US$1 in the USA. Suppose that at the same time the £/$ exchange rate was £0.7/US$. In these circumstances bread is relatively expensive in the UK. Someone in the UK with £0.80 could exchange £0.70 for US$1, buy a loaf of bread in the USA and still have £0.10 left over. This compares with spending the whole £0.80 on a loaf of bread in the UK. The relative price of a loaf of bread in the two countries is obviously not the only consideration in an individual's decision on where to purchase bread, however. There are the costs and time involved in searching out information on the prices in the first place and then of travelling between the two countries to complete the purchase. Purchasing power parity is thus more likely to be exhibited where prices are easily obtained on goods in different countries and where the costs of transporting products is low. The sort of goods this might apply to are financial products and, increasingly, entertainment products, such as music, which can be delivered electronically. Interestingly the Internet may have a significant part to play in increasing purchasing power parity around the world by making information gathering regarding prices cheaper and easier.

A further complication with purchasing power parity is deciding which goods to apply the idea of parity too. The example given above is much simplified in only considering the valuation of currencies in relation to one good, bread. In reality, even if purchasing power parity were to hold absolutely, we would need to consider the costs of a range of goods in order to establish the value of one currency in terms of another. What is normally done is to compare the amount of two currencies required to buy a representative basket of goods. Deciding on a representative basket is not, however, straightforward, as the range of goods typically bought in one country tends to differ from that in another country.

Exchange rates and interest rates

Exchange rates and interest rates in different countries are linked by investors' ability to place their funds in the currency and country which offers, overall, the highest return.

Imagine, for instance, a UK investor with funds in sterling considering a choice of investing his or her money in either the UK or the USA. Suppose too that the spot and one year forward exchange rate is US\$1.6/£, while the rate of return on US government securities is 5 per cent and on UK government securities is 3 per cent. It would make sense for our UK investor to convert his or her money into dollars, invest it in US securities and at the same time enter a forward agreement to convert the whole of the proceeds of the investment back into sterling in a year's time. By doing these transactions, the investor locks in a 5 per cent return which compares favourably with the 3 per cent return which would be earned by keeping the money invested in sterling. This situation in the markets could not last for long, because investment money would flow out of sterling and UK investment products and into dollars and US investment products. Exchange rates, in particular the relationship between spot and forward rates, and the rate of return available on investment products would have to alter so that the overall rate of return in the two countries became equal.

Activity 7

If the spot \$/£ exchange rate is \$1.6/£ and the one year forward rate is \$1.65/£, what should American one year interest rates be, assuming that investment in the two countries yields the same reeturn, if UK rates are 5 per cent?

Let us consider this question from the point of view of a UK investor. If he or she keeps money in sterling, the rate of return earned will be 5 per cent; £1 invested will become £1.05 in one year's time. If money is converted into dollars, interest will be earned at an as yet unknown rate, say x per cent. Money will need to be converted into dollars in the spot market and then an arrangement made to convert them back through the forward market in one year's time. For each pound converted, conversion now gives \$1.6. This earns interest for a year, giving at the year end $\$1.6 \times (1 + x)$. Conversion back in the forward market gives:

$$\frac{£1.6 \times (1 + x)}{1.65}$$

For the market to be in equilibrium, the sum converted back should provide the same sum in sterling as investing the money in the UK. Thus:

$$\frac{£1.6 \times (1 + x)}{1.65} = £1.05$$

Rearranging this:

$$1 + x = \frac{1.05 \times 1.65}{1.6} = 1.0828$$

US rates should be 8.28 per cent if the markets are in equilibrium.

For exchange rates and interest rates to be in equilibrium between two countries, the currency of the country with the higher interest rates should stand at a forward discount to the currency of the country with the lower interest rates. That way, rates of return to investors in the two countries will be equalized. If you choose to invest in the country with the high interest rates you will win in terms of the percentage return you obtain but lose in experiencing some currency depreciation as well. If you invest in the low interest rate country, your percentage return will be less attractive but you will enjoy some currency appreciation as compensation.

The idea that the relationship between spot and forward exchange rates will need to be in equilibrium with relative interest rates in two countries is known as 'the interest rate parity theorem'. Unlike purchasing power parity, which is attractive in theory but not observed fully in practice, interest rate parity is apparent in forex and investment product markets. Interest rate parity is likely to hold because of the relative ease of obtaining information about rates of return and exchange rates and because funds can be reasonably easily and cheaply transferred between countries.

Before we leave the idea of interest rate parity, one further thing the theorem shows is that in an open economy financial authorities cannot control interest rates and exchange rates. If you set out to control interest rates, you have to leave exchange rates to find their own level and to equalize rates of return available to investors in other countries. If, on the other hand, you commit to maintain a particular exchange rate, you will have to adjust interest rates in order to achieve that and give up setting interest rates to meet any other targets.

Expectations of future exchange rates

The forward rate of exchange is, as explained above, the rate at which you can arrange now to exchange currency in future. There would be a discrepancy in the forex market if this forward rate did not accord with what people expected the future spot rate to be. This is probably best illustrated with an example. Suppose that the current spot dollar/sterling rate of exchange is US$1.6/£ but that the three month forward rate is US$1.65/£. If everyone expected that the spot rate of exchange in three months' time would actually be US$1.58/£, the forward rate quoted would not make sense. Why would anyone enter a forward contract now to purchase pounds for US$1.65 when the general expectation was that those pounds could be purchased in the spot market in future for US$1.58? What traders in the market would be likely to do would be to undertake transactions to profit from the discrepancy between forward and expected future spot rates. They would enter forward contracts to sell sterling for dollars at the rate of US$1.65/£, hoping to fulfil the contract in three months' time by buying sterling for US$1.58/£. This action should act as a pressure to reduce the forward price of sterling, which should then approach the expected future spot rate of exchange.

The contribution of expectations to exchange rate theory is thus to show that the forward exchange rate should represent the average expectation of what the future spot rate will be. This does not mean that the future spot rate will turn out to be exactly the same as a previously quoted forward rate, because unexpected events can always affect exchange rates in the meantime. What it does mean is that the forward rate should be an unbiased predictor of future spot exchange rates.

What we now have are three theories which have something to say about the setting of exchange rates:

- *Purchasing power parity.* Spot exchange rates should be such as to ensure that different currencies can purchase comparable amounts of goods and services. Expected future spot rates of exchange will reflect the different inflation rates anticipated in countries. Countries with a relatively high inflation rate will have currencies which are expected to depreciate in order to maintain purchasing power parity.
- *Interest rate parity.* The relationship between spot and forward rates of exchange will reflect the different levels of interest rates in countries. A country with relatively high interest rates should have a currency which stands at a forward discount to others; thus investors in the country obtain a relatively high rate of return but experience some currency losses as an offset.
- *Expectations theory.* The forward rate of exchange should represent what the market expects, on average, the future spot rate of exchange to be.

These three theories concern current spot rates of exchange, expected future spot rates of exchange and forward rates. The way they link together is shown in Figure 8.2.[4]

Figure 8.2 The interrelationship between exchange rates, inflation and interest rates

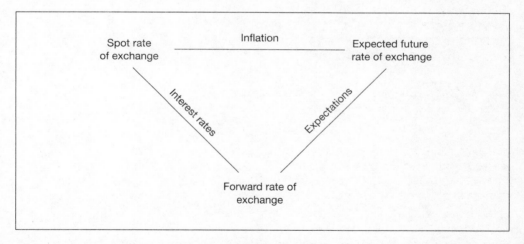

The relationship at the top of the figure between the spot and expected future rates of exchange is derived from the purchasing power parity theorem. The interest rate connection between spot and forward rates on the left-hand side of Figure 8.2 comes from interest rate parity, and the relationship on the right-hand side of the figure between forward rates and expected future rates comes from expectations theory.

Figure 8.2 shows the delicate balance that equilibrium in financial markets represents. Exchange rates must reflect not only the prices of goods and services, represented by the general inflation rate, but also rates of return on financial assets in different countries. The figure also gives an indication of how complex adjustment to any disequilibrium could be. If any of the relationships in Figure 8.2 did not hold, adjustment could be through changes in any one or a combination of the spot rate of exchange, the forward rate, the prices of goods and services or the prices of financial products, which would in turn affect financial rates of return. When you also think that markets should theoretically be in equilibrium not only between a single pair of countries but between each and every country, the process of adjustment becomes extremely difficult even to contemplate.

One final point to make before we leave the determination of exchange rates is that the discussion so far relates to the setting of exchange rates in response to open market forces. As is discussed below, in some countries and under some financial regimes governments and financial authorities attempt to control or at least influence exchange rates instead of leaving their determination to global forex markets. If this happens, the theoretical relationships between inflation, interest rates and exchange rates may be weakened or cease to hold at all.

The forex markets

The forex markets, in accordance with the nature of the products they trade, are truly international. They operate around the world throughout 24 hours, with the centres of trading moving to coincide with the business hours of different global areas. Most trading takes place during the afternoon in Europe and the morning in the states on the east coast of the USA, these two time zones coinciding. Trading then moves progressively west to the western states of America and then Asia. The relative importance of different countries in hosting forex trading is shown in Table 8.1.

Table 8.1 Geographical distribution of foreign exchange market activity in April 1998

	Per cent share of market
UK	32
USA	18
Japan	8
Singapore	7
Germany	5
France	4
Hong Kong	4
Switzerland	4
Other	18

Source: The Central Bank Survey of Foreign Exchange and Derivatives Market Activity, 1998, Bank for International Settlements

The relative importance of London in the forex market, which has also increased in the past ten years, is due to a number of factors. The location of London in a time zone which coincides with both Asia (in the morning) and the USA (in the afternoon), allows London-based traders to do business with both markets during normal working hours; English, which is the language commonly used in the forex market, is a further advantage. A number of historical factors have also encouraged forex business to come to the UK, in particular American regulation of lending, which led to the setting up of international and multicurrency debt markets (the Euromarkets) based in the UK.

While London remains the most important centre for forex trading, sterling is not the most important currency in the markets. The US dollar is the dominant currency, followed in importance by the yen and, from 1999, the euro. The importance of different currencies in 1998 (which is before the euro was introduced) is shown in Table 8.2.

Table 8.2 Currency distribution of global foreign exchange market activity in April 1998

Currency	Per cent
US dollar	43.5
Deutschmark	15.0
Japanese yen	10.5
Pound sterling	5.5
French franc	2.5
Swiss franc	3.5
Canadian dollar	2.0
Australian dollar	1.5
ECU and other EMS currencies	8.5
Other	7.5

Source: The Central Bank Survey of Foreign Exchange and Derivatives Market Activity, 1998, Bank for International Settlements

Tables 8.1 and 8.2 give an idea of where forex trading is centred and on which currencies. How significant is forex market turnover overall, though? Table 8.3 shows the estimated daily global turnover in the forex markets in the period from 1973 to 1998.

Table 8.3 Estimated daily global forex market turnover from 1973 to 1998 (US$ billion)

Year	Turnover
1973	10
1986	300
1989	590
1992	820
1995	1,190
1998	1,500

Source: Arnold (1998) and The Central Bank Survey of Foreign Exchange and Derivatives Market Activity, 1998, Bank for International Settlements

What is interesting to note is, first, how rapidly the markets have grown (500 per cent in the twelve years from 1986 to 1998) and how large the turnover now is. Arnold (1998) provides some useful comparisons which put the forex market turnover in perspective. The total annual turnover in global equity markets in 1994 was US$21,000 billion and the total annual volume of trade in goods and services in the same year US$4,315 billion. The first represents just 17 days and the second 3.5 days of turnover in the forex markets.

The introduction of the euro

The euro was introduced at the start of 1999 at an exchange rate of about US\$1.19/euro. It then dropped in value over the next seven months by about 10 per cent and at one point looked close to reaching the psychologically important level of parity, i.e. a one for one exchange, with the dollar. Since then it has recovered, on the basis of better economic news from countries within the euro zone, to trade at about US\$1.05/euro in September 1999.

Will the introduction of the euro reduce the turnover of the foreign exchange markets? On first thoughts, this would be something we might expect, as a significant number of European individuals and companies will no longer have to exchange currencies in order to carry out transactions with each other. The impact of the euro may not be immediate, however. Until 2002, euros will not actually circulate as a currency. A German person going on holiday to France, for instance, will still need, for the next few years, to convert Deutschmarks into French francs in order to buy things in France. What is absent though, since the locking of currency values at the start of 1999, is the exchange rate risk resulting from the previous variability of European exchange rates. Even now, therefore, there is likely to be some reduction in forex business because people will have less need to cover exchange rate risk in the forward or future foreign exchange markets. From 2002, there should be a further reduction in forex business once euros become a common physical currency, as there will be less need for exchange of currencies to meet commercial or personal cross border transactions. The impact may still be relatively small, however. The vast majority of foreign exchange trades relate to inter-bank investment/speculation rather than to currency exchange to meet non-financial needs. Speculation business will not necessarily reduce just because there are fewer currencies to trade. Speculators may, instead, divert their business to different currencies but still carry out the same volume of business as before. Overall, therefore, the introduction of the euro is likely not to be good news for the forex markets, but its impact may not be too dramatic. It will be interesting to see the detailed effect of the currency when forex statistics become available over the next few years.

The introduction of the euro has encouraged European capital issues. Euro denominated bond issues more than trebled in 1999 and the first Europe-wide issue of shares aimed at retail investors was launched by Deutsche Telekom during the year (*The Economist*, 18 September 1999).

Uses of the markets

Use of the forex markets can be split between companies and individuals buying and selling currencies in order to complete other unassociated commercial or personal transactions, and individuals and institutions trading currencies solely in order to make money in the forex markets themselves. In addition, governments and financial authorities may intervene in the markets, as discussed above, in order to try to influence the value of a country's currency. Most of the trading (an estimated 90 per cent; Howells and Bain, 1998) results from inter-bank trading rather than purchases or sales of currency by individuals or companies to satisfy commercial or personal requirements.

The three types of trading of financial assets that we noted in Chapter 2 – speculation, hedging and arbitrage – are all identifiable in forex markets. Speculation involves buying a foreign currency spot or entering into a forward contract in the hope of making a profit if exchange rates move in the way you expect. For example, if I were a forex market speculator and expected the US dollar to appreciate against the pound over the next year by more than the markets currently indicated, I could either sell pounds for US dollars in the spot market and then invest the dollars over a year, or enter a forward or futures contract again as a buyer of US dollars. In either case, if my hunch proved correct, I would make money on my transactions.

Activity 8

Let us put some figures on the situation just described above. Imagine that you are a speculator with £1 million of funds at your disposal. The forex market is quoting the US$/£ spot and one year forward exchange rates as US$1.6/£ and US$1.58/£ respectively, and one year US and UK interest rates are 3.69 per cent and 5 per cent respectively. You, however, expect that the exchange rate in one year's time will be US$1.55/£.

Show that, if the future exchange rate turns out to be as predicted by the forex markets, it would make no difference whether you invested your money in pounds or dollars. Find out how much money can be made, conversely, if your expectations turn out to be correct.

Dealing first with the situation where the future rate turns out to be as predicted by the forward rate:

1. Investing in sterling.

£1 million invested at sterling interest rate of 5 per cent for a year will produce £1.05 million at the year end.

2. Investing in dollars.

Convert £1 million into dollars at spot rate.

£1 million = US$1.6 × 1 = US$1.6 million

US$1.6 million invested at dollar interest rate of 3.69 per cent for a year will produce US$1.659 million at the year end.

Convert US$1.659 million to pounds at the spot rate at the end of the year, i.e. US$1.58/£.

US$1.659 million/1.58 = £1.05 million.

Thus it makes no difference to my wealth whether I invest in dollars or pounds.

Now let us consider what happens if the future spot rate ends up at US$1.55/£.

1. Investing in pounds.

As above.

2. Investing in dollars.

As above up to the point where dollars are converted to sterling at the end of one year. The amount of sterling produced on this conversion is now:

US$1.659 million/1.55 = £1.07 million

An additional £20,000 has been earned by my speculation in dollars.

An alternative method of speculating would be to enter a forward contract to sell sterling for dollars in a year's time. If the dollar appreciated in the way expected, the following transactions would be undertaken at the end of a year to earn a profit.

> Sell sterling for dollars under the forward contract: £1 million would be exchanged for US$1.58 million.

> Convert dollars back to sterling in the spot market: US$1.58 million converted at US$1.55/£ = US$1.58 million/1.55 = £1.019 million.

A profit of £19,000 has been earned. At first sight this makes the use of the forward contract route seem less attractive than buying currency at the outset. With the forward contract option, however, the £1 million could of course have been invested prior to being exchanged at the end of one year. Many speculators would in fact prefer to back a view of exchange rate movements through the forward or futures markets than by buying a currency in the spot market, because the former requires less capital than the latter.

Forex speculation has proved to be a profitable business for many institutions and individuals in recent years. Large banks have done particularly well, as have some rich individuals, such as the American speculator George Soros. A notable opportunity to make money has presented itself at times when central banks have entered the markets to try to support currencies. One classic example of this was in September 1992, when sterling was in the Exchange Rate Mechanism – just. The problem was that the DM/£ exchange rate under the system of DM2.9/£ was appearing increasingly untenable in view of the relative economic positions of the UK and Germany. In a free market, selling pressure would have led to the pound depreciating immediately, and there would have been no sustained opportunity to make money. Under the ERM, however, European central banks, and in particular the Bank of England, were obliged to support sterling by buying pounds, even when everyone else wanted to sell them. This presented a golden opportunity for speculators. By selling sterling for foreign currency, they could make a bet that sterling would stay at the same value or depreciate, in the almost sure fire knowledge that they could not lose money by doing this, as there was virtually no chance of sterling appreciating, since it was already considerably overvalued. In the end, even concerted central bank buying of sterling and several hikes in UK interest rates (up to a rate of 15 per cent) were unable to stem the flight out of sterling, and the currency was forced to come out of the ERM and float freely. The support exercise cost the Bank of England a supposed £7bn, money that presumably made its way into the pockets of institutional and individual speculators around the world.

Hedging is the activity that is most likely to be undertaken by commercial companies through the forex markets. A forex hedging transaction will be the purchase or sale of foreign currency in order to offset foreign exchange risk arising in the commercial operations of a company. For example, suppose a UK company had arranged to acquire equipment abroad. The price to be paid for the equipment might be set in foreign currency, say DM1 million. If the equipment takes some time to be manufactured and delivered, there may be some time between the acquisition being agreed and the purchase price being paid. The risk for the UK company is that during this period the Deutschmark might appreciate against the pound, making the equipment more expensive in sterling terms than originally anticipated. The way the company can hedge this risk through the forex market is by buying DM1 million forward, so that the currency will be available exactly at the time payment is required.[5] By doing this, the company fixes exactly the sterling cost of the machine to it, and foreign exchange risk has been removed. Other foreign exchange risk that companies might seek to hedge would be where funds were raised in a foreign currency or business activities located abroad. Sophisticated foreign exchange risk management might also involve undertaking forex transactions to try to neutralize any advantage foreign competitors might obtain from changes in the value of currencies.

The final type of trading which is undertaken in forex markets is arbitrage. This has been mentioned above in connection with exchange rate equilibrium. Arbitrage trading would seek to profit from any discrepancies in market pricing. Discrepancies could arise in the exchange rates quoted for the same currencies in different locations around the world, in inconsistencies in cross rates and in any divergence of forward rates and futures. Discrepancies are likely to be small and short-lived, since market information is generally good and there are many active traders. Forex arbitrage, as is typical of arbitrage in general, is therefore characterized by large-volume, low-risk trades.

Exchange rate systems

At various times in the twentieth century, attempts have been made to manage exchange rates around the world or on a more limited basis. This final section looks at why such attempts should have been undertaken and at the degree of success they enjoyed.

Fixed versus floating exchange rates

A system of fixed exchange rates sets a particular value for the exchange rate of two currencies. It is then up to the institutions committed to managing this system of exchange rates to ensure that the rate remains unchanged. They could do this by making it illegal to exchange currencies at any different rate. However, in open foreign exchange markets where there are not such laws, a particular rate can only be sustained either by the institutions themselves acting as buyers or sellers in the market to counteract any forces tending to bring about a change in exchange rates or by altering other economic variables so as to influence market forces which affect exchange rates. The primary economic variable that can be changed to alter demand for or supply of a currency is interest rates. If interest rates rise, money will tend to flow into a currency, and if interest rates fall the effect will be the opposite.

A system of floating exchange rates is where governments and financial authorities leave exchange rates to find their own value in forex markets. Leaving the exchange rate to find its own level means that other economic variables, such as interest rates, can then be set to achieve domestic economic aims, such as a desired inflation rate.

Between fixed and floating exchange rate systems are partially fixed systems, where currencies are not permitted to float freely but are instead managed so as to remain within given bounds around an agreed central rate. The two most influential exchange rate systems of modern times, the Bretton Woods system and the European Monetary System (EMS), which led up to the introduction of the euro, were partially fixed exchange rate systems.

Why should governments seek to restrict exchange rate movements?

There have been a number of attempts at global or at least regional management of exchange rates because exchange rate movements have been considered potentially damaging to world trade and to the achievement of central economic goals such as high employment and growth.

Fluctuating exchange rates discourage trade between nations, because potential losses that can be incurred on currency conversion add to the general risks of a commercial transaction. As we discussed in Chapter 1, most investors and business people try to avoid risk, and so the presence of exchange rate fluctuations deters the buying and selling of goods abroad. A detailed examination of the benefits of external trade is outside the scope of this text, but it is generally accepted that trade increases the welfare of all countries participating in it. One reason, therefore, for governments trying on a number of occasions to restrict exchange rate movements was to encourage trade in the expectation that this in turn would increase economic welfare around the world.

A second motive for fixing or partially fixing exchange rates was to prevent countries using currency devaluations to solve their own economic problems at the expense of neighbouring countries. If you refer back to Activity 3, we noted that a depreciation in a home currency tended to make exports cheaper and imports more expensive. The temptation for the government of a country experiencing lack of demand for goods at home and a generally sluggish economy is thus to devalue the country's currency. This will make it easier for exporters to sell goods abroad and also easier for producers to sell goods at home, because of lesser competition from more expensive imports. Overall, demand for home produced goods and services should increase, boosting the country's economy. The problem with this solution to the country's economic problems is that it might cause exactly the same economic problems then to be experienced by trading partners. While the first country's exports and home production are boosted by devaluation, trading partners' imports rise and exports reduce. If these partners themselves were experiencing weak demand in the first place, what they will be tempted to do will be to devalue their currency in response. In the end, you have a series of competitive devaluations which bring about an uncertain environment in which companies have to try to operate, and no long-term economic benefit to anyone.

Exchange rate systems

The gold standard

Up to the First World War, the value of currencies was fixed in terms of how much gold each could be converted into. Convertibility into gold effectively meant that the value of currencies *vis-à-vis* each other was also fixed. Britain was the first country to adopt the Gold Standard and sterling was central to the system in being held as a reserve currency by many countries to support the convertibility of their currency into gold.

The Gold Standard was abandoned at the time of world recession in the 1930s. Many countries were tempted to try currency devaluation at this time in order to stimulate domestic demand, although this proved to be ineffective in the long term because of retaliatory action by others.

The Bretton Woods system

An attempt was made to return to a system of fixed exchange rates towards the end of the Second World War. The damaging results of competitive devaluations had been noted during the period of floating exchange rates following the demise of the Gold Standard, and in 1944 representatives of 44 countries, including John Maynard Keynes from the United Kingdom, met to design a new exchange rate system.

What emerged from the Bretton Woods meeting was a partially fixed exchange rate system centring on the US dollar. An exchange rate for each participating currency against the dollar was agreed upon, but a 1 per cent fluctuation of the actual exchange rate around this central rate was permitted. The dollar in turn was pegged in value against gold, with an agreed conversion rate of $35 per ounce of gold. The idea of the system was thus to produce exchange rate stability and to prevent inflation by indirectly pegging all currencies to gold.

The agreed values of currencies in the Bretton Woods system were to be maintained by central banks intervening in forex markets to buy currencies in order to support demand should this be weak. An institution was set up to assist individual countries with this task, named the International Monetary Fund (IMF). A country needing to buy up its currency in order to prevent depreciation could borrow funds from the IMF to do this. The IMF also lent to countries so that balance of payments deficits could be financed in the short to medium term, while economic policy was applied gradually to correct the deficits in the longer term and therefore to eliminate any underlying pressure for a change in currency value.

While the Bretton Woods system was designed to allow only minimal fluctuations of currencies, i.e. within the permitted 1 per cent above or below the central fixed exchange rate, occasional devaluations or revaluations were allowed if a country's underlying economic position changed substantially. In such an instance, the government of a country would have to persuade the IMF that a change of exchange rate was not designed simply to cure short-term economic ills but was instead necessary to represent the true economic position of the country.

The Bretton Woods system delivered a period of relative exchange rate stability from the mid-1940s until the late 1960s. The system eventually had to be abandoned in 1972 because of pressures on the dollar. The USA had huge balance of payment deficits, partly because of the demands of funding the Vietnam War, and convertibility of the dollar into gold was no longer sustainable.

The EMS and the euro

The political will in Europe to create a closer economic union of countries than elsewhere in the world has always encouraged a particular focus on stabilizing intra-European exchange rates. Exchange rate stability is viewed as desirable in order to promote the most free trade and resource mobility possible within EU countries and to encourage a zone of low inflation.

The EMS was set up in 1979 and central to it was a system of partially fixed exchange rates known as the Exchange Rate Mechansim, or the ERM. A central rate of exchange for each currency in the system against the European Currency Unit (the ecu) was established, and currencies could then fluctuate around this central rate by given percentages. The ecu was not a currency as such, but was calculated as a weighted average of all the currencies in the EU. The permitted fluctuations of currencies around the central ecu value was, until autumn 1992, ±2.25 per cent for fully participating ERM members and ±6 per cent for countries wishing to have a greater degree of flexibility.

The ERM, in having centrally agreed exchange rates with permitted fluctations around this, was in many ways similar in design to the Bretton Woods system. However, there was no single currency in the ERM acting as a peg, but instead an average of currencies in the form of the ecu. It was also intended that any divergence of exchange rates from the central, or parity, rate should lead to action by the governments of both countries with currencies represented in the divergent rate. One of the problems with Bretton Woods was that all the pressure for acting to support exchange rates fell on the government of the weaker currency country. Another difference between the ERM and the Bretton Woods system was that the latter allowed for relatively frequent realignments of currencies, whereas in the ERM centrally agreed rates were supposed to be maintained long term.

It was always envisaged by the system's designers that the EMS should be an intermediate step in the progress towards a single European currency. The formal process of introducing the currency was then set out in the Treaty of European Union, signed in Maastricht in December 1991. It was agreed that countries should participate in a single European currency, later named the euro, when it was introduced in 1999, provided certain convergence criteria were met. The criteria can be summarized as follows:

1. *Inflation convergence.* A country's inflation rate to be within 1.5 per cent of the average rate of the three countries with the lowest inflation rates.
2. *Interest rate convergence.* A country's long-term interest rate to be within 2 per cent of the average interest rate of the three countries with the lowest inflation rates.
3. *Sustainable government borrowing.* A country's budget deficit to be less than 3 per cent of gross domestic product (GDP), and the outstanding public debt less than 60 per cent of GDP.
4. *Exchange rate stability.* A country's exchange rate to have operated within the narrow bands of the ERM (i.e. ±2.25 per cent) for two years without devaluations.

Activity 9

Referring back to the section above on the determinants of exchange rates, can you see the logic for the convergence criteria introduced for participation in the euro?

We noted above that two factors with which exchange rates are integrally connected are inflation rates and interest rates. If two countries had very different inflation rates, this would be adjusted for, were exchange rates freely floating, by the currency of the high inflation country depreciating over time. The depreciation of the country's currency allows its producers to remain competitive globally even though prices at home are rising faster than those abroad. Fixing exchange rates between two countries removes this adjustment mechanism and could set up pressures which would be difficult to handle were countries performing at different levels economically. The country with the high inflation rate would find itself becoming increasingly uncompetitive. In time the fixed exchange rate regime could force inflation to come down, but the cost in the meantime of high unemployment and the loss of businesses could be very high. It would therefore seem to make sense only for countries with similar inflation rates to fix their currencies.

If a country were experiencing strong inflationary pressures, the way the financial authorities would be likely to combat this would be by raising interest rates. If countries had similar inflation rates but very different interest rates, the latter might be showing that the underlying inflationary pressures in the two countries were in fact quite different. With a single currency, only one interest rate can be adopted, and the interest convergence criterion is meant to ensure that this single rate is likely to be adequate to control inflationary pressures in all participating countries.

The government debt criteria were designed to ensure that participating countries did not manage to meet disciplines of low inflation and interest rates only by boosting domestic demand with high government borrowing. A high level of borrowing by one or more members participating in the single currency would be likely to reduce confidence in that currency and increase interest rates attaching to it.

The final criterion of recent exchange rate stability really embodies the former three. If a country had been unable to maintain partial fixing of its exchange rate in the period leading up to the adoption of a single currency, then this could be taken as an indication that the pressures of participating in the currency could be great.

The events of the latter stages of the ERM are well known. By September 1992, pressure for realignment of some exchange rates due to divergent economic performance had built up. This coincided with referenda being undertaken in a number of countries on the single currency, with considerable doubt as to their outcome. Together, these factors gave speculators the one-way bets referred to above that currencies would either stay at their same level or be devalued. Eventually sterling and the lira were forced out of the system when their governments were unable to defend the parity rates of their currencies. Criticism of the ERM was levelled at the time in that, despite its original design, all pressure for intervention to maintain rates fell on the financial authorities of the weaker currency countries, rather than action being taken jointly by weak and strong countries. Subsequently, other currencies in the system were permitted to fluctuate in a band of ±15 per cent around their central rate – hardly a fixing of exchange rates at all.

Despite the traumas of the system in the early 1990s, exchange rates were still irrevocably fixed between a core group of countries in the EU, and the euro was introduced at the beginning of 1999. Many argued that the convergence criteria insisted on by the Maastricht Treaty had not been met or at the very least had been fudged. Whether this will lead to unmanageable economic imbalances between countries in future only time will tell.

Summary

An exchange rate is the price of a unit of money used in one country or area expressed in the money of another country or area. Exchange rates can be quoted on a direct or indirect basis. A direct quotation expresses the price of one unit of a foreign currency in home currency, and is the quotation method used in most countries other than the UK. An indirect quotation expresses the value of one unit of home currency in foreign currency. The cross exchange rate for two currencies is a rate derived from exchange rates for each of the currencies against a third common currency.

Exchange rates are important to individuals in affecting the purchasing power of their money abroad, and to companies in influencing their competitiveness in international markets. Governments and financial authorities may be concerned about exchange rates either because those rates may be a specific policy target or because monetary policy might otherwise be thrown off course by its incidental effects on the exchange rate.

Data are provided in the financial press on spot and forward exchange rates. Spot exchanges are where currency is delivered straight away, while in forward exchanges the exchange rate is fixed now but for delivery of currencies at some time in the future.

There are three principal theories relating to the determination of spot and forward/future exchange rates. The purchasing power parity theorem suggests that spot exchange rates will be set so as to equalize the power of different currencies to purchase goods and services. Expected future rates of exchange will then reflect inflation rates in different countries, so that future purchasing power parity will be maintained. The interest rate parity theorem states that the relationship between spot and future exchange rates in two countries will reflect the difference between those countries' interest rates. To equalize expected returns to investors, currency premium or discount in the forward market should offset differences between return earned by way of interest. Finally, expectations theory suggests that the forward exchange rate should be an unbiased predictor of the future spot exchange rate.

Combining the three theories of exchange rate determination shows how a country's prime economic factors – its inflation rate, interest rate and exchange rate – are all linked together. Any imbalance in the relationships between them will lead to adjustment either through the rates themselves or through the value of financial products traded in different countries' financial markets.

The forex markets are 24-hour international markets, the turnover of which dwarfs that of other financial and real asset markets. The markets are used by companies and individuals requiring foreign exchange or to hedge foreign exchange risk. Around 90 per cent of turnover, however, represents inter-bank trading.

Governments and financial authorities have operated a number of exchange rate systems at different times in the twentieth century; the purpose of these systems has been to fix, or partially fix, exchange rates so as to promote world trade, reduce the possibly damaging effects of competitive currency devaluations and, in some cases, encourage an environment of low inflation. The Bretton Woods system operated from 1944 until 1972. Currencies were tied in value to the dollar, which in turn had its value fixed in terms of gold. The system broke down because budget deficits in the USA made the convertibility of the dollar into gold unsupportable. Europe has operated its own exchange rate systems, notably the Exchange Rate Mechanism, which is an integral part of Economic and Monetary Union. The ERM is a system of partially fixed exchange rates, with member currencies being permitted to move within specified margins around a central exchange rate, which is established against a basket of European currencies.

Notes

1. Somewhat confusingly, the rates in the 'dollar spot' part of the table for the UK pound, the Irish punt and the euro are given in the direct form, i.e. how many US dollars are needed to acquire one unit of these three currencies.
2. Currencies traded spot are in fact traded for delivery within two working days. It takes this time for the administration of the transaction to be conducted.
3. In the case of some currencies, the value of the most prominent unit of that currency is particularly small *vis-à-vis* the units of other major currencies, such as the pound or dollar; an example is the Italian lira. In these cases the quotations in the cross rates part of the data are either for 10 or 100 units of the currency with the particularly low value per unit. A note at the bottom of the cross rates table makes clear the relevant number of currency units.
4. Figure 8.2 could be expanded to show in addition the theoretical relationship between interest rates and inflation; this is included in some texts in discussions of this subject area. The interest rate–inflation relationship is discussed in Chapter 7 but has not been included here in order to keep the discussion as straightforward as possible.
5. An alternative method would be to buy Deutschmarks now and put the money on deposit until payment was required. The money acquired now, plus interest, would be designed to come exactly to the DM1 million required.

References

Arnold, G. (1998) *Corporate Financial Management.* London: Financial Times Professional Limited.

Howells, P. and Bain, K. (1998) *The Economics of Money, Banking and Finance.* London: Addison Wesley Longman.

Questions

Note: suggested solutions are provided for questions marked *

1. Discuss the importance of exchange rates for individuals, companies and governments.

*2. The rate of exchange between Swiss francs and sterling is quoted in the UK financial press as SF2.4/£, while the exchange rate between Australian dollars and sterling is A$2.5/£. Explain the meaning of these exchange rates and calculate a cross SF/A$ exchange rate, expressed in the direct form from the point of view of an Australian resident.

*3. The US$/£ spot exchange rate is US$1.56/£. Inflation in the UK over one year is expected to be 5%, in the US 3%. Assuming that purchasing power parity holds, what will be the expected spot $/£ exchange rate in one year's time? What premium or discount does this rate represent as compared to the current spot rate?

*4. Spot and forward exchange rate data is provided in the UK financial press for the Deutschmark against sterling as follows:

	Spot	3 month forward
DM	2.98	2.97

If the rate of interest obtainable in the UK for investing sterling over three months is 1.5 per cent, what should the equivalent DM interest rate be in order to bring about interest rate parity?

5. Imagine a country which starts from a position of equilibrium in which its current and expected future spot rates of exchange and its forward rate of exchange are in line with anticipated inflation and interest rates. The forecast rate of inflation then unexpectedly rises. Discuss how equilibrium could be restored by an adjustment in exchange rates and interest rates in the country, and consider how prices of other financial assets, such as shares and bonds, may also be affected.

9

Areas of change and issues for the future

THE FINANCIAL SECTOR has been no stranger to change in the last few decades. New financial products have been devised and existing ones altered to suit new circumstances. Markets too have not stood still, and many would be difficult to recognize from their predecessors of, say, the 1960s. Last but not least, participants in financial markets, be they institutions or financial authorities, have altered in the functions they carry out and the means they use to achieve their ends.

In this final chapter, we will look at the factors which have tended to spur on change in the past few decades and at the types of change that each has produced. We will then examine probable trends in these change-producing factors in future and deduce from this study how financial products and markets are likely to adapt over the next few years. At the end of the chapter, some general and critical issues facing the financial sector are also discussed.

Learning objectives

This chapter examines a number of factors which tend to promote change in the financial sector and then considers the types of change which follow. This analytical framework is then applied to study change in recent decades and to forecast future change. Particular points to note are:

- the influence of technology, regulation and the political/economic environment in promoting financial sector change;
- the manifestation of change in product innovation and institutional and market restructuring;
- likely future financial sector developments affecting both individuals and companies;
- the issues of the trustworthiness of the financial sector, and its stability and manageability.

Change-inducing factors

Three factors can be identified as being especially significant in bringing about change in the financial sector in the past. These factors are technology, regulation and the political/economic environment.

Technology

Advances in technology bring about change in the financial sector by making it possible to carry out the business of the sector in different ways, or by altering the areas that institutions and markets can cover. The first financial markets, for instance, which were developed in the seventeenth century, focused exclusively around a single geographical location; the UK Stock Exchange, for example, along with a number of other London markets, started life in a coffee house in the City area of London. In order to participate in such a market, individuals had to attend the market location, because there was no means otherwise of knowing what was going on in the market and of carrying out transactions. Technological advances can, however, reduce the importance of a central trading location. If systems record data on transactions within a market and this information can be accessed instantaneously from a remote site, then there is no need to be present physically in the market in order to know what is going on. If other systems allow trades to be input remotely, then there is also no need for end users of the market to attend a market location in order to effect trades. If the systems which accept trading instructions remotely also carry out those trades automatically, then there is a questionable need for market professionals to be involved with the processing of trades. Removing the need for a geographical 'home' for a market drastically changes the costs of operating in that market and also makes its scope of operations that much wider. Why should a market limit its trading sphere by national boundaries when geography is no longer a factor in the way the market does business?

Regulation

A second factor that has tended to be significant in bringing about change is financial sector regulation. In some ways it seems obvious that new types of regulation should cause change in the financial sector. If a new regulation is introduced which makes the way a product was previously being supplied illegal, for example, then a market or institution will have to cease supplying that product simply to comply with the new law; in one sense, then, the relationship between regulation and change is direct. The impact of regulatory change is, however, often more far reaching and subtle than this. When authorities attempt to regulate the sector, either through taxation or through limits placed on market or institutional activity, the sector response is often to create new products or new ways of delivering services in order to *get round* the new regulations. Product and market innovation are thus often the more long-lasting result of financial sector regulation, rather than the restriction of some activities that the regulation might originally have been designed to achieve. It should be noted too that it is not just regulation but also deregulation, i.e. the removal of laws and practices restricting the freedom of activity within a market, that acts as a catalyst for change in the financial sector. Deregulation was a particularly significant influence on Western financial markets in the 1980s.

The economic/political environment

The third factor that we need to recognize as stimulating change in the financial sector is, at first sight, an extremely broad one; the political and/or economic environment in a country or area can stimulate or restrain change. To define the influence of the economic and political environment more closely, let us consider a few examples. For instance, if financial authorities are successful in keeping inflation low, there will be little call for the financial sector to develop inflation resistant savings products. If, on the other hand, exchange rates are particularly volatile, new financial assets may be required in order to offset the risks that this environment automatically places on individuals and companies. These are two examples of the economic environment influencing product development in the financial sector. The political environment too can have a profound effect on the sector. Political alliances or, conversely, disagreements can affect where and how financial transactions are carried out. In these sorts of instances the political environment has a very direct effect on the financial sector. A more indirect effect can also be exerted, rather similar to that of the economic environment discussed above. The political stability or otherwise of an area can affect the demand for financial products designed to insulate investors from the effects of political risk, so again product development can be affected by the overall investment environment at any time.

Areas of change

We can analyse the changes that arise in the financial sector in response to the factors noted above under three headings: product innovation, market development and institutional restructuring.

Product innovation

New financial products are normally devised by market professionals seeking to exploit some gap in the current product provision and therefore to earn a profit for themselves or their organizations. As financial markets are probably the most closely observed markets of all in an economy, there is often only space for a new product if something in the sector changes to produce a product gap.

New technology can stimulate product innovation by making it possible to produce and deliver a product in a way that was not feasible before. If the new delivery method is cheaper or quicker or covers a wider geographical area than previously possible, there may be profit in innovation for market professionals. Regulatory changes can make existing products inefficient; perhaps they attract a new tax or are subject to a restriction that limits the profits that an organization can earn from them. The spur is then to produce a new product which fulfils a customer's needs but is more profitable to the professionals supplying it. Developments in the economic or political environment can in turn create a need for products which fit that environment in terms of their return or risk reducing characteristics; examples of this were given above.

Market development

It is not just financial products which are created or adapt in response to changes in underlying factors. Markets too cannot stand still. New markets may be created to trade new types of financial product, and in such cases product innovation is the cause of market development. Existing markets may also change their mode of operation, either to reduce costs to remain competitive or to expand their area of operation beyond their original domestic field.

Technology affects markets, in that it determines what systems can operate to disseminate price and turnover information, and also to settle trades. Regulation and deregulation also have an impact, in that, if markets in one country are highly regulated, trade will tend to drift to other less regulated markets, as these will probably be cheaper. On the other hand, a complete lack of regulation in a market may put investors and fund raisers off using that market, because they may fear that their funds will not be secure and they may not be able to trade fairly. Some balance of regulation which is designed to protect market users but otherwise to leave market operation as unfettered as possible is thus likely to promote the greatest level of market activity. The political and economic environment may also have a significant influence on market fortunes. If, for instance, a market is operating in a politically hostile or unstable environment, market participants may divert trade to other centres in order to avoid risk or other political problems.

Institutional restructuring

Finally, the way organizations which participate in financial markets are structured will tend to change in response to movements in the underlying factors we have identified.

Advances in technology have enabled organizations, both financial and commercial, to operate on a global scale. As financial markets have become more international, institutions which are active in the markets have felt the pressure to operate worldwide too. Technology also puts pressure on institutions to keep their structures as up-to-date as possible. If new ways of organizing offer cost advantages as compared to older structures, institutions will be forced to keep on changing in order to remain competitive. Regulation has had its influence as well. In the past, regulation has tended to restrict the activities of particular financial institutions to specific product areas. As such regulations have been removed, the possibility of widening business to encompass several types of financial market has arisen. Restructuring of commercial organizations, together with change in the economic and political environment, has in turn brought about alterations to the way financial authorities operate. As commercial institutions have become more global, and the economic thinking of the day has favoured free markets with less distorting governmental intervention, the structure of some authorities has changed, while others have remained largely in the same format as before but now perform different functions.

Recent financial sector change

The past twenty years have witnessed change in the financial sectors of the major developed countries on a scale rarely witnessed before in any other sector and at any other time. Why should this have been and what does it suggest for the future?

Technology

The most significant factor promoting change in the past twenty years has probably been technology. Relevant technology has developed so quickly that it has brought about more change in this time in the way the financial sector operates than has been experienced in any comparable period.

Advances in computer and information technology have allowed financial information to be gathered, analysed and disseminated much more easily and quickly than in the past. This has affected the range of products that can be valued and traded, and the methods used to make trading decisions. For example, financial options can only be accurately valued using computer programs; without such technology it would be difficult for professional traders to make decisions as to the underlying value of such assets. Computer programs are also used by market professionals not just to value financial assets but to trigger sales or purchases of them. In some computerized trading, trading of assets is triggered whenever a market index rises or falls by a certain amount; in other cases, vast amounts of data are analysed by computer in order to determine pricing trends that would not be noticed through casual observation. Technology has also transformed the way trades can be carried out and settled in financial markets. Information systems have been developed which give real-time, screen-based information on market trading to professionals in geographically dispersed sites; increasingly, through the Internet, such information is also being relayed equally instantaneously to non-professional users of the markets. Technology also allows trades to be matched automatically without any input from professional market-makers. Finally, settlement, both of trades in securities and of non-market transactions, has been transformed by recent technological advances. The time taken to effect transactions like share sales and the making of loans has been shortened, and electronic records have made paper evidence largely superfluous.

Developments in computer and information technology have, in fact, so changed the possibilities open to markets and companies that they have in some cases forced change in other factors fundamental to the financial sector. New regulation, for example, has often had to be introduced in response to developments in markets prompted by advances in technology. The overall impact of technology is thus much wider even than the highly significant direct effects noted above.

Regulation

The story on regulation in the past twenty years has been principally one of deregulation of the financial sector, coupled with the introduction of new forms of supervision.

The financial markets of the 1970s were relatively tightly regulated. Financial markets, such as markets for shares, concentrated mostly on domestic business, exhibited barriers to entry in respect of foreign traders and were relatively small in terms of the amount of capital which backed them. Financial institutions were restricted in the types of business they could carry out, and were subject to forms of taxation being imposed on them by financial authorities seeking to manage the economy. For example, UK building societies were, until 1986, limited by law to lending to individuals to buy houses and could not offer current accounts in competition with banks. UK banks were subject in turn to a monetary policy tool known as 'the corset', whereby penalty interest had to be paid on any deposits created above a given level; the idea behind this was to control the growth of the money supply. A similar system operated in the USA, known as 'Regulation Q'. This regulation restricted the amount of interest that US banks could offer to their customers, and again artificially limited the growth of bank deposits. Many countries also applied 'exchange control' regulations, which limited the movement of capital across national boundaries.

Deregulation of the financial sector happened in different countries at different times. Broadly, the USA was the first to deregulate, towards the end of the 1970s, although some restrictive rules survived the process. The UK followed, deregulating banking at the end of the 1970s and other institutions, such as building societies, and markets in the mid-1980s. Most other European markets have been somewhat slower to deregulate, but carried out actions of the same kind in the late 1980s and early 1990s. Former communist countries have taken longer still, because financial markets had to be developed from scratch in these instances.

What prompted authorities to deregulate at all? In part there was a political recognition that free markets were likely to perform better than closely regulated ones and that this would then assist growth and employment in a country. It was also accepted that regulations such as the corset and Regulation Q were somewhat ineffective, in that financial institutions tended to find ways to get round the regulations to meet unsatisfied market demands. At the same time, commercial organizations were becoming increasingly global, partly as a result of technological advances. Trying to enforce domestic regulations, such as exchange controls, where these were at odds with the forces of international markets was becoming increasingly difficult.

The form deregulation generally took was to remove restrictions on the nature and amount of business undertaken by financial institutions. Thus, limits on deposits created by banks were abolished, and instead financial authorities attempted to control the monetary side of the economy through changes in interest rates, which affected all lenders and borrowers equally; the methods used are discussed in Chapter 3. Banks in the UK were permitted to enter the home lending and securities dealing markets, while building societies in turn were able to compete with banks for current account business. Markets were deregulated to encourage easier entry for market professionals. Restrictions on the charges made for services were also removed. The deregulation of the UK stock market, 'Big Bang', took place in 1986 and is discussed in Chapter 4. Deregulation was not limited purely to individual countries. In Europe, Economic and Monetary Union has played a part, with the EU Second Banking Directive (1989) and the Investment Services Directive (1992) promoting Europe-wide financial business by allowing organizations recognized in one member country then to operate without restriction in other member countries.

The freeing up of institutions and markets as a result of deregulation was accompanied by the introduction of more comprehensive systems of financial sector supervision. In the UK, for example, prior to the introduction of the Financial Services Act 1986, formal supervision was concentrated particularly on retail banks. This was because these banks had been the main providers of current account deposits, and these were considered crucial in the monetary management of the economy. The blurring of the divisions between the types of business carried out by different institutions made the old system inappropriate, and the new Act regulated the financial sector according to the type of financial product or service offered rather than the title of the institution doing business. Supervision also became more international in recognition of the increasingly global nature of markets and institutions. Banks, for example, became subject from 1988 to the Basle capital adequacy ratio, as discussed in Chapter 3. In addition, non-lending activities had to satisfy risk management requirements from 1994.

The economic/political environment

There have obviously been a huge number of economic and political events over the past few decades which have had their particular influence on the financial sector. What we can do here is to pick out the main trends in order to see how notable developments in the financial sector may or may not have been connected to them.

The 1970s was a decade of high, and largely unanticipated, inflation rates in many countries. Interest rates, in line with inflation, rose to historically high levels and also showed considerable variability between years. Savers with money in fixed rate investment products found their returns on money eroded in an unexpected fashion. Borrowers, on the other hand, found the true burden of fixed rate debt repayments reduced by rising prices. Exchange rates were also variable following the demise of the Bretton Woods exchange rate system, as discussed in Chapter 8.

By the 1980s, financial authorities had become more aware of the damaging consequences of high inflation. Economic policy was oriented towards controlling inflation, but with mixed outcomes. In some countries, such as West Germany, authorities were reasonably successful in hitting money supply targets and inflation was kept fairly well in check. In other countries, such as the UK, the inflation performance, while better than in the 1970s, was still variable. Interest rates fluctuated over the period in line with inflation, varying from around 10 to 15 per cent. Some exchange rates were partially fixed, notably those relating to currencies in the European Exchange Rate System, but other currencies floated, leading to exchange rate fluctuations.

What of the 1990s? The latter part of the decade exhibited considerably greater economic stability than in many earlier years. Inflation in most developed countries was at relatively low levels – around 3 or 4 per cent. Interest rates too were low and fairly stable, and exchange rate movements were limited towards the end of the decade by the locking of many European currency values following the introduction of the euro at the start of 1999. This picture of stability in many countries at the end of the decade has been a close run thing, however. In 1992, European countries were in some turmoil following the near break up of the ERM and the exit of the lira and sterling from the system. In October 1998, the whole world seemed to hang on a knife edge of economic crisis, following the collapse of Asian financial markets in the preceding months. The Asian crisis involved a collapse of currency and stock market values following the bankruptcy of some Japanese financial institutions which had over-invested in financial and property assets. The crisis deepened when Russia defaulted on some of its debts in August 1998. The fact that other financial markets around the world dipped sharply but then recovered seems to be attributable to surprising resilience and deep rooted confidence on the part of investors, particularly individuals, and to swift action taken by financial authorities to reduce interest rates to boost economic demand. The Asian markets had by the end of 1999 recovered much of the ground lost in terms of their currency and financial market values.

On the political side, there have been a number of notable events which have had a particular influence on financial markets. The whole European integration movement has been influential, as noted at various stages in this book. Its effect has been felt through the encouragement of greater cross-border trade, the development of European financial sector regulation and the removal of considerable currency risk. The political goodwill towards free markets and individual share ownership has also had an effect in most countries. The demise of communism in Eastern Europe has led to a wide recognition that free markets and privately managed businesses tend to provide the greatest economic prosperity. Institutions which were previously in public ownership have been sold off to private investors in order to improve their performance and, perhaps, to raise money for cash strapped governments. Companies have been encouraged to remunerate their employees partly by giving them a stake in their enterprises. Both these movements have promoted the fortunes of capital markets around the world.

Activity 1

Referring back to the chapters on different financial products and their markets earlier in this book, give examples of recent product innovations or market and institutional developments that can be related to the changes in technology, regulation and the economic/political environment discussed above.

A number of product innovations and developments in market and institutional organizations are set out in Tables 9.1 to 9.3.

Table 9.1 Some recent product innovations and their connection to change-inducing factors

Product innovation	Factor inducing change
Automated teller machines, debit cards	New technology: cost reduction, consumer convenience
Financial derivatives: futures, options, swaps	Economic environment: variability in interest and exchange rates: demand for risk management products. New technology: valuation programs
Asset backed securities	Regulation: avoid capital adequacy requirements

Table 9.1 shows product innovations related to all three change-inducing factors. Financial derivatives, for example, were developed because the economic climate in the 1970s and early 1980s was one of considerable interest rate and exchange rate variability. The products answered a need for financial market users to be able to adjust the amount of financial market risk they were exposed to. As discussed in Chapter 7, hedgers could reduce their risk by using derivatives, while speculators could buy assets which had more risk attaching to them than other financial products. Technological advances also played a part. As noted above, computer programs, building on financial models, are necessary in order to value such products.

Changes in technology, regulation and the economic/political environment have brought about the birth of new financial markets and considerable change in existing ones (see Table 9.2). Domestic market regulation had a significant influence on the financial sector in the 1970s and early 1980s; new markets, notably the Euro debt markets and the UK inter-company money market, were established in order to get round regulations such as the corset in the UK and Regulation Q in the USA. Technology, then, had a huge impact in the 1980s and 1990s. Markets such as the UK stock market, which prior to 1986 was a small domestically oriented market with a physical trading floor, have been transformed into electronic market places with new trading systems and greatly expanded turnover and capital value.

Table 9.2 Market developments in relation to change inducing factors

Market development	Factor inducing change
Existing markets adapted	
Euro markets	Regulation: avoid domestic regulation Political environment: political influence of Cold War
UK parallel money markets	Regulation: avoid monetary regulation
Derivatives markets	Trade new products
Existing markets adapted	
Abandonment of physical locations	New technology: cost reduction, wider and longer sphere of operation
Trading and settlement systems, e.g. SEAQ, Crest	New technology: cost reduction, wider and longer sphere of operation
Increased scale, e.g. UK stock market	Deregulation Political environment: privatizations, shareholder culture, globalization from new technology

Table 9.3 Institutional restructuring in relation to change inducing factors

Institutional restructuring	Factor inducing change
Cross-functional mergers, e.g. banks/insurance companies/building societies	Deregulation
Cross-border mergers, e.g. international/pan-European banks	Deregulation New technology: globalization, Political environment: EMU
Change of status, e.g. building societies becoming banks	Deregulation
New entrants to financial sector, e.g. supermarkets	New technology: branchless banks Deregulation
New financial authorities, e.g. Financial Services Authority, European Central Bank	Regulation Political Environment: EMU
Separation of authorities conducting monetary policy and sector supervision	Economic environment: importance of inflation Regulation: market wide, comprehensive regulation required

Both commercial and public financial organizations have experienced change as a result of developments in the factors we have identified as being particularly influential in the sector (see Table 9.3). New organizations have entered the financial sector, such as supermarkets (e.g. Tesco and Sainsbury's in UK banking) and conglomerates (e.g. Virgin offering personal financial products and British Gas marketing Goldfish, a credit card). Existing financial institutions have undergone huge change, some changing their legal status and many others merging either domestically or internationally. New technology has often been at the root of many changes. Whereas the key to success in the financial sector, certainly in the retail segment of the market, was once to have a network of physical locations which provided easy access to people, developments in electronic communications now may make such facilities a costly burden. Just as markets have increasingly had to abandon physical locations to reduce costs, so institutions are also having to make the same adjustments as new competitors enter the sector with structures designed to exploit the latest technological advances.

Future trends

Using the preceding framework of analysis, can we spot trends in factors producing change in the financial sector which will then give an indication of what the sector will be like in years to come?

Technology

The dominant technological change would seem to be at present, and probably for a number of years ahead, the all-pervasive and ever growing Internet. The Internet is already having a notable effect in the financial sector. It is estimated that in the USA one in six share transactions now takes place over the Internet, this volume being five times higher than such trade only two years ago (*The Economist*, 8 May 1999). Other technologies may offer similar advantages. Digital TV is likely to allow people to tap information and implement financial transactions in a way similar to the Internet but by means of a TV set rather than a personal computer. HSBC announced a personal banking service based on digital TV in September 1999.

What does the Internet and, in some aspects, similar competitive technology make possible that was not so in the past? First of all, it provides much wider access to the most up-to-date financial data than was previously possible. For instance, someone dealing in shares, on however small a scale, can now have access to up to the minute share prices from a home computer; in times past, this sort of information was only available to market professionals participating in exclusive market systems and paying a high price for the privilege. Second, the Internet provides a means for end users of the financial sector to communicate with each other directly and without going through financial institutions or formal financial markets. This sort of communication has in many senses been possible for a long time. A company, for instance, wishing to borrow money could phone round other companies likely to have spare funds to lend. This is likely to be a laborious process, however, in that possible fund providers have to be contacted individually to determine their willingness to lend. The Internet potentially makes the whole process much simpler and less time consuming, in that it provides a facility for financial needs to be registered and for other parties accessing the appropriate part of the network then to respond. Third, the Internet provides a means for people to implement financial transactions without human contact. With the development of the right systems, payments can be made from a bank account or shares bought and sold, all through action at a keyboard rather than via discussion over a phone, in print or in person. Overall, what the Internet thus offers is the facility for people around the world to receive the most up-to-date financial information and then to get together and make financial transactions with the minimum input required from market professionals.

As soon as you eliminate market professionals and expand the sphere of operations of a market, the result is likely to be lower costs per transaction – and, possibly, fewer market professionals employed.

Quite how far and how fast the Internet will develop is difficult to predict; the considerable variability of the share prices of Internet companies, be they financially oriented or otherwise, bears out the uncertainty that surrounds the future prospects of Internet-based business. Will people want to retain personal contact in conducting their financial affairs, and will the cost advantage of the Internet and other electronic services not sway them to give this up? Will problems be experienced with Internet transactions, perhaps relating to security or to the accuracy of prices, and will this tilt the trend for doing business back to more traditional methods? It is impossible to determine this, but the fact that Internet-based financial business is likely to offer a significant cost advantage and the fact that the Internet is making people think increasingly on a more global basis than before means that the chances are that it is likely to grow in importance in the financial sector in years to come.

Regulation

Regulation has tended in the past to lag behind technological and institutional change. This seems to be so too today. While the Internet is making global financial markets even more of a reality and while many financial institutions already operate on an international basis, financial sector supervision is still organized largely on domestic lines. This will need to change in years ahead. Whether and how fast it will actually change will, however, be influenced by politics and national interest.

There is still some way for regulation in many countries to go to recognize the multi-functional nature of most financial institutions. In the UK until the beginning of 1998, banking regulation was under the control of one authority, the Bank of England, while other financial services were supervised by another body, the then Securities and Investments Board (SIB). As discussed in Chapter 3, regulation of the whole sector now comes under a new body created from the old SIB, the Financial Services Authority. The new structure should make regulation more even handed between institutions and less cumbersome than before, but detailed provisions on how it is to operate are still awaited.

Domestic regulation, however well organized, is likely to face difficulties in efficiently monitoring a sector which is organized on global lines. Attempts have been made to ensure both fair competition between institutions of different countries and a safe investment environment through the introduction of regional or global aspects of regulation. The Basle system of capital adequacy requirements has been discussed earlier in this chapter and in Chapter 3. This system is the closest thing we have to a global system of regulation, but it is limited in imposing detailed requirements only on lending operations. Even then it is not uncontroversial or wholly satisfactory. The system requires lenders to have capital to back lending according to the riskiness of the borrowing customer. In order to produce a simple system, borrowers have until now been categorized in very broad ways; less capital has been required to be set aside to back a loan to OECD governments, for example, than is required for commercial loans, the argument being that countries are generally less risky borrowers than companies. This system fails to recognize the diversity of country and company borrowers, however; lending to some countries, like South Korea, may in reality be considerably more risky than lending to the largest companies in the world, such as Microsoft. The inadequacies of the Basle accord have been recognized in new proposals issued in June 1999. Among other changes, the proposals provide for the credit rating of borrowers, determined by credit rating agencies, to dictate the amount of capital that needs to be evident to support different loans; it also suggests that capital backing should be imposed for wider risks, including market risk such as that arising in connection with interest rate changes. Reaching agreement on the new proposals has been tortuous. There was disagreement between the Germans and the Americans on how some German lending products were to be treated. The slow progress of even limited global regulation indicates how difficult it may be to develop a more comprehensive system when national interests are at stake.

Although the development of a full global system of regulation, however much warranted, may be some way off because of the lack of political integration on a worldwide basis, there is already discussion of the establishment of a single European system of regulation in line with the progress of Economic and Monetary Union. For some time there have been provisions in place to try to bring some commonality into the financial sectors of different European countries: the Second Banking Directive (1989) is intended to bring a level playing field and impose minimum capital standards on banking operations in the EU; and the Investment Services Directive (1992) extends similar regulations to other financial services. Even so, myriad different domestic regulations apply in individual markets; for example, regarding takeover and share listing rules. In order to create a truly European financial market, there have been calls for a single regulator, perhaps on the lines of the UK Financial Services Authority, to oversee all financial activities in all areas of the European Union. Creating such an authority and setting aside domestic arrangements is likely to be highly controversial, again because of politics and consideration of individual countries' national interests.

The economic/political environment

What sort of economic and political influences are likely to be exerted on the financial sector at the start of the twenty-first century?

The recent success of many countries in producing stable, growing economies gives reason to hope for an extended period of low inflation, low interest rates and relatively unchanging exchange rates. This happy situation could be expected to pertain if governments and financial authorities are believed to have got policy right in targeting inflation and in having found the right tools to deliver the inflation rates they want. Certainly, economic policy does seem to have become more effective, both in damping down economies when demand threatens to set off unwanted inflation, and, during the recent Asian crisis, in stimulating more economic activity when deflation appears to be the greater peril. Damaging cycles of boom and bust, may, on the most optimistic interpretation, be a thing of the past.

Perhaps the greatest fear for the world economy in the near future lies in the current level of the prices of financial assets, particularly shares. Share prices, particularly in the USA, are at record highs in relation to underlying factors such as company profits and dividends. These prices can be justified if the prospects for company profit growth are much rosier over the next few years than they have proved to be in the past; another explicatory factor could be that investors have changed their attitude to risk, and are therefore happier to invest in relatively risky shares, even for modest returns, than they were in the past. The alternative explanation is that shares are overpriced, and perhaps drastically so. A share price bubble, fuelled by investors expecting share prices to keep rising just because they have done so consistently in the recent past, could eventually lead to a market realignment, with share prices falling to historically standard levels in relation to company earnings and the yields on alternative products. Such a realignment could have a major effect on the feeling of wealth of millions of people, and that in turn could dramatically affect economic demand.

Politically, it looks likely that in Europe EMU will continue the process of economic integration. Although the introduction of the euro has not been without problems, notably the almost uninterrupted fall in the value of the currency over the first few months of its trading, there have been no serious calls for the currency to be abandoned. The euro looks likely, therefore, to be here to stay, and more countries can be expected to join it provided its relative success continues.

What results can be expected to flow from the changes envisaged in factors traditionally affecting the financial sector? We will consider this under the three categories noted before, but starting with market development and institutional restructuring, in that these seem to dictate product innovation in future, rather than the other way round.

Market development

Markets are perhaps the elements of the financial sector likely to go through the greatest change in the next few years. The unrelenting advance of technology is forcing formal financial markets to adapt significantly in order to stay competitive and to retain business.

Already change is happening apace. Existing markets are, first, moving inexorably from physical locations to screen-based trading. LIFFE, the UK derivatives market and one of the last physically based financial markets, was some way down a planned relocation to new premises with an expanded trading floor, only to have to change course late in the day because competition from screen-based markets made the new set-up uneconomic.

Even wholly screen-based markets are feeling the effects of electronic competition, however. The threat to traditional stock exchanges comes particularly from ECNs, 'electronic communications networks'. These are networks, mostly between large investors, which allow shares to be traded without going through a recognized exchange. Institutions using the networks save costs in terms of dealers' spreads and commission. At present the ECNs operate on the backs of more formal exchanges in using the asset prices determined in those markets; shares, for instance, will be exchanged between two institutions at the prices ruling in a formal market, but the actual trade will not go through the market and will therefore not be subject to its costs. If enough trade goes through ECNs and circumvents traditional markets, the concern is that formal market prices may cease to be reliable. In the face of such competition, markets are being forced to do everything they can to cut costs to meet those of the electronic competition. Some markets are being forced to merge, both to reflect the international nature of companies and investors using them, and to keep costs to a minimum. Derivatives exchanges are linking up – for example, the two Chicago exchanges with LIFFE and Eurex – as are markets for shares, notably the German and UK stock exchanges, latterly accompanied by six other European exchanges. Markets are also looking to change their organizational structures in order to be able to respond to change more quickly. Stock and derivatives exchanges, including the London Stock Exchange and LIFFE, are seeking to remove structures of ownership by members and to replace these with share-owning companies. The aim is to enable funds to be raised to invest in new technology as well as to make decision-making less cumbersome.

The change in formal markets brought about by technology is so dramatic that it leads us to ask what we need in future from an exchange. Will we need a special market place, physical or computerized, in order to act as an intermediary between the end providers and users of funds? Will we need to rely on particular market systems to trade securities and on market professionals to accept and execute orders? What is certainly likely to be required is some form of financial market regulation to prevent abuse of investors and to promote market stability. There may then, however, be no reason why transactions should not be completed in a number of ways and using a number of different systems, provided that in all cases regulation is complied with.

Overall, what can we expect financial markets to be like in future? Possibly we will end up with single, global markets for different financial products, such as a global market for shares, for derivatives and for government bonds. Such markets will be computer rather than geographically based but governed by a worldwide set of regulations. What might stop this sort of development is the difficulty of reaching agreement on regulation or market mergers on such a large scale; even the linking up of the German and UK stock exchanges has met with difficulty on this front. If such global markets were to be created, however, they might be accessed through a variety of providers of information and trading services. Thus, on the one hand, financial markets will get smaller in number, reducing at the limit to a single one for each type of product, but, on the other hand, the number of ways of accessing such markets could multiply as formalized market systems lose out to numerous technologically advanced electronic trading methods.

Institutional restructuring

Financial institutions merged in the 1980s and 1990s at a rate never witnessed before; the value of banking sector mergers in the USA alone in 1998 was $250.8 billion, more than three times the value in 1997 and more than ten times the annual value at the start of the decade (*The Economist*, 28 August 1999). In some cases, institutions from different parts of the financial sector have got together, notably retail and investment banks in the 1980s and insurance companies, investment institutions and retail banks in the 1990s. The intention behind these mergers is often to create a financial 'supermarket', i.e. a single financial institution which can meet all the financial needs of its customers. Other mergers have been between institutions in the same field of business, based either in the same country or in different countries or world regions. The impetus here is to save costs, with duplicated structures such as bank branches and support centres often being cut out to exploit economies of scale.

Is this trend of mergers likely to continue and will it result in a dramatic reduction in the number of organizations offering services in the financial sector in years to come? One factor militating against the trend in financial mergers continuing is that there are considerable doubts as to the profitability of some of the current financial mergers. The most tangible potential benefits of some mergers come in the form of cost cutting, as noted above. Yet in practice it often proves difficult to achieve the potential savings that joining firms, particularly those in different countries, at first seems to offer. One problem is that regulation in different countries varies, so often a variety of products is still needed to serve different markets. Customers in different countries also become used to different products, so again rationalizing products and services is harder to do than it might first appear. The justification for cross-functional institutional mergers is even more questionable. The idea of many banks and insurance companies getting together is for each part of the business to use its customer contacts to sell the other's products. It is not wholly clear, however, that customers want to be sold products in this way; they may prefer the idea of 'financial boutiques', opting to buy their financial products from perceived specialists with particular expertise, and independence, in their field. If the financial outcome of the current wave of mergers proves less rosy than was at first imagined, the appetite for further link-ups, even among the institutions themselves, may wain. Set against this is the intensely competitive environment many institutions now find themselves in, which encourages them to do something, anything, to survive in the new world of financial services. Existing institutions face competition both from other institutions abroad and from new entrants to the markets, and to fend off the threats this imposes they may see merit in getting ever larger, both to enable significant capital to be invested in new technology and to prevent the institutions involved from being swallowed up by bigger enterprises. Mergers among financial institutions may thus continue to be a significant factor, but shareholders may require them to be more precisely justified than in the past.

The merger of current financial institutions may not lead to a reduction in the number of operators offering financial products and services. New technology has made it much easier for new entrants to set up in business in the financial sector and, in particular, to deliver financial products cheaply and quickly. Non-financial firms have joined the market, notably supermarkets and retail stores, and Internet companies have been created originally to deliver a particular financial service but then latterly have widened their range to offer broader financial services. Charles Schwab is an example of the latter: it is the leading Internet share broking firm, but is now looking to sell wider financial services to its customers, such as insurance. The financial sector of the future may thus be characterized by a large number of service providers with a range of original business backgrounds.

A trend that does seem likely to continue is for financial institutions to be increasingly divided more by who they serve than by the type of product they sell. Supermarkets, for instance, are well placed to sell financial products to individuals as long as shoppers still regularly visit their premises, or websites, in order to buy their groceries. These shops are not well positioned to cut in on the traditional financial institutions' corporate business, however; no current line of communication exists between companies and supermarkets which is open to exploitation through selling financial services. Internet share broking firms like Charles Schwab may also build up a retail rather than wholesale trade because their current contacts are mostly of this type. New entrants may thus be particularly relevant on the retail side of the financial sector, while traditional institutions may maintain their role of providing intermediation services, as far as these are required, to wholesale financial customers.

The financial sector of the future may thus include a number of huge, international financial institutions and a variety of other financial services providers concentrating particularly on retail customers. Which type of institution will win out in the war to provide financial services to individuals is difficult to predict. Are people likely to choose to do business with traditional institutions, such as banks, albeit through new media such as the Internet or digital TV, or are they likely increasingly to drift to other providers such as shops or new Internet firms? The answer may depend on other social changes, such as whether the practice of physically shopping at supermarkets still continues or whether all transactions, financial and otherwise, migrate to the ether.

Product innovation

Innovation concerning financial products, certainly as far as individuals are concerned, may come more in the form of how existing products are delivered than in new products being devised. This factor has really already been covered in the consideration of institutional and market change above. Thus, investing in shares has been an option for centuries for individuals; current innovation lies not in changing the nature of shares themselves but in allowing individuals to access real-time information about them and to carry out transactions through their computer screens. Similarly, personal banking is undergoing a delivery revolution. People may choose even now to carry out banking transactions by personally visiting a bank branch, by telephone, Internet or digital TV. Which of these delivery systems will dominate the market in future only time will tell, but the latter ones are likely to offer a cost and convenience advantage.

On the corporate side, the development of technology making markets ever cheaper will probably only further the trend for disintermediation, i.e. for companies to raise money through markets rather than financial institutions. Large companies have been doing this on an increasing scale for a number of years and this will probably continue. Financial markets may also open up to small and medium-sized companies. In Chapter 2 it was noted that one barrier to small and medium-sized companies using markets came in the form of costs involved in publicizing any market offering. The Internet, by providing a means for a company to communicate with millions of potential investors easily and cheaply, possibly removes such barriers. The result may be a widening of the sources of finance open to smaller companies, to include bonds, for instance. The result of all this for financial institutions is that they will need to move their business increasingly towards participating in markets as investors and dealers, and to offering advice on market strategies, and reduce their dependence on direct lending and investment.

Some critical issues for the financial sector

From the foregoing, we can deduce that the financial sector is going to face considerable, continuing change in the years ahead. As well as coping with this, there are a number of critical issues which the sector must face up to. Three of these are discussed briefly below.

The regard in which the financial sector is held

The financial sector in many countries, certainly the UK, is not the economic sector held in the highest affection or esteem among the population at large. Following a number of financial scandals, including bank collapses and the misselling of financial products, and on the back of publicity about huge institutional profits and the accompanying pay packets of financial employees, the sector is often perceived to be characterized by avarice and a total lack of scruples. Hostility towards the financial sector became most evident on 4 June 1999 when institutions in the City of London were attacked by thousands of protesters. The action, which had been organized through the Internet, was intended to show public anger about the profits made by financial institutions and their power over so many people's lives. Such protesters are not typical of the citizens of the UK, yet it may be significant that such protests, however extreme, should be aimed at financial institutions rather than at commercial companies or public bodies.

Does it matter that people often think poorly of the financial sector? It matters to the sector itself, in that such attitudes may be reflected in political actions which may be unfavourable to the business of the sector. In discussion of the UK joining EMU, for example, the financial sector has made clear its preference for participating in the single currency so as not to lose out on financial business to Frankfurt. These opinions are likely to carry more weight the greater the popular support for the sector. The standing of the sector also matters in a wider sense; as we saw right at the start of this book, the financial sector has an important role to perform in channelling funds from savers to borrowers and it is important for the wealth of an economy that people trust the financial sector enough in order fully to participate in it. In fact, the financial sector has probably never had a more important role now that many developed countries have ageing populations. Individuals need to save and save profitably in order to provide for their old age without being an unacceptable financial burden on future generations.

What can the financial sector do to improve its reputation? In part, nothing, because some of the criticism of financial institutions and organizations may be unjustified. Retail banks, for instance, are criticized for withdrawing loan finance from some borrowers or for insisting on planned repayments from others, even when they are struggling. The implication here is that such financial institutions should act like public, or even charitable, bodies. Yet these institutions are, unashamedly, share-owned companies. Their first duty is to provide the greatest return they can for their owners; relief for those who get in financial difficulty should perhaps instead come from truly public bodies. There can, however, be no excuse for customers being misled or exploited by a market-instituted lack of competition, and this is where a good system of regulation comes in. The problems of putting together a comprehensive, non-distorting and global system of regulation have been discussed above. It is probably some way off, but it is what is needed to make the financial sector a safe and fair sector to participate in, and it is probably this that will ultimately raise the sector's popular standing.

The stability of the financial sector

Referring back again to where we started at the beginning of this book, it was noted that the financial sector is unique among all sectors in an economy in having a particularly wide economic influence. If the value of securities in the financial sector falls, this will tend to affect all economic demand, in that consumers will suddenly feel less wealthy. If a large financial institution were to experience financial difficulties, this could affect a large number of other enterprises, as their financial resources, the lifeblood of their business, could be reduced. Stability in the financial sector could thus be vital to the well-being of a whole economy.

How stable are financial sectors around the world? The answer is, at times, not very. In 1987, stock markets around the world crashed; roughly 30 per cent of the value of share capital around the world was eliminated in a few days, though value was restored in subsequent years. When markets dipped at the time of the Asian crisis in 1998, £2,100 billion was wiped off the value of world stock markets in a single day, the equivalent of the whole GDP of Canada for a year. The possibly precarious underlying support for current share prices, particularly those in the USA, has been discussed above. While economists try perplexedly to explain and justify current share valuations, is another stock market crash in fact waiting just around the corner?

The potential instability of markets in the financial sector is probably something that no one can do anything about. If share values are currently at an insupportable level and the majority of investors come to the same conclusion, then share values in free share markets will inevitably fall. What financial authorities can do, and indeed did to some effect in 1998 in the aftermath of the Asian crisis, is take economic action to dampen the effects of any financial sector instability. Monetary policy might thus be loosened or tightened to counterbalance a significant fall or rise in stock markets. Authorities also have to stand prepared effectively to guarantee the financial institutions whose collapse would cause the greatest economic damage, such as clearing banks. In that way, problems experienced by one institution may be contained rather than leading to a general collapse of financial confidence.

The manageability of the financial sector

This final issue follows on from the first two mentioned above: can the financial sector be managed by the sector itself or at least influenced by external financial authorities in order to ensure that it does its job in an economy in the most effective way possible?

As should be evident from the foregoing discussion in this chapter, the financial sector is becoming, or has even become, so international in its business and so unreliant on a demand for physically based premises that it is almost impossible for any domestic financial authority to seek to control it closely. A government may be unhappy, for example, with share prices going up and leading to a feeling of wealth among consumers which stimulates domestic demand and inflation. There is probably nothing that government can do about this, however. The level of share prices is probably determined as much by the value of shares in stock markets in other countries as it is by domestic factors, and any attempt to tax gains to try to depress values will only lead to share business migrating abroad. Financial authorities may increasingly find themselves powerless to control interest rates as well; the very shortest-term interest rates may be under their influence, but longer-term rates will be influenced by international supply and demand. As even individual borrowers become more global in their outlook, borrowers in a country may be increasingly insulated from the actions of their domestic financial authorities, as borrowings may be in currencies other than their home one.

The management of financial markets in the future is thus likely to need to be organized on a global scale to be effective. Influence may be exerted through a comprehensive regulatory system (that again!) and by the buying and selling of financial securities in markets by a global financial authority, or by a number of lesser authorities acting in concert. There is, without doubt, a lot of work to be done by world politicians and central bankers to bring this about.

Summary

The three factors that have been particularly significant in bringing about change in the financial sector in the past are advances in information and computer technology, sector regulation and aspects of the political/economic environment, such as the variability of exchange rates and inflation. Change has been induced in the form of product innovation, developments in the way markets operate and the restructuring of institutions active in the financial sector.

In recent decades, advances in technology have probably been the greatest change-producing factor. They have transformed the way financial information can be accessed, acted upon and recorded. The advances have been so fundamental that they have brought about developments in other change-producing factors, such as regulation.

The trend in regulation over recent years has been for domestic markets and institutions to be progressively deregulated, but with wider but less economically distorting systems of supervision then being introduced. The economic environment has been one of historically high inflation and variable exchange and interest rates in the 1970s and 1980s. In the late 1990s, inflation rates were at their lowest levels in most developed countries for many years. Exchange rate fluctuations are also limited in Europe by Economic and Monetary Union.

The influence of technological advances, regulatory change and the economic and political environment of recent years can be seen in product innovations, such as the introduction of different derivative products, market developments – for example, new information, trading and settlement systems in stock markets – and commercial restructuring, such as the mergers of institutions with different product backgrounds.

Looking to the future, technological advances in the form of the growth of the Internet and digital TV are likely to be the basis for further change. International regulation is also going through some change, with capital adequacy rules being adjusted and some call for the development of a European regulator. The economic environment is one of stability in many developed countries, but with financial assets prices, which are at historically high levels, potentially presenting a threat.

Markets are likely increasingly to abandon physical locations and reform as companies because of cost competition from electronic exchanges. Financial markets of the future may be characterized by many different organizations providing alternative trading and information systems, but all subject to a common system of regulation.

Financial institutions are likely in the future to be defined more by who they serve than by the type of products which they supply. Financial mergers to reduce costs may well continue, as institutions find themselves up against ever greater competition from service providers using new technology. Cross-functional mergers with no obvious cost savings may become fewer because their economic justification is more questionable.

Product innovation may be more in the form of how traditional products are delivered than in new types of products being supplied. Small and medium-sized companies may find access to finance supplied through markets, such as bond finance, being opened up by better market technology and a lowering of market costs.

Three critical issues for the financial sector in future are the regard in which the sector is held, its stability and whether or not it can be managed or influenced to any significant extent in order to ensure that its job of channelling funds is performed in an efficient way. A global system of regulation may be required to bring about a satisfactory resolution of all three issues.

Suggested solutions to end-of-chapter questions

Chapter 1

1. When you compare the prices of different goods, you are using money as *a unit of account*. The value of each is set via the common denominator of money. Comparing value without money would be difficult. The comparison of the quality of possible gifts each costing £10 and the marking of the prices of goods on supermarket shelves reflect money being used as a unit of account.

    When money is used to pay for goods it acts as *a medium of exchange*. This means that goods can be exchanged without direct barter, i.e. without one good being exchanged directly for another. Payment using a bank debit card is an example of a form of money (a deposit account) being used as a medium of exchange.

    The third function of money is to provide a means of storing value. Saving money now to increase spending power later is an example of money being used *to store value*. Paying money into a deposit account is an example of money being used to store value.

2. The six characteristics that make money efficient are divisibility, homogeneity, recognizability, portability, acceptability and durability. We can analyse the money alternatives under each of these headings and then decide whether they are likely to make efficient forms of money.

    a) Shells
        Shells have been used in some primitive societies as money, and also in more developed economies in limited circumstances, for example in holiday resorts, perhaps to promote the feeling of getting away from normal financial pressures.

        The main drawback of shells as money is their lack of exclusivity; if everyone can collect shells they may lose their value and fail on the grounds of acceptability. However, small and rarer shells meet the requirements of portability and recognizability. Divisibility would be a problem if only one type of shell were used – you would then have only a single denomination. Paying for large value items would be cumbersome if the money unit had a small value, but paying for small value items would be impossible if the money unit had a large value. One solution would be to use different types of rare shells to represent different money units. Recognizability and durability would remain problems. Shells vary naturally and can deteriorate over time.

b) Cattle

Cattle have been used as a measure and store of wealth in a number of more primitive societies. For example, in some African countries, cattle are offered as a dowry.

Cattle have obvious shortcomings as a unit of money. They are neither portable nor divisible. As a store of value they fare rather better. Their durability and homogeneity are, however, uncertain. Healthy cattle are a useful long term asset, but weak and ailing stock may not last as long as the recipient might hope.

c) Gold, jewellery and precious stones

Precious metals, stones and jewellery have tended to be used as money in times of political turmoil, for instance during persecution and war when people are forced to flee their homes or at times when confidence in other financial assets fails. Even in the most developed financial economies, people still talk of a 'flight to gold' when there are fears about the value of other assets, for example when a crash in financial markets seems imminent.

One of the main drawbacks of precious metals and jewellery as a form of money is their lack of divisibility. Even a single item is likely to have a relatively high value, and therefore using such items as a means of exchange for everyday goods will be difficult. Recognizability will also be a drawback, with the non-experts finding it difficult to distinguish the real from the fakes. Where jewellery and precious stones win as a form of money is in their durability and almost universal acceptability. These qualities make this money unit popular at times of greatest uncertainty.

d) Cigarettes

Cigarettes have been used as money around the world, for instance among soldiers and people serving prison sentences.

Cigarettes are divisible, reasonably uniform and recognizable. They are also widely acceptable. Their main drawback is that they are not durable – their physical condition deteriorates over time. Like shells, they are also single denomination forms of money and are unlikely to have the scope to enable both high- and low-value items to be measured and paid for in money terms.

e) An 'IOU' (i.e. a note promising future payment) for a large sum of money, say £100,000

An IOU is actually the form that a number of financial securities take, such as the short-term borrowing instruments discussed in Chapter 6. In financial markets, IOUs are issued below their face value (i.e. below £100,000 in our example), and the difference between the issue price and the price paid when the IOU falls due provides a return to the person acquiring the IOU.

One problem with an IOU as a form of money is that its value depends on the reputation of the institution or person issuing it. If a respected and financially sound government or large corporation issues the IOU, then it should certainly have a substantial value. However, if a bankrupt issues the IOU, it will in all likelihood not be worth the paper it is written on. There are immediate problems with homogeneity and recognizability – one IOU is not worth the same as another, and some financial acumen is required to evaluate the differ-ence. Another difficulty with an IOU for a large amount of money is its lack of divisibility; the IOU will not be suitable as a unit of account or medium of exchange.

Where the IOU has definite benefits as a form of money is in its function as a store of value. Unlike many forms of money, financial securities of the IOU type offer their holders a return over time. This means that an IOU may be a better store of value than notes and coin.

4. The position of each sector, showing inflows as positive numbers and outflows as negative numbers, is:

Overseas sector	£bn
Imports	25
Exports	−30
Deficit	−5

Commercial and industrial firms	£bn
Government spending	250
Consumption	450
Expenditure on real assets by individuals	40
Exports	30
Imports	−25
Wages and dividends	−600
Surplus	145

Government	£bn
Income tax	200
Expenditure tax	170
Transfers	−150
Government spending	−250
Deficit	−30

Personal sector	£bn
Wages and dividends	600
Transfers	150
Income tax	−200
Disposable income	550
Expenditure on real assets	−40
Consumption	−450
Expenditure tax	−170
Deficit	−110

Chapter 2

2. The function of most financial markets is exactly the same as that of financial institutions, that is to facilitate the flow of funds from units in the economy with a financial surplus to those with a financial deficit. This is illustrated in Activity 3 (pp. 25–6) where the role of a market for shares in transforming size, maturity and risk is discussed. Some financial markets have a function other than the channelling of funds around the economy, in particular the derivatives markets (which are

primarily concerned with the transfer of risk between different economic units) and the foreign exchange markets (which allow the exchange of the money used in one country or geographical area for that used in another country or area).

The qualities required from primary and secondary financial markets are discussed on pp. 16–18.

4. a) Alexandra is undertaking arbitrage. She is buying French francs in a market in which they are relatively cheap and selling them in a market in which they are relatively expensive. Alexandra makes a profit because of pricing discrepancies between the two currency markets. The arbitrage transactions of Alexandra and others like her should remove the pricing discrepancies, the price of French francs being pushed up by buying pressure in New York and pushed down by selling pressure in Paris.

   b) Bob is undertaking investment/speculation. He is buying a financial asset with the hope of making a profit from future price rises or from the income generated by the financial asset over the period he holds it. If Bob's intention is to hold Microsoft shares for some considerable time, say a few years, then his transaction would popularly be described as investment. If his intention is to hold the shares only for a short time with the hope of making a quick profit, then his actions would be described as speculation.

   c) Carol is participating in a hedging transaction by acquiring a derivative product. The purpose of a hedge is to remove risk by buying a financial asset whose value moves inversely with the value of other assets already held.

Chapter 3

3. The bank needs to have capital equal to 8% of its risk adjusted assets. The amount required can be calculated as follows:

	£bn	% risk weighting	capital required (£bn)
Cash and government debt	35	0	0
Bank loans	40	20	0.64*
Corporate debt	30	100	2.4
Minimum capital required			3.04

* capital required $= 40 \times 0.2 \times 0.08 = 0.64$

Chapter 4

1. The fact that corporate bonds, as investments in the debt of a company, have yielded on average less than shares of a company is not surprising. As explained in the chapter, shares are a riskier investment than debt, since the income on a share (its dividend) and the capital value of a share (its market price) are uncertain. As investors generally try to avoid risk, the expected return on shares needs to be higher than on debt to compensate for risk.

   Another point to make is that what Mrs Jackson should really be interested in is what returns she can expect on different financial securities in future. The returns such financial assets have yielded in the past are not necessarily a good indicator of future performance.

From the information given, we cannot say whether corporate bonds or shares will be right for Mrs Jackson. In order to make a decision, factors such as Mrs Jackson's attitude to risk would need to be taken into account, and evidence on the way returns on the alternative assets would be likely to move in the future.

2. In order to calculate the BLD dividend yield and p/e ratio, we first need to work out how many shares the company has in issue, since this information is not given directly in the question. The extract from the BLD balance sheet has an entry against 'share capital' of £12.5 million; this is the total par value of the company's shares in issue. The notes to the accounts state that each individual share has a par value of 25p, so there must be 50 million shares in issue (12.5m x £1/£0.25).

The dividend per share = $\frac{£10m}{50m}$ = £0.2 or 20p

The dividend yield = $\frac{£0.2}{£16.5}$ = 0.01 or 1%

The earnings per share = $\frac{£46m}{50m}$ = £0.92 or 92p

The p/e ratio = $\frac{£16.5}{£0.92}$ = 18

4. a) You would expect the share price of Bargate to fall. All share prices are likely to fall on the announcement of an unexpected rise in interest rates since this is likely to dampen demand for products and will increase the cost of borrowing. House builders such as Bargate might be especially affected, since most house buyers take on considerable borrowing, thus making housing demand particularly sensitive to interest rates.

Although a fall in share prices would normally be associated with an unexpected rise in interest rates, it does not always have to be so. Imagine a situation, for example, where there was concern in the markets that the financial authorities were operating too lax a monetary policy and letting inflation run out of control. A rise in interest rates might actually lead to an increase in share prices as the evidence of some firmness on the financial authorities' part was welcomed.

b) We might expect little or even no change at all in Bargate's share price because the reduction in interest rates had been signalled and should already have been built into share prices. This lack of response to the interest rate change relies on the stock market pricing efficiently.

c) The abolition of mortgage tax relief would be expected to bring about a reduction in Bargate's share price. As with an increase in interest rates, the tax change would be expected to reduce demand for new homes because the cost of buying them has become more expensive after tax. One difference between this piece of news and a change in interest rates is that the mortgage tax change could be expected to affect only a limited number of companies - those in the business of supplying homes or associated goods and services. An interest change is likely to affect all companies in the stock market.

d) The departure of Bargate's Managing Director is another piece of news that is likely to affect only Bargate and its close rivals. In this case, as Ms Littledale's performance seems to have been something short of sparkling, the price of Bargate's shares might be expected to rise and that of Stanton to fall.

Chapter 5

1. a) On all three bank loans, a total interest of 8% per annum is charged. The equivalent annual cost of each is different, however, because the 8% is charged on the loan at different intervals. The most expensive loan is the one that charges 0.67% every month, because you will pay interest on loan principal plus accumulated interest from month two onwards. The loan which charges interest at 2% quarterly is the next most expensive. A rational borrower looking for the cheapest loan, other things being equal, would be advised to go for the third loan, where interest is charged at 8% but only at the end of each year.

   b) The unsecured bank loan is likely to be preferable. With h.p. finance, the lender takes security in the form of the asset financed. The borrower would be advised to obtain money without offering security, other things being equal, in order to preserve capacity to offer security for future borrowing.

   c) The bank loan is likely to be preferable to the debenture finance because the loan offers flexibility on repayment but at no extra cost to the borrower.

2. The interest yield on a bond is calculated as follows:

$$\frac{\text{coupon}}{\text{market value}}$$

For Bond A:

$$\text{Interest yield} = \frac{6}{110} = 5.45\%$$

For Bond B:

$$\text{Interest yield} = \frac{4}{95} = 4.21\%$$

The interest yield gives a measure of the percentage income return that an investor can expect on a bond. The redemption yield shows the overall return a bond offers, taking into account both income and capital gain/loss. Interest yields on similar risk and similar maturity bonds can differ markedly, but their redemption yields should not vary much, as investors will look for bonds to be priced competitively so as to offer comparable overall returns.

4. The most important factor in pricing a bond is the redemption yield. The bond needs to be priced, once a coupon and maturity have been set, so that the redemption yield is competitive with investments of a similar maturity and risk. As companies are normally considered to be more risky as borrowers than govern-

ments, a starting point would be to look at the redemption yield on government debt of the same maturity as your company's bond. Your bond redemption yield will need to be higher than this reference rate, but the tricky bit is deciding how much higher.

If there are companies of a similar size to yours and in a similar business, the yield on which their bonds trade might be a help, but other complicating factors will come in, such as how well known your company is in the international bond market compared to companies with bonds currently traded. You can imagine how difficult it must be to price some of the more innovative bond packages involving equity conversion rights and various forms of indexation, etc.

Once you know the redemption yield your bond needs to offer, you can determine a selling price. The price should be such that the income the bond generates plus any capital gain or loss to the purchaser will provide a return equal to the required redemption yield. This is reflected in the calculations set out in Activity 5 (p. 110).

Chapter 6

3. a)   A bank borrowing money for three months would pay an annual rate of interest of 5½%.

    b)   A bank lending money overnight would earn an annual rate of interest of 5%.

    c)   The spread on one month money is ¼ % (5⅞ – 5⅝).

4. To compare the two investments, we need to convert the discount rate quoted on the bank bills to an interest rate comparable with the CDs. Considering a bill with a maturity value of £100, the one month discount on the bill will be:

(6% of £100) × 1/12 = £0.5

The issue price of the bill will be £99.5. We can then convert the discount rate to an interest rate using equation (5) on p. 133:

$$1 \text{ month interest rate} = 1 \text{ month discount rate} \times \frac{\text{maturity value}}{\text{issue price}}$$

.06 × (1/12) × (100/99.5) = .005025

To find the annual interest rate, multiply the one month rate by twelve, giving 6.03%. This rate can now be compared with the annual interest rate quoted for CDs, 6⅛% or 6.125%. The CDs offer a higher rate than the bank bills.

Chapter 7

2. a)   The contract will be worth +£1,500 to Gregory and –£1,500 to Sophie. The value to Gregory as the buyer is 30p per share, that is the difference between the value he can obtain the shares for from Sophie (£7) and the value he can then realize in the open market (£7.30). Sophie's loss is the reverse of Gregory's gain.

    b)   The contract in this instance is worth £1,000 to Sophie and -£1,000 to Gregory. The value to Sophie is 20p per share, the difference between the value for a Halifax share that she can obtain under the forward contract and the value of a share in the open market.

c) The contract has neither positive nor negative value for either party, since the contract price equals the value of the shares in the open market.

3. a) An option to buy a share is a call option. From the table, an investor would have to pay 75p to acquire an April call with an exercise price of 500p.

   b) The calls with an exercise price of 500p and the puts with an exercise price of 600p are in-the-money. An option holder would make money on all these options if they were exercised now.

   c) The intrinsic value of the July 600p puts is 50p (the option exercise price of 600p less the current share price of 550p). The remaining value of the option – 43p – is time value.

   d) July calls are worth more than January calls because they have a greater time to maturity. There is a greater chance with the July calls that share prices will go up during the life of the option and make a larger profit for the option holder.

4. a) With the price ending up at 480p, 20p less than the exercise price of the call, the option is not worth exercising. Samantha's loss is the whole of the premium paid, or $1000 \times 75p = £750$. This is the maximum loss Samantha can incur on her option purchase.

   b) The option produces a profit on exercise of 50p per share, £500 in total. Overall Samantha still makes a loss on the transaction as she paid a premium to acquire the options of £750, as in a) above. Her net loss is £250.

   c) The option produces a profit on exercise of £1 per share or £1,000 in total. After taking into account the premium payment, Samantha makes a net profit of £250.

   d) The option produces a profit of £1,500 on exercise, giving a profit net of premium paid of £750.

Chapter 8

2. Exchange rates for sterling are expressed in the UK in the indirect form. The two rates given thus show how many units of Swiss and Australian currency can be exchanged for £1.

   A direct SF/A$ quotation from the point of view of an Australian resident will express the price of one Swiss franc in Australian dollars.

   SF2.4 = A$2.5

   SF1 = A$2.5/2.4 = A$1.0417

   The direct quotation is thus A$1.0417/SF.

3. If purchasing power parity holds, then currently goods worth US$1.56 in America can be bought for £1 in the UK. Over one year, the price of those goods will rise to US$1.607 ($1.56 \times 1.03$) in the US and to £1.05 in the UK. For purchasing power parity still to hold in one year's time, the spot rate at the end of that period should be US$1.607/£1.05, or US$1.53/£. The US$ is at a 1.9% premium ([1.56-1.53]/1.56) against sterling over one year.

4. Consider a UK individual, and the results that that individual could obtain by investing £100.

If the money was invested in sterling, the £100 would produce £101.5 (£100 x 1.015) over three months.

If the £100 was converted into DMs, it would produce DM298 now. This sum could then be invested at the DM 3 month rate of interest, say r, and then converted back into sterling at the forward exchange rate of DM2.97/£. The sterling sum resulting is given by:

DM 298 × (1+ r)

DM 2.97

and if interest parity holds, this sum should equal the amount produced by investing in sterling i.e. £101.5.

298 × (1+r) = 101.5

2.97

Rearranging, we have r = 1.16%. It makes sense that the German interest rate is less than the UK one, because, for a UK investor, a lower German interest rate is offset by an appreciation of the DM against sterling.

Index